## The Living Wisdom of
# TREES

FRED HAGENEDER  *with photographs by Edward Parker*

# THE LIVING WISDOM OF
# TREES

NATURAL HISTORY • FOLKLORE • SYMBOLISM • HEALING

DUNCAN BAIRD PUBLISHERS
LONDON

**The Living Wisdom of Trees**

*Dedicated to all the trees shown in this book*
*And to those that are not.*

First published in the United Kingdom and Ireland in 2005 by:

Duncan Baird Publishers Ltd
Sixth Floor
Castle House
75–76 Wells Street
London W1T 3QH

Conceived, created and designed by
Duncan Baird Publishers

Copyright © Duncan Baird Publishers 2005
Text copyright © Fred Hageneder 2005
Commissioned artwork © Duncan Baird Publishers 2005
For copyright of photographs see page 224 which is to be regarded as an extension of this copyright

All rights reserved. No part of this book may be reproduced in any form or by any electronic or mechanical means, including information storage and retrieval systems, without permission in writing from the publisher, except by a reviewer who may quote brief passages in a review.

The right of Fred Hageneder to be identified as the Author of this text has been asserted in accordance with the Copyright, Designs and Patents Act of 1988.

Commissioning editor: Naomi Waters
Editor: Ingrid Court-Jones
Managing designer: Manisha Patel
Designer: Allan Sommerville
Picture editor: Julia Brown
Commissioned artwork: Jeremy Sancha

British Library Cataloguing-in-Publication Data:
A CIP record for this book is available from the British Library

ISBN-10: 1-84483-164-7   ISBN-13: 9-781844-831647

10 9 8 7 6 5 4 3 2

Typeset in Optima
Colour reproduction by Colourscan
Printed in Singapore by Imago

PUBLISHER'S NOTES:
This book is printed on paper produced from pulp obtained from managed sustainable forests, and from paper mills, which meet environmental standards 15014001.

The following abbreviations are used in this book:
BCE (Before Common Era), the equivalent of BC
CE (Common Era), the equivalent of AD

The three taxonomic divisions this book deals with are the family, genus and species. A family contains one genus or two or more genera, and each genus contains one or more species. Most chapters in this book are about a genus and the main species contained within it, but some cover a family, or focus on a particular species.

The publishers and the author cannot accept any responsibility for any damage incurred as a result of any of the therapeutic methods contained in this work. If you have a medical condition and are unsure of the suitability of any of the therapeutic methods mentioned in this book, or if you are pregnant, it is advisable to consult a medical practitioner.

PAGE 2: *Coastal redwood forest, near San Francisco, USA.*

LEFT: *Douglas firs, Scotland.*

# contents

| | | | | | |
|---|---|---|---|---|---|
| Introduction | 6 | Common fig | 90 | Cottonwood | 160 |
| Guide to early history | 12 | Sycomore fig | 94 | Cherry | 164 |
| | | Banyan | 96 | Blackthorn | 166 |
| Acacia | 16 | Pipal or Bo | 100 | Pomegranate | 168 |
| Maple | 20 | Ash | 102 | Pear | 170 |
| Baobab | 24 | Ginkgo | 106 | Oak | 172 |
| Horse chestnut | 26 | Holly | 110 | Willow | 178 |
| Kauri | 30 | Walnut | 112 | Elder | 182 |
| Alder | 32 | Juniper | 116 | Redwood | 186 |
| Almond | 34 | Larch | 120 | Rowan | 190 |
| Monkey-puzzle | 38 | Laurel | 122 | Tamarisk | 194 |
| Birch | 40 | Apple | 124 | Montezuma cypress | 196 |
| Hornbeam | 46 | Mulberry | 128 | Yew | 198 |
| Sweet chestnut | 48 | Myrtle | 130 | Linden | 206 |
| Cedar | 52 | Olive | 132 | Elm | 210 |
| Orange | 60 | Date palm | 138 | | |
| Myrrh | 64 | Spruce and fir | 142 | Botanical glossary | 212 |
| Hazel | 66 | Pine | 146 | Introduction to natural healing | 214 |
| Hawthorn | 68 | Terebinth | 150 | | |
| Cypress | 72 | Plane | 152 | Further reading | 216 |
| Quince | 78 | Totara | 154 | Index | 220 |
| Eucalyptus | 82 | Poplar | 156 | Acknowledgments and picture credits | 224 |
| Beech | 86 | Aspen | 158 | | |

RIGHT: "Rizzio's tree" at Melville Castle, near Edinburgh, Scotland – a sweet chestnut said to have been planted by Mary Queen of Scots' secretary, David Rizzio (1533?–66), as a token of his love for her.

# Introduction

Trees and humankind have always had a symbiotic relationship. Throughout the centuries, trees have offered us shelter from the cold and the heat. They have provided us with a multitude of nutritious fruits, leaves, flowers and roots for food and medicine. They have given us wood with which to make our tools, weapons and toys, not to mention timber for houses, fences, boats and bridges. But perhaps most significant of all, trees have provided fuel for fire, which, once it was tamed hundreds of thousands of years ago, became the engine of civilization. Trees are our strongest allies.

The entire spectrum of human existence is reflected in tree lore through the ages: from birth, death and rebirth to the age-old struggle between good and evil, and the quest for beauty, truth and enlightenment.

Our ancestors recognized that there is a vital balance in life: you take *and* you give. So they *celebrated* the forces of nature by offering them gifts, songs, prayers and blessings to revitalize the natural world – a world of which they felt themselves to be an intimate part. Many cultures saw (and still see) everything in creation as imbued with spirit, which means that all living things are regarded as sacred.

Whatever our personal beliefs regarding nature spirits, and the question of whether God exists *inside* creation or only outside it (or at all), one thing is certain: the ability to extend compassion to other life forms, to feel gratitude and give thanks for sharing in the miracle of life, to respect, if not to love, all fellow inhabitants of this planet, makes us better human beings and helps us to triumph over ignorance and greed. The living wisdom of trees shows us that life is worth so much.

ABOVE: The Green Man is a symbol of the regenerative powers of nature, often depicted with foliage emerging from the mouth, like this example from a church in Sutton Benger, Wiltshire, England.

## The Tree of Life

Native North Americans call trees "our standing brothers and sisters". Humans and trees share an upright, vertical orientation. We walk, they stand. We move and change, they remain the quiet centre of *being*.

*RIGHT: An illuminated manuscript depicting Fenrir, the wolf of Norse myth, and the World Tree, Yggdrasil (Icelandic school, 1680).*

According to many of the teachings of ancient wisdom, the universe comprises a spiral or circular movement around a central axis, the *axis mundi*. And this centre pole has often been depicted as the *Tree of Life* or *Universal Tree*. Essentially, the Tree of Life is an image of the whole universe, or at least of our planet, that embodies the notion that all life is interrelated and sacred. It portrays the universe as much more than a lifeless, clockwork mechanism that blindly follows the laws of physics; rather, it presents our world as a living, evolving organism, imbued with divine spirit.

The Tree of Life is a concept that can be traced back to Neolithic times. From there it developed as part of the philosophy of most ancient cultures, whether it was early civilizations and city-states, such as those of Egypt, Persia and Greece, or tribal societies which remained closer to nature.

During the Bronze and Iron Ages different cultures developed their particular characteristics, their sets of moral and law codes, aesthetics, languages, customs, and so on. And as part of the process, the ancient concept of the Tree of Life also evolved into a multitude of forms – for example, the *Haoma* tree in Zoroastrian Persia, the *Tooba* Tree at the centre of the Islamic paradise, the World Tree *Yggdrasil* in Norse myth, *'Ez Chajim* in Judaism and *Ts'ogs-shing*, the "Assembly Tree of the Gods" in Tibetan Buddhism. And it appears elsewhere in world mythology under many more guises.

However, one aspect of tree-related traditions remained the same throughout the largely patriarchal ages which followed the Neolithic: a clear sense of the *female* side of the divine. The Tree remained linked with the notion of female deities and the ancient Mother Goddess. For example, in the pre-hieroglyphic script of ancient Egypt, the word for giving birth is derived directly from the word for tree. This was no coincidence. The Tree of Life *is* the great mother of creation: all-encompassing, all-birthing, all-healing. The tree symbolism goes back to a time that coincides with the worldwide cult of the Great Goddess.

The cosmic "womb" is also all-devouring, but only to transform life and *rebirth* it. In ancient cosmology, death is not a polar opposite of life, just an important part of its cycle. Most peoples believed in reincarnation or some other form of afterlife. An ancient druid saying that has come down to us from Gaul (modern France) states, "Death is nothing but a gate in a long journey."

The living wisdom of trees tells us that we are all travelling together through the cycles of life.

## The Tree of Knowledge

In the Germanic languages, most terms for learning, knowledge, wisdom and so on are derived from the words for tree or wood. In Anglo-Saxon we have *witan* ("mind, consciousness") and *witiga* ("wisdom"), in English "wits", "witch" and "wizard", and in modern German *Witz* ("wits, joke"). These words all stem from the ancient Scandinavian root word *vid*, which means "wood" (as in forest, not timber).

A druid was a most knowledgeable person. The word is made up from two Gaulish Celtic words *dru* ("very, highly, most") and *vid* ("knowledge"). And this very knowledge came from the woods, not only because a druid trained for up to 20 years in remote forest academies, but also because *all* original knowledge came from the trees. (This does not threaten God's elevated position as the highest being: God is the source, trees are but channels.) All ancient cultures,

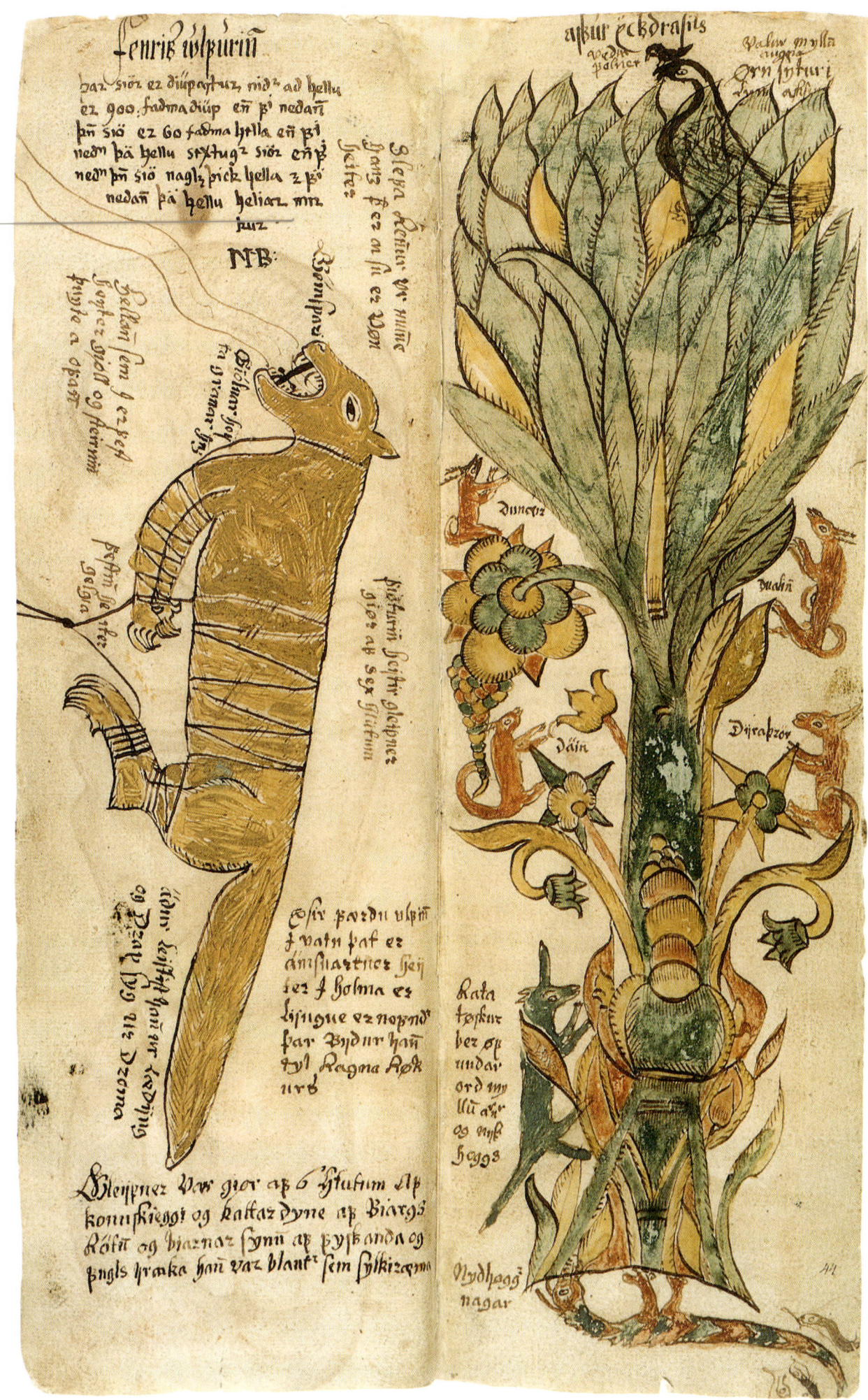

whether they prayed to one god or many, acknowledged trees as being able to elevate the human consciousness to higher forms of perception, and to receive messages from the higher planes (or the deeper Self). Hence the worldwide abundance of traditions of tree oracles and sanctuaries. Some divine messengers, such as birds, might have wings, but most have leaves.

And the leaves of the Tree of Knowledge are the letters of the old sacred alphabets, which early humans plucked from the tree, and which gave them writing to enable them to preserve the word. Writing was regarded as magical because it empowered the word to travel through, and even defeat, time. Primarily, early alphabets functioned as systems for divination (for example, the Norse runes), with every symbol representing a certain aspect of the primeval life force. An ancient Irish alphabet, the *Ogham* (pronounced "oam"), comprises 20 letters, each named after a local species of tree. Using such alphabets as tools, humankind began to write on birch bark, walnut or beech tablets, and to carve spells in yew, rowan and other woods.

In the seventh century BCE, the Buddha searched under a sacred pipal tree for the *highest* knowledge, the "ultimate and unconditioned truth". He found it. The living wisdom of trees reminds us that learning starts with *listening*.

## Sacred groves

The notion of the spiritual nature of trees had a very real effect on people and on the landscape. On every continent, certain trees and groves were protected as "sacred". To different peoples of the world, different tree species represented

**LEFT**: *Egyptian 19th-Dynasty wall painting from the tomb of Sennedjem, Deir el-Medina, Thebes, Egypt. The heavily laden date palms and sycomore fig trees are testament to the care with which Sennedjem and his wife tended their land, thereby pleasing the gods.*

the Tree of Life (or aspects of it), according to which species grew locally and – as all species have different characteristics and qualities – which tree character resonated most strongly with the spiritual ideals emphasized by a particular culture. For example, in ancient Sumer it seems to have been the cedar of Lebanon; in pre-historic Persia it was the plane tree; and in Siberia the birch is the World Tree of shamanic tradition.

Most religions began beneath sacred trees. A simple altar marked the sanctuary. Later, a roof or enclosure might have been added, and eventually the sanctuary became a man-made temple.

A "sacred" status also has a very direct impact on ecology: such a tree, or even a species, is protected. For example, the persea (*Mimusops schimperia*) was one of the sacred trees of ancient Egypt. However, with the disappearance of the ancient religion, it lost its special status and became a source of timber and fuel in a hot country where trees are rare. Sadly, by about 900 years later it was extinct in Egypt, and only a few specimens still survive today in Ethiopia. In medieval Europe, almost the only ancient yew trees to escape felling and being made into longbows were consecrated trees that grew in churchyards.

## Sustainability

But people had to survive, and they needed the products of trees of all kinds. Growing populations and increasing farming slowly changed the face of the earth.

Some contemporary writers have accused early civilizations of thoughtless deforestation and overexploitation of trees. In fact, there is increasing archeological evidence that effective resource management was employed all over the ancient world. The sustainable methods of coppicing and pollarding, which were once thought to have been introduced by the medieval metal, glass and salt industries to feed their vast charcoal requirement, has actually been shown to go back as far as the Neolithic. Similarly, the lopping of branches for leaf fodder to feed livestock is a sustainable technique of ancient farmyard management.

An example of good ancient timber management is the cypresses of Crete, which were highly valued by the ancient Minoans, but also exported to Egypt and Greece. Yet these trees continued to flourish in Crete until the Middle Ages when the Venetians overexploited the cypresses' suitability as timber for ships until they became extinct on the island. But the exploding populations of Europe in the Middle Ages, with their large wooden cities that repeatedly burnt down and had to be rebuilt, created higher demands for wood than millennia of ancient cultures in the Near East had done – they used mostly mud-bricks, even to build palaces. And any modern skyscraper requires more wood (for encasing the cement) than an ancient palace ever did.

Wood trade and construction in the Old World were part of everyday life, as they are today. But in ancient times trees were respected as living beings with *equal* seriousness. Around 3,500 years ago, an ancient Egyptian, Treasurer of Pharaoh Thutmosis III, led an expedition to find cedar timber in the Lebanon. The inscription on his tomb tells how he made offerings, until – from a source beyond our modern reasoning – he knew he had permission to take *certain* trees. This is one of many ancient examples of respect triumphing over greed to ensure harmony with nature.

# Guide to early history

**Angles** Germanic people who, with the Jutes and Saxons, invaded Britain in the fifth century CE.

**Aryans** A people who, in prehistoric times, settled in Iran and northern India. The Indo-European languages of southern Asia are descended from their language.

**Assyria** Kingdom of northern Mesopotamia (modern northern Iraq and southeastern Turkey). Emerged as an independent state in the 14th century BCE; was a major empire until its fall in 612BCE.

**Babylonia** Kingdom of southern Mesopotamia. The city of Babylon became the commercial and administrative centre c.1850BCE. Babylon was destroyed in 689BCE.

**Canaan** Area west of the Jordan River, later known as Palestine. The Canaanites' religion was similar to that of the Phoenicians.

**Celts** A diverse group of early Indo-European peoples who, from the second millennium BCE to the first century BCE, spread over much of Europe. The Halstatt period (c.700BCE) was followed by the La Tène culture (from the mid-fifth century BCE). Most of the Celtic territories in Europe were annexed by the Roman Empire in the first century BCE.

**Dorians** An ancient Greek people, originating from northwestern Greece (Macedonia and Epirus). During the 11th century BCE, they invaded the Peloponnese peninsula. They swept away the Mycenean and Minoan civilizations, and plunged Greece into a dark age until the city-states emerged about 300 years later.

**Egypt** One of the earliest urban and literate societies. Its millennia of continuous cultural history began in c.3100BCE.

**Gauls** An agricultural Celtic society based in a region comprising what is now France and parts of Belgium. Gaul was conquered by the Roman general Julius Caesar in 58–50BCE.

**Germanic peoples** A diverse group of early Indo-European peoples who, in the Bronze Age, inhabited what is now southern Sweden, the Danish peninsula, and northern Germany. During the Iron Age and the Dark Ages the Germanic population experienced many expansions and migrations. Peoples include Saxons, Angles, Frisians, Lombards, Burgundians and Goths.

**Hebrews** Ancient northern Semitic people, the ancestors of the Jews.

**Ionians** The eastern division of the ancient Greeks who gave their name to Ionia on the western coast of Anatolia (modern-day Turkey). The Ionians are said to have migrated from Attica (southeastern Greece) after the invasion of the Dorians. The Ionians were later (from the fifth century BCE) identified with the indigenous population, the Pelasgians. The Ionian contribution to Greek culture was of major importance.

**Israelites** The descendants of the Biblical patriarchs, during the period from the conquest of Canaan (c.2,000 BCE) to their return from the Babylonian Exile (late sixth century BCE), from which time on they became known as the Jews.

**Jericho** Possibly the oldest city in the world. Jericho was transformed from a settlement of Mesolithic hunters in c.9,000BCE to an organized community which built a massive stone wall around the town in c.8,000BCE. The size of this settlement (estimated at 2,000–3,000 inhabitants) suggests that it had developed an early form of agriculture and a method of irrigation.

**Mesopotamia** The "Land of Two Rivers", the so-called "fertile crescent" between the Euphrates and Tigris rivers (modern Iraq). Location of the ancient civilizations of Sumeria, Babylonia and Assyria.

**Native Americans** The Americas are believed to have been settled first by Asiatic peoples from c.10,000 BCE. Originally from northeastern Siberia, the first Americans probably entered Alaska via the Bering Strait, and then dispersed southwards. Many Native North American cultures retained their hunter-gatherer lifestyle until the post-Columbian colonization by Europeans.

OVERLEAF: *A stately common oak standing amid a sea of bluebells in a hazel coppice in Dorset, England.*

**Old World** A term used by commentators in the New World – the Americas, Australia and New Zealand – to denote Europe, whence their forebears had originated. The term has been used here to refer to the old civilizations of the Near East (Egypt, Canaan, Phoenicia, Syria, Arabia, Persia, Mesopotamia, Anatolia, Greece, pre-Christian Rome, plus their colonies), and their complex political, social and economical relationships. The tribal societies of Europe's northern peoples (the Celts, Germans, Finno-Ugrians) are omitted from this definition.

**Palestine** Later name for Canaan. The word is derived from Philistia, the term used by Greek writers for the land of the Philistines. The name was revived by the second-century Romans for the southern part of their province of Syria, "Syria Palaestina".

**Pelasgians** Aegean population of Greece before the 12th century BCE. *Pelasgoi* is the term the Greeks used for the indigenous culture that preceded them. It is not known what the Pelasgians called themselves, or whether they were one homogenous group at all. The Greeks incorporated a great number of local Pelasgian myths and legends into their culture, which made it is so rich and diverse.

**Persia** The Parsa, an Indo-European people arrived on the Iranian plateau in around 1000 BCE. Their power slowly grew into the Persian Empire which lasted until the conquest by Alexander the Great in the third century BCE. Zoroaster (c.628–c.551 BCE) was an important cultural and religious reformer.

**Philistines** People of Aegean origin who settled on the southern coast of Canaan (between modern Tel Aviv-Yafo and the Gaza Strip) in the 12th century BCE, about the time of the migration of the Israelites.

**Phoenicia** Ancient region on the eastern coast of the Mediterranean (modern Lebanon). The Phoenicians appeared in the area in around 3000 BCE and were seafarers, merchants and colonizers. Their coastal territory reached up into the mountains of Lebanon with its famous conifers (cedars). Religion was centred around the forces of nature, such as the spirit of the land (Baal) and the mother goddess Astarte.

**Phrygia** Ancient district in west-central Anatolia. The Phrygians dominated Asia Minor between the 12th and fifth centuries BCE. They engaged in agriculture, and sheep and horse rearing. Their principal cult – of the mother goddess Cybele – was passed on to the Greeks.

**Roman Empire** By the late first century BCE, the Roman Empire was established and covered almost all the Mediterranean countries, extending northward as far as Britain. It began to crumble in the late third century CE, and ended in 395CE, when Rome split into Eastern and Western empires.

**Saxons** A Germanic people who in ancient times lived in the area of northern Germany and the Baltic coast. They invaded and settled in Britain in the fifth century CE.

**Sparta** Greek city-state. From the fifth century BCE its ruling class devoted itself to war and diplomacy, neglecting the arts and philosophy. The single-minded focus on militarism performed a great service to Greece in times of national defence but precluded any hope of a political unification of classical Greece, eventually spurring the Roman conquest of Greece.

**Sumer** Southernmost part of Mesopotamia. Site of the earliest known civilization. Twelve independent city-states flourished from c.3000 BCE until c.1900 BCE.

**Ur** Ancient city of southern Mesopotamia (Sumer), about 200 miles (300km) southeast of Baghdad, founded by Chalcolithic farmers in the fourth millennium BCE. In c.2000 BCE, the Biblical Abraham and his clan migrated from Ur to Canaan.

# Acacia *Acacia*

Acacia is a very large genus of 800 to 1,000 species of shrubs and trees, found throughout the subtropical and tropical regions, particularly of Africa and Australia (where they are known as wattles). They are mainly shrubs, but several species reach tree size. The leaves are often bipinnate. The flowers are usually yellow and appear in small, rounded heads, mostly in winter or spring. The fruits are ovate to linear legumes.

The common acacia (*A. raddiana*) grows 16–26ft (5–8m) high, and its leaves divide bipinnately into small oblong to elliptical leaflets. The main flowering season is in spring, with a second season in late summer. The twisted pods contain many seeds, which, after falling from the tree, are eaten by various animals. *A. abyssinica* is native to Ethiopia and has 3–5in (7.5–12.5cm) long fruits.

The locust tree or false acacia (*Robinia pseudoacacia*) is not a species of this genus but, like the true acacias, a member of the pea family (*Leguminosae*).

## Practical Uses

The acacia was of great importance in ancient Egypt, both practically and spiritually. Of the native trees, it was the most widespread and also the most useful. Roof-timbers up to 12 cubits (17ft 9in/5.4m) long could be cut from the low-hanging, curved branches, and the wood was strong enough to form the main timbers of the hulls and ribs of small ships. Shorter pieces of wood were used to make the common

RIGHT: *The beautiful, feathered leaves of acacia trees seen here in mixed woodland in Provence. It is thought that fragrant acacias were introduced to southern France to support the perfume industry.*

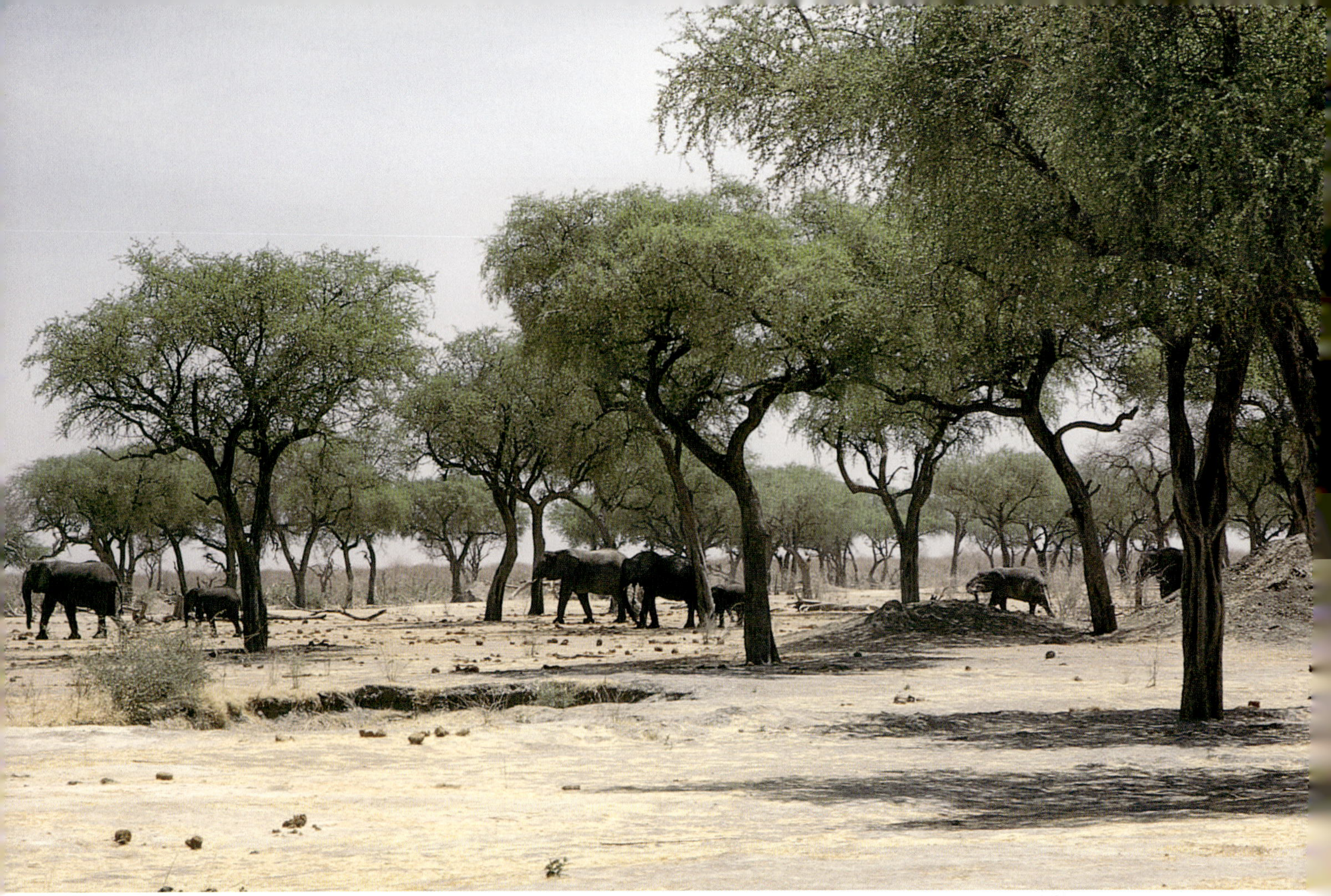
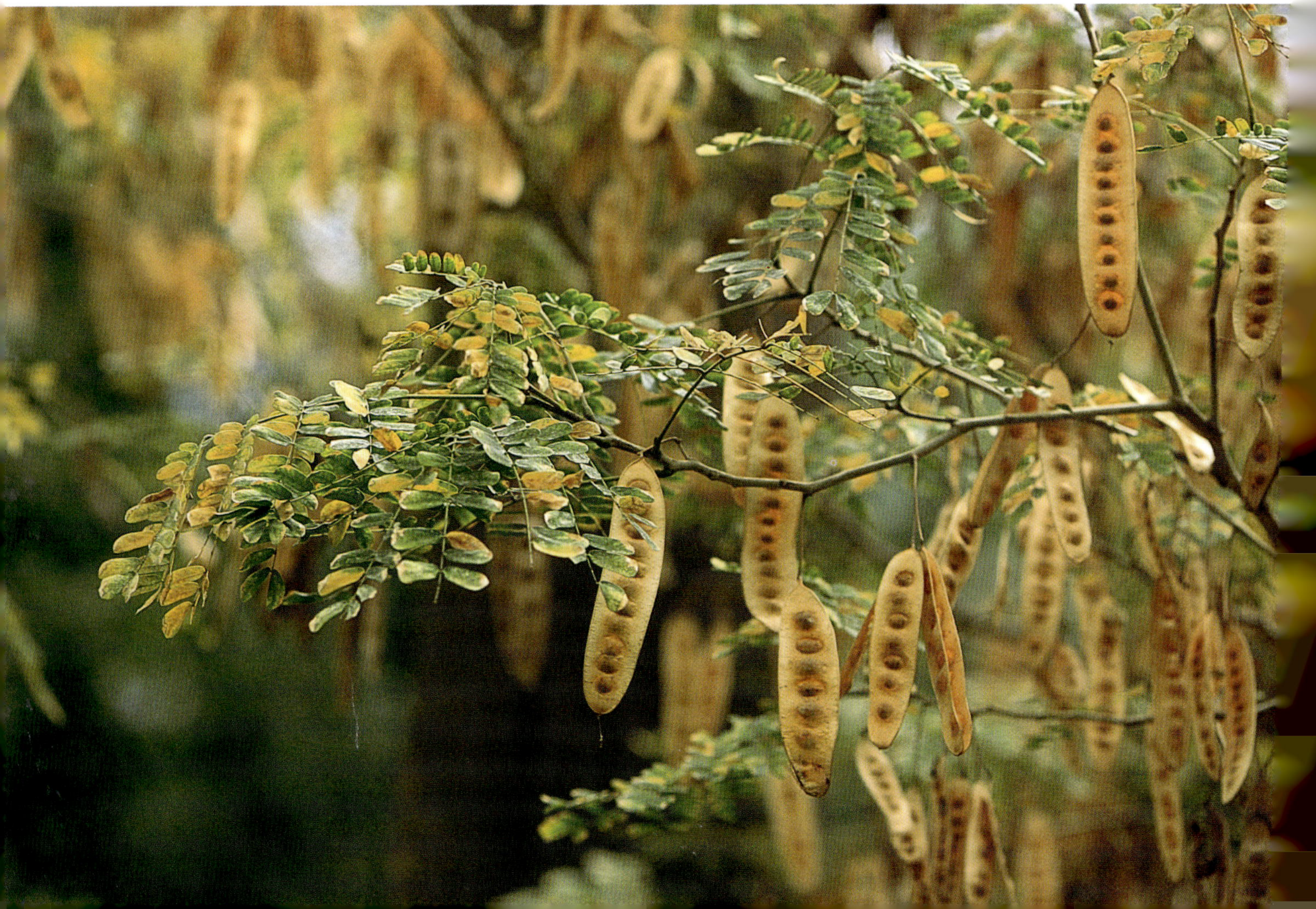

**OPPOSITE, ABOVE**: *Elephants on their way to a water hole pass through an acacia grove in Waza National Park, northern Cameroon.*

**OPPOSITE, BELOW**: *The pods of pea-like acacia seeds are a food source for many animals and human hunter-gatherer peoples.*

Nile cargo barge. This boat was constructed from pieces 2ft (60cm) long, fitted together like bricks. Acacia was also used for making furniture, chests, coffins and bows.

In the southwestern USA, the Cahuilla and the Pima tribes eat the pods or seeds of catclaw acacia (*A. greggii*) either raw, or ground and cooked in cakes. In Hawaii, the wood of the koa (*A. koa*) was used to make canoes.

## Natural Healing

Hawaiians apply koa ashes to the insides of infants' mouths to give them physical strength. They also place the leaves on a sick person's bed to encourage him or her to sweat.

## Culture, Myth and Symbol

To the mind of the ancient Egyptian, a boat was not only a physical object but also a mirror image of the barge of consciousness on which the soul floated through life. Viewed in this way, boats and coffins have something in common, and many cultures developed ship or boat burials. In the five boat burials discovered near the pyramid of Cheops (c.2590BCE) the boats were made from acacia and cedar.

Most importantly, the original sacred barge of Osiris at the temple of Thebes was made from acacia. This ancient nature god "died" every year when the plants withered, only to be "reborn" in spring. By overcoming death and achieving eternal life, Osiris personified the promise of redemption in the afterlife. The ancient Egyptians' spiritual goal was to transcend the boundaries of personality and merge with Osiris. The acacia was the guardian of this promise, for it protected Osiris' mummy while his soul embraced the universe. Inscriptions call him "the solitary one in the acacia", and inscribed images show the god as a mummy sheltered by the tree.

The tribes of Israel made the Ark of the Covenant, the Tabernacle, the table and altar from common acacia wood (*A. raddiana*). This tree has no other sacred history in Jewish tradition and it was probably used for the Ark simply because Moses was familiar with it from having lived in Egypt. Of the three acacia species that survive the harsh conditions of Sinai, only the common acacia would have been suitable for construction timber.

In Arabia, the acacia tree is still revered, and anyone who even breaks a twig is expected to die within a year.

Elsewhere, in ancient China, the great earth god was said to live in a pine tree, while the other earth deities resided at the four points of the compass in other species of trees. The homes of the gods of the north were acacia trees.

**Symbolism:** Sensitivity and protection

**Divine Association:** Osiris (ancient Egyptian)

**Astrological Association:** Sun, Pluto

**Historical Spotlight:** When travelling through Patagonia (southern Chile and Argentina) in 1833, Charles Darwin came upon a sacred tree between the Rio Negro and the Rio Colorado. The native peoples referred to this solitary acacia as the Altar of Walleechu, and visited it to hang votive offerings in its branches. Poor people just added coloured threads, while richer people poured alcohol and *maté* into a hole in the tree. The visitors made smoke offerings that carried their gratitude to the spirit world.

# Maple  *Aceraceae*

The maple family (*Aceraceae*) comprises more than 100 species found throughout the northern temperate regions, with a large number in eastern Asia. In the main, they are deciduous trees and shrubs with opposite leaves, which are palmately lobed in most species. The flowers are small but often attractive and they usually open at the same time as the leaves. The insect-pollinated flowers ripen into the winged seeds which children love to play with.

The field maple (*Acer campestre*) is a medium-sized tree, frequently found in fields and rural hedges in Europe; it also grows in western Asia. In autumn, the leaves turn a pure yellow, sometimes red. The Norway maple (*A. platanoides*) is a handsome, fast-growing tree of great size. The sycamore (*A. pseudoplatanus*), another species of maple, can grow in exposed positions in almost any soil. Native to the European mountain areas, it has been planted and naturalized widely. The silver maple (*A. saccharinum*) is a large, fast-growing tree in eastern North America. The shape and colour of its leaves create a delightful effect in the breeze. The sugar maple (*A.saccharum*) resembles the Norway maple, and is one of the most spectacular North American trees in autumn when its leaves change colour.

## Practical Uses

The tough and fine-grained maple wood is suitable for high-quality carving – for example, of musical instruments – or for turning work, such as ornamental bowls. In the UK,

RIGHT: *An attractive and recognizable feature of the handsome maple family is the autumnal transformation of the trees, when their leaves display a wide range of hues, from pale golds to deep reds.*

Anglo-Saxon maple harps have been excavated from a barrow at Taplow in Berkshire; they were also found, wrapped in a sealskin bag, as part of the Sutton Hoo ship burial treasure in Suffolk. The pale and clean sycamore wood has been popular for kitchen tables and furniture because it has no scent to taint food and a fine grain that can be cleaned easily. Further west, in southwest England, sycamore leaves were once used as bases on which to bake Easter or harvest-time buns, their distinctive veins giving a beautiful pattern to the undersides of the buns.

In North America, many indigenous tribes have traditionally used maple wood to make paddles and oars, and in building, basketry and furniture-making.

The popular maple syrup is produced mainly in Canada. For centuries, Native North Americans have cut into the trunks of sugar maples in late winter to collect the sap. Today this is done on a commercial scale. If the trees are not over-bled and hence damaged, they can be tapped again the following year. But it takes 40 gallons (182 litres) of sap to make just 1 gallon (4.5 litres) of syrup.

Pure maple syrup is precious because it contains balanced sugars, minerals such as potassium, calcium, magnesium and manganese, vitamins A, B2, B5 and B6, folic acid, niacin, biotin and also proteins. But beware – some cheaper products might only contain a fifth of maple syrup in a mixture otherwise made up of corn syrup and various artificial additives, so always check the label before buying.

## Natural Healing

Maples of all varieties have a long tradition of use in herbal medicine, particularly among Native North Americans. For

ABOVE: *The adoption of the distinctively shaped maple leaf as the national symbol of Canada derives from the tree's multiple uses.*

example, the Tsalagi tribe uses the bark of the silver maple to make remedies for sore eyes, gynecological problems and cramps. The Chippewa use it to treat sores, the Mohegan to cure coughs and the Ojibwa to combat gonorrhea.

## Culture, Myth and Symbol

The sycamore in the Alps and the field maple in the lower-lying regions of Europe were both intimately associated with farming. People ate the spring leaves in salads and other dishes, and the leafy branches were a common cattle fodder. The trees provided shade, stabilized slopes or damp ground conditions and could almost be regarded as part of the working "staff" of the farmyard.

The old Welsh tradition of carving love spoons utilizes sycamore, but apart from a rich tradition of being made into musical instruments (maple wood has qualities excellent for

*A tale among the Salteaux tribe of North America relates how the fiery autumn colours of the maples saved the grandmother of Nanahboozhoo, the Creator, from malevolent spirits of darkness.*

sound transmission), the European maples hardly ever left the farmyard.

However, in North America it is a different story, particularly with the sugar maples. A tale among the Salteaux tribe relates how the fiery autumn leaves of the maples saved the grandmother of Nanahboozhoo, the Creator, from malevolent spirits of darkness. Nanahboozhoo was so grateful, and also so taken with the maples' beauty, that he decided to live among them. One day, some tribespeople came and asked him how to collect maple sap and he showed them how to do so without harming the trees more than necessary.

The maple features in the myths and legends of many other Native North American tribes. In a story told by the Chippewa people about a hero called Mishosha, the maple was once an evil magician. However, Mishosha's courageous and skillful deeds turned a most malevolent man into the most benevolent tree.

The Iroquois legend of "The Hunting of the Great Bear" relates how four brothers were hunting Nyahgwaheh, an enormous bear. After a long and arduous chase, they finally struck him down at the top of a mountain. They made a fire, cooked the bear and ate. When they were replete they looked down and saw thousands of small sparkling lights beneath and around them. They were no longer on the mountain top, but up in the sky! The bones of the bear came back to life and started to run, and the four brothers grabbed their spears and followed him across the skies. And they still do – because the four brothers make up the constellation of the Great Bear. Every autumn, when they kill him, so the legend says, the bear's blood falls down from the heavens and paints the maple leaves scarlet.

The Kiowa nation uses the wood of the box elder (*A. negundo*) to burn on the altar fire at the sacred *peyote* ceremony (peyote is an hallucinogenic cactus).

**Symbolism:** Expansion

**Divine Association:** Nanahboozhoo (Salteaux Indian)

**Astrological Association:** Jupiter

**Superstition:** The Roman grammarian Servius noted in c.400CE that, as the Trojan horse had been made from maple wood, the maple was a tree that brought bad luck.

**Historical Spotlight:** The sycamore tree was first recorded in England in 1578, possibly brought from Europe by the Crusaders. Its English name is a misspelling of "sycomore" fig – a tree native to Egypt and Palestine.

# Baobab *Adansonia*

*Adansonia* is a genus of eight species of deciduous trees native to Africa, six endemic to Madagascar and one endemic to Australia. The most common species of baobab (*A. digitata*) grows in most of Africa and Madagascar. It has a short but massive trunk of up to 60ft (18m) tall, which can reach half that height in diameter. The leaves at the ends of the stout branches have five to seven oblong-elliptic leaflets up to 5in (12.5cm) long. The flowers often open before the leaves, with white obovate petals up to 4in (10cm) long. They are pollinated by various nocturnal creatures, including bats. The largest living specimen stands in Northern Province (South Africa) and measures 45ft (13.7m) in diameter. It is estimated to be over 3,000 years old.

## Practical Uses

The enormous trunks of the largest baobabs can contain more than 30,000 gallons (136,000 litres) of water. Over millennia, this special ability to store water in their spongy wood has facilitated the survival and well-being of many tribes during periods of drought or in riverless areas.

The inner bast layer underneath the bark of the trunk yields a strong fibre, which can be used for making ropes and nets, and woven into cloth. In some parts of Africa, the white fibrous fruit pulp is burnt to repel the insects that plague domestic cattle.

**Symbolism:** the Tree of Life

**Divine Association:** the spirit world

**Astrological Association:** Moon

## Natural Healing

The large, woody, egg-shaped fruits, rich in protein and oil, are an important source of nutrition for local populations. The big, black seeds are eaten on their own, mixed with millet, or pounded into a paste; their oil is also extracted. The white pulp of the fruit is a base for a lemonade-like drink. The young shoots and leaves are eaten too, by domestic and wild animals as well as humans.

The baobab has a long history of medicinal use. Both leaves and seeds are high in vitamin C and calcium, which strengthen the immune system. Bark and seeds can be used to treat fevers and even malaria.

## Culture, Myth and Symbol

A large corpus of myths, legends and folklore surrounding the baobab has been collected, particularly during the early 20th century. First of all, the gift of water has made this tree a true "Tree of Life" for many peoples, and the appropriate respect and thanksgiving rituals go back to time immemorial. Furthermore, some countries have tribal burial rites in which the bodies of people of special note, such as medicine people and shamans, and sometimes poets and musicians, are placed inside (cracked) hollow baobabs that are no longer used for water storage. Like the birch in Siberia, the baobab is perceived as a powerful gate to the spirit world that will facilitate the soul's ascent – and, if called upon, also its return.

OPPOSITE: *Baobabs are among Africa's oldest and most venerated trees. An entire community can survive by drawing from the vast store of water a single ancient tree can hold in its mighty trunk.*

OPPOSITE: *The splendid sight of a mature horse chestnut in flower. These trees are often planted in parks and avenues for their ornamental beauty.*

# Horse chestnut *Aesculus*

The horse chestnuts, and the American buckeyes that belong to the same genus, comprise about 13 species in southeastern Europe, North America and eastern Asia. All have compound palmate leaves. The flowers occur in panicles. These trees are easily cultivated and thrive in any soil, hence their wide distribution in parks and cities.

In Europe, the best-known member of this genus is the common horse chestnut (*A. hippocastanum*), a native of the border region between northern Greece and Albania. This tree was introduced to Europe in 1576, and to Britain in 1633. It can grow up to 90ft (27m) tall. It produces sticky buds and looks exceptionally beautiful when its flower "candles" blossom in May. The flowers are creamy-white with a yellow patch that later turns magenta.

The large, brown, shiny seeds or nuts are encased in green, spiny husks. On close inspection, the surface of the nuts reveals tree-like rings, making them resemble polished wood. They are very popular with adults and children alike for their sheer beauty and tactile appeal.

The American members of the horse chestnut or buckeye family (*Hippocastanaceae*) include the Ohio buckeye (*A. glabra*), the state tree of Ohio. The only buckeye that grows in the west is the California buckeye (*A. californica*), a small tree with an abundance of showy flowers.

## Practical Uses

The timber of the horse chestnut is not used much but the living tree is highly ornamental, hence it is planted in parks and avenues all around the northern temperate zone. The nuts are rich in saponins and in the past were used for making soap. They are poisonous to humans if eaten raw. The flower buds make an effective substitute for hops in the brewing of beer.

## Natural Healing

Early pioneers in the United States carried an Ohio buckeye seed in their pocket to ward off rheumatism.

Creams, ointments and tincture of the seeds of horse chestnut are an important remedy for the treatment of varicose veins and hemorrhoids. They appear to work by supporting the microcirculation and by decreasing capillary permeability, while also having an astringent and anti-inflammatory effect. Traditionally, the horse chestnut was used to relieve congestion in the veins. It has also been

LEFT: *Horse chestnut leaves are palmate. In the autumn they display a wide range of hues, from bright yellow to deep brown.*

**OPPOSITE**: *Fallow deer at dawn on a frosty morning under a solitary horse chestnut tree foraging for seasonal fallen fruits to eat.*

reported to reduce symptoms of leg pain, edema and itching. Recent research suggests that aescin, a chemical that can be extracted from the nuts, is a good remedy for sprains and bruises – exactly the ailments for which the Turks treated their horses with the fruits (see Culture, Myth and Symbol below). The tree essence of horse chestnut eases an agitated mind, enhancing clarity of thought and intuition.

## Culture, Myth and Symbol

In Britain horse chestnut seeds are known popularly as "conkers" and since the late 18th century children have used them to play a game of the same name. They pierce the nut through the middle and thread it onto a long piece of string, knotted at the end. Two children then take turns in swinging their conker to hit their opponent's, which has to be held still, dangling on its string – until one of the contestants wins by breaking their opponent's nut into pieces.

There are no ancient traditions concerning the horse chestnut. This is because, like all trees, the species retreated south in order to survive the last Ice Age; however, as the climate slowly warmed up again, the horse chestnut found itself stuck in a remote valley in eastern Europe. While birch seeds can travel fast on the wind, and rowan and other berries migrate with the birds that eat them, the large horse chestnut fruits did not succeed in crossing the mountain ridges for about 10,000 years!

However, eventually their turn came. In the 16th century, Ogier Ghislain de Busteq, Flemish ambassador to Turkey from 1556 to 1562, visited the court of Suleman the Magnificent and saw Turkish soldiers feeding the fruit to their horses – hence the name "horse" chestnut. They are also so-

**ABOVE**: *The horse chestnut's flower "candles", which appear in May.*

called because, after the leaves fall, they leave scars on the twigs in the shape of a horse-shoe.

Busteq tracked down the trees that produced the fruit the Turkish soldiers fed to the horses and sent a young specimen to the Botanical Gardens in Paris. In 1576 the first horse chestnuts were planted in Vienna, and from there this tree spread quickly all over Europe and North America.

**Symbolism:** Patience

**Astrological Association:** Jupiter

**Historical Spotlight:** The fruits contain aescin, which is poisonous if eaten raw. However, during rationing in World War II, many civilians roasted and ground horse chestnut fruit or "conkers" to make a rather bitter substitute for coffee.

# Kauri *Agathis australis*

The genus *Agathis* belongs to *Araucariaceae*, the same family as the monkey-puzzle, and comprises about 20 species of tall, evergreen, coniferous trees native to New Zealand, Australia and the Philippines. Their leaves are broad, undivided, smooth and leathery. The seeds, one sitting behind each scale of the cone, mature during the second year.

The kauri (*A. australis*) of New Zealand is one of the world's largest and most beautiful trees. Its juvenile leaves are opposite, linear-oblong, and up to 2½in (6.5cm) long. The adult leaves are elliptic to broadly oblong, sessile, and ½in to 1½in (1.3–3.8cm) long.

### Practical Uses

The canoes, meeting houses and shrines of the Maori were traditionally made of kauri wood. The resin of this tree, the "gum", was much sought after – the hardened resin was burnt and provided the dye for ceremonial tattoos.

Sadly, during the last 150 years the ancient and majestic kauri forests of New Zealand's North Island have been reduced from an estimated four million acres (1.6 million hectares) to barely 18,420 acres (7,455 hectares).

---

**Symbolism:** a sacred relationship

**Astrological Association:** Saturn, Moon

**Divine Association:** Tane Mahuta, Lord of the Forest (Maori)

**Historical Spotlight:** When Captain Cook "discovered" New Zealand in 1769, he noted enthusiastically, "The banks of the river were completely clothed with the finest timber my eyes have ever seen ... "

---

### Culture, Myth and Symbol

The indigenous people of New Zealand, the Maoris, believe that everything in the natural world, such as trees, animals, birds, insects, and stones, possesses a spirit. At the beginning of time, heaven and earth were one, and among their children was Tane Mahuta, the Supreme Being and Lord of the Forest. When heaven and earth separated, he offered to serve as a column to keep them apart and in balance.

In the forest Maoris consider themselves to be among relatives, because they believe that humans and trees are both descendants of Tane. Whenever the younger branch of the family (the humans) have to slay a member of the older branch (a tree) to obtain timber for the building of houses or boats, solemn ceremonies have to be performed. Before this the *tohunga* – the wise men or priests – take into account the phase of the moon and the spirits of the forest.

An ancient Maori myth expresses the intimate relationship of the kauri with another creature that is essential to Maori life – the whale. From its place inside the forest, the tall kauri tree observed and admired the whale in the sea. One day, the whale swam to the shore and the giants met and made friends. Each wanted to be with the other but neither of them could leave their own world. So the two found another way of expressing their friendship: the whale took off its gray skin and gave it to the kauri; and the kauri took off its skin (the bark) and gave it to the whale.

*OPPOSITE: "Tane Mahuta" in Waipoua Forest, North Island, New Zealand, is the largest living kauri with a height of 169ft (51m) and a girth of 45ft (13.8m). It is thought to be 2,000 years old. A kauri twice as old and three times larger was destroyed by fire in the 1880s.*

OPPOSITE: *Veteran alders acquire great character and this unusual specimen – with its massive, wide bole – at Sheepscombe in Gloucestershire, England, is one of the oldest alder trees in Europe.*

# Alder *Alnus*

A genus of about 35 species, *Alnus* consists of deciduous, monoecious trees and shrubs that grow mainly in northern temperate regions. The male catkins are long and drooping, the females short, later turning into woody cones. The common alder (*A. glutinosa*) is widely found near lakes and rivers and in wetlands. The bark of the young tree is smooth and greenish brown, later turning a very dark brown or gray and becoming deeply fissured. The empty cones often stay on the tree throughout winter, while the seeds fly off or float away on water, for which they are equipped with tiny airbags.

## Practical Uses

Protein-rich alder wood is attractive to woodworm and hence not used much in building. But under water it comes into its own, being most durable when constantly wet. Many river- or lakeside buildings and bridges have foundations made from alder poles. Traditionally, this wood was also used for water pipes, pumps and sluices, and charcoal.

## Natural Healing

In European herbal medicine, it was customary for country people to use alder bark to treat inflammations, rheumatism and diarrhea. Bags filled with heated alder leaves were known to help with chronic skin diseases, while the leaves and bark were used to make a gargle to cure mouth ulcers. The tree essence is invigorating, and it also reduces nervousness and anxiety.

## Culture, Myth and Symbol

In Greek tradition, the alder is sacred to Phoroneus, the inventor of fire. In German tradition we meet the Alder Woman under various names – *Else*, *Elsa*, *Elise* are all forms of Anglo-Saxon *alor* and Gothic *alisa*, meaning "alder". She appears first as a seductive woman, but then teaches all-too-lustful males a lesson by changing into a hairy or bark-like creature. In the *Wulfdietrich Saga* she is a wild-looking woman called "Rough Else". She enchants the hero who goes mad (like Merlin in Welsh tradition), and lives for six months in the forest, feeding on herbs. Then, she takes him on a boat to another land where she is queen. She bathes herself in a magical well, which changes her into the most beautiful woman imaginable. In her new guise she is called Sigeminne, which means "Victory of Love".

The Alder Woman's tale is reminiscent of that of the ancient Celtic goddess who marries a mortal king. She is the spirit of the surrounding land. This connection with the land also appears in the alder's Greek name, *klethra*, which comes from *kleio*, meaning "I embrace, I surround".

According to Welsh myth, King Bran (meaning "Raven") was forced to go to war against Ireland to rescue his sister Branwen. Mortally wounded, he instructed his loyal followers to cut off his head, which then sang and uttered prophecies. After seven years the head was buried at the site on which the Tower of London was subsequently built, and this is said to explain why there are ravens resident there.

---

**Symbolism**: Release

**Divine Associations**: Bran (Welsh), Phoroneus (Greek)

**Astrological Association**: Neptune

# Almond *Amygdalus*

The genus *Amygdalus* comprises about 40 species, mainly confined to southwestern and central Asia. About 15 species occur throughout Iran, and there are two bitter-seeded and one sweet-seeded species found in Israel. The latter (*A. communis*) is the almond that features so strongly in Jewish tradition. It is a wild, deciduous, medium-sized tree with oblong, lanceolate leaves, flowering from mid-February to mid-March. The abundance of snow-white blossom appears mainly before the leaves. The bell-shaped flowers are pollinated by bees.

Commercial nut production employs a cultivar, the common almond (*Prunus amygdalus, P. dulcis, P. communis*), a small tree with lanceolate, long-pointed, finely-toothed leaves. The pink flowers are borne singly, or in pairs, in March and April and measure 1–2in (2.5–5cm) across.

The soft husk of the fruit encloses a hard shell that protects the kernel – the actual almond. It is covered by a brown seed coat which contains antioxidants to prevent the nut from turning rancid.

## Practical Uses

Sweet almonds (*P. amygdalus dulcis*) have an oval, flattened or roundish shape and a sweet flavour. They are eaten raw or roasted, on their own or in pastries, cakes, confectionery and marzipan.

Bitter almonds (*P. amygdalus amara*) are smaller and more pointed in shape, and have a bitter, astringent taste. They contain two to four percent of the glycoside amygdalin,

RIGHT: *Almonds and lavender are traditional products in Provence – this tree on the edge of a lavender field is on the Valensole Plateau.*

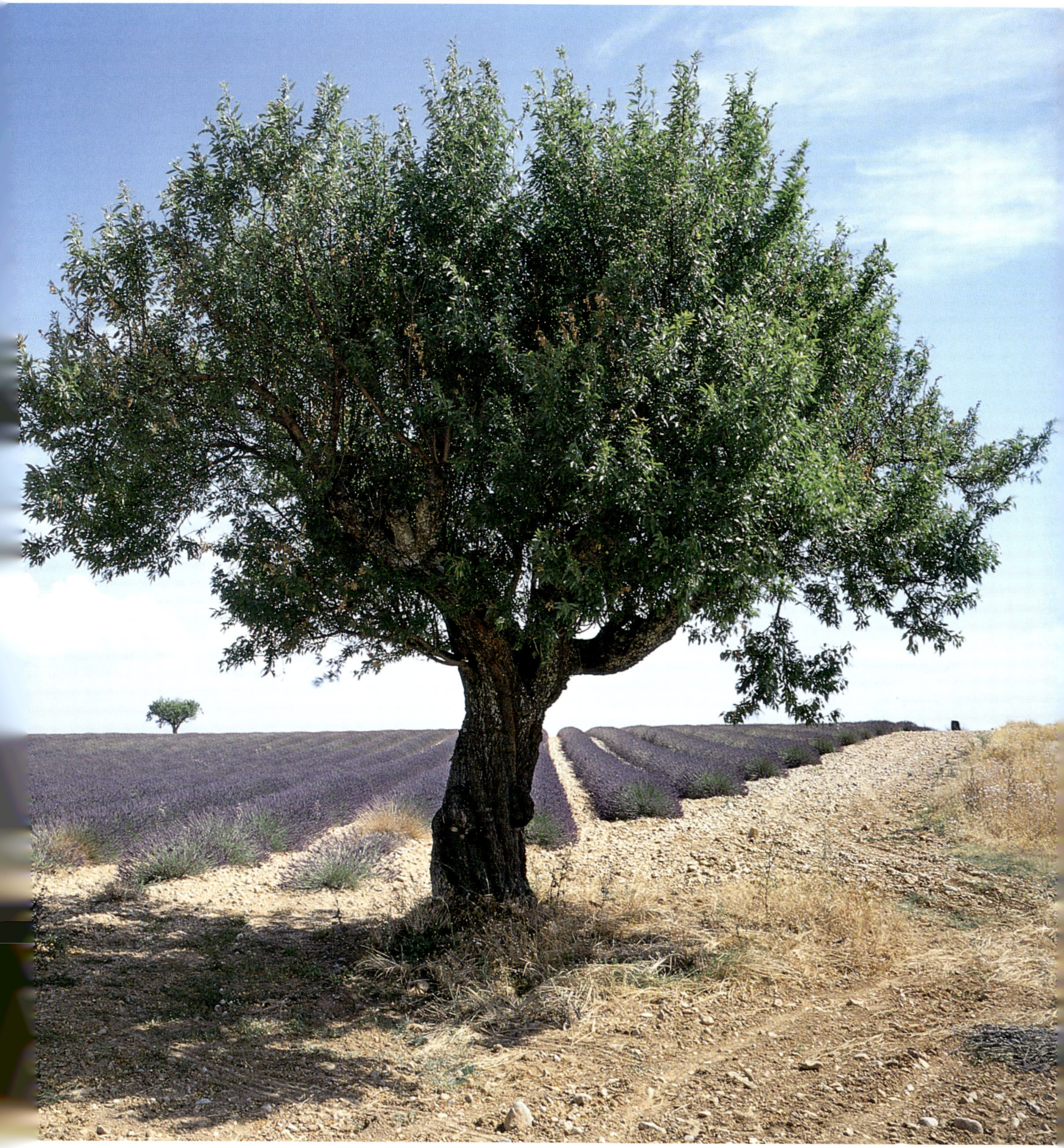

RIGHT: *Almond trees are grown across southern Europe and in Morocco, Israel, Iran, China, Australia, Argentina and the USA (California). The fruits yielded are high in monounsaturated fat.*

which releases harmful prussic acid when eaten by humans. Seven to ten bitter almonds eaten raw can cause severe problems in adults and could be fatal to children. Boiling or baking the nuts destroys most of the harmful acid. However, it is from bitter almonds that most almond oil is extracted.

## Natural Healing

Almond oil is one of the most important cosmetics oils, as it softens, smoothes and nourishes the skin. Nutritionally, sweet almonds are a good source of potassium, calcium, magnesium, vitamin E and protein.

In ayurvedic medicine the nuts are viewed as a balancing food: ten peeled almonds eaten daily will help to settle the body's energy system. The protein content aids in the stabilizing of blood sugar levels, while the potassium, magnesium and calcium strengthen the nervous system and provide energy.

## Culture, Myth and Symbol

From the beginning of civilization, the white-blossoming almond heralded spring and provided an emblem of the archetypal White Goddess. Its archaic Semitic name, *amygdala*, can be traced back to the Sumerian *ama ga*, which means the Great Mother.

For the ancient Phrygians, too, the almond was the parent of all things on earth. In their creation myths, Agditis, a hermaphrodite monster, appeared and terrified the gods. They castrated it and turned it into the Great Mother, Cybele, causing the original unity of opposites – male and female – to disappear from creation. But from the spilled blood rose two trees, an almond and a pomegranate. Many cycles later, Attis, the divine child of the goddess Cybele, was magically conceived by the daughter of a river spirit as she ate an almond or a pomegranate seed. Such ancient tales illustrate how much the almond reverberates with the primeval forces of creation.

Among the tribes of Israel, the almond was originally conceived as a Tree of Life. Moses' (and Aaron's) staff was of almond (Numbers 17:8) and was described as the "rod of God" (Exodus 17:9). It was said to have been handed down from Adam via Abraham, Isaac and Jacob to Joseph who took it to Egypt where Moses obtained it. That Moses should bear the almond of the Great Mother is ironic, because in the Old Testament he is instructed to destroy the ancient cult

# ALMOND

**RIGHT**: *The delicous kernel, the actual "almond", is protected in a hard shell, which in turn is housed in a soft but inedible husk.*

of the Goddess (Exodus 22:1 and 34:13). However, his staff became the sceptre of the kings of Israel for many generations. Much later, the "shepherd staffs" of Christian patriarchs followed this tradition. And even today the Pope carries a crosier. The irony returns when we remember that in the first millennium or so of Christianity, many people were accused of heresy for carrying pieces of "pagan" sacred wood, such as talismans. The staff, like the magician's wand, is obviously an instrument of power, for its carrier can claim some form of divine justification for his rulership.

However, the true symbolism of almond has nothing to do with power or rulership, but with the divine light that embraces us all equally. This is demonstrated in the other of the almond's ancient names, *luz*, which in Aramaic means "light". It is also the name of the mythical City of Almond of the Canaanites (who worshipped the goddess Astarte). Judaism adopted these traditions. Jacob slept at Luz, an almond sanctuary in Canaan, where the Lord appeared to him (Genesis 28:11–19). In Judaism, the divine light that shines mystically from the almond came to be celebrated in the Tree of Light. In ritual, this is the *menorah*, the candlestick which has a light for each of the seven planets. The menorah in Solomon's Temple at Jerusalem had almond-shaped sconces to represent Aaron's rod when it broke out in buds. And in rabbinic legend, the mystical quality of the almond is even more refined. We hear of a paradise city whose only entrance can be found in "a hole in an almond tree". In that place, "the angel of death has no power".

In Aramaic the word *luz* means both the almond tree and the vertebra at the end of the spinal column – the coccyx. The notion that this part of the body serves as the nucleus for life overcoming death has a direct parallel in the Djed-pillar of Osiris in ancient Egypt. And, of course, this also makes sense in the light of the teachings of Kundalini yoga, as well as in Taoist practice, which both describe an energy gate at the base of the spine where the life force or kundalini enters the physical body.

In the Old Testament (Jeremiah 1:11), the Hebrew for almond, *shaqed*, is linked in a word game with *shoqed*, "to watch over". This connects the almond, the tree of divine light, with the omnipresence of the divine.

**Symbolism:** Purity and perfection

**Divine Association:** the White Goddess, Cybele (Phrygian), Astarte (Phoenician)

**Astrological Associations:** Venus, Mars and Mercury

**Historical Spotlight:** Almond sanctuaries were common in ancient Israel and Judea, until the religious reforms of King Josiah in 621BCE. He focused all religious life on the Temple to withstand the infiltration of the Assyrian invaders.

OPPOSITE: *The volcanic slopes of the Andes, on the borders of Chile and Argentina, are the true home of the monkey-puzzle tree.*

# Monkey-puzzle *Araucaria araucana*

The genus *Araucaria* comprises about 15 species of tall, evergreen, coniferous and usually dioecious trees, native to the southern hemisphere. Old trees usually have flat heads above rather bare trunks. Juvenile leaves may differ from adult ones in size, shape and arrangement. The large and woody female cones house the winged seeds, one to each scale, which take two to three years to mature.

The monkey-puzzle tree or Chilean pine (*A. araucana*) has closely overlapping, leathery, sharp-pointed leaves 1–2in (2.5–5cm) long. The erect male cones are large but still outsized by the female ones which measure 4–7in (10–17.5cm) in height and 3–5in (7.5–12.5cm) in diameter.

## Practical Uses

Originally an important food source for native people, the monkey-puzzle became the most important coniferous timber tree in Chile. Over-exploitation catapulted the Chilean and Argentinian trees into the World List of Threatened Trees, and trade in Chilean monkey-puzzle timber is now banned according to the Convention of International Trade in Endangered Species. During the 1980s, the indigenous people fought to save the trees, but when the Chilean government conceded to this pressure, it not only limited access for the logging companies but also restricted the native peoples' rights to collect the seeds for food.

## Natural Healing

The indigenous people remove the outer skin of the nutritious seeds and eat them boiled or roasted. The seeds taste similar to sweet chestnuts. They are also ground into a flour for making bread, or producing a nutritious drink. The resin is used in various external and internal medicines.

## Culture, Myth and Symbol

Around 190 million years ago the monkey-puzzle was a dominant species in the southern hemisphere, but today it only grows in a small area. One tribal group in south-central Chile, the Pehuenche, have a special relationship with the trees, even calling themselves after them (*pehuen*, monkey-puzzle; *che*, people). Every late summer and early autumn they live as food-gatherers in the high volcanic forests where they collect monkey-puzzle seeds, both to eat and to store. They burn dead wood but never fell a living tree.

To the Pehuenche, the monkey-puzzle is a sacred tree. They regard the female trees as "mothers" and the monkey-puzzle forest as part of their extended family. The male tree, *domopehuen*, and the female tree, *wentrupehuen*, are believed to reproduce through their extensive root systems. Their deities, Pehuencha and Pehuenkuze, live in the forest. A special ceremony held at the summer solstice includes prayers and dances around a monkey-puzzle tree, which is seen as a bridge between the earth and the spirit world.

---

**Symbolism:** Care

**Divine Associations:** Pehuencha and Pehuenkuze (native Chilean)

**Astrological Associations:** Saturn and Mars

**Historical Spotlight:** Early European observers apparently wondered how a monkey could climb the sharp spikes of the trunk and branches. However, there are no monkeys in the forests of Chile.

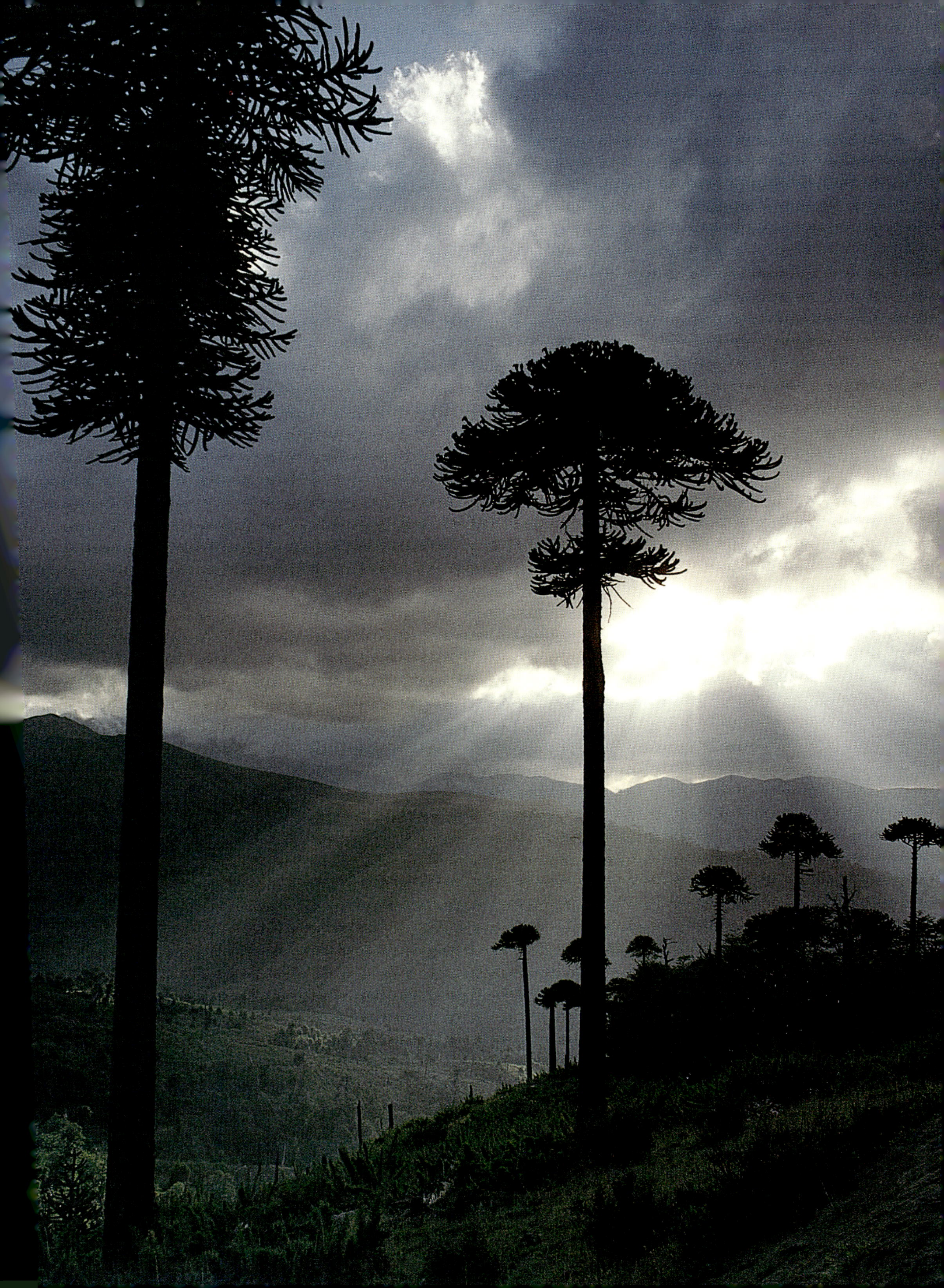

OPPOSITE: *Birch trees such as these at Aberfeldy in Perthshire, Scotland, were immortalized in 1787 by the poet Robert Burns (1759–96) in his poem "The Birks of Aberfeldie".*

# Birch *Betula*

Birches comprise about 60 species of deciduous, monoecious trees and shrubs of the northern temperate regions. They thrive on most soils, whether damp or dry, but need plenty of light. The male catkins are pendulous and elongate in spring; the female catkins are shorter and erect. The birches are some of the most graceful and attractive trees because they have a slender shape, bright bark and their leaves turn yellow in autumn.

The common silver birch (*B. pendula*) is a medium-sized, white-stemmed tree that thrives in drier soils than the common white birch (*B. pubescens* or *B. alba*), from which it is distinguished by its rough, warty shoots and diamond-shaped leaves. The white birch, which is less pendulous in shape, has rounder leaves and smooth downy shoots. Old silver birches develop a rough black bark at the base, while old specimens of the white birch retain their white bark.

## Practical Uses

Everywhere in the boreal and temperate forests, birch has been a welcome contributor to human life. The indigenous peoples of North America, Russia, Siberia, northern Europe and Scandinavia have used the durable bark to make a whole array of items essential to life, including boats and canoes, coverings for wigwams and *yurts*, roof tiles for houses, all sorts of containers, writing paper and even shoes.

## Natural Healing

In Russian and Scandinavian tradition, birch twigs are used to "beat" the body during a sauna, which is an old method to stimulate circulation and increase the vitality of the skin. Similarly, birch is used in Native North American sweat-lodge cleansing ceremonies, by tribes such as the Ojibwa who also cover their tipi floors with birch boughs.

Tea from the young leaves or leaf buds stimulates the gall bladder, kidneys and liver, and can be drunk over three weeks as a spring "detox". The leaves are collected in April

LEFT: *A rare surviving fragment of ancient deciduous birch forest at Glen Finglass, Scotland.*

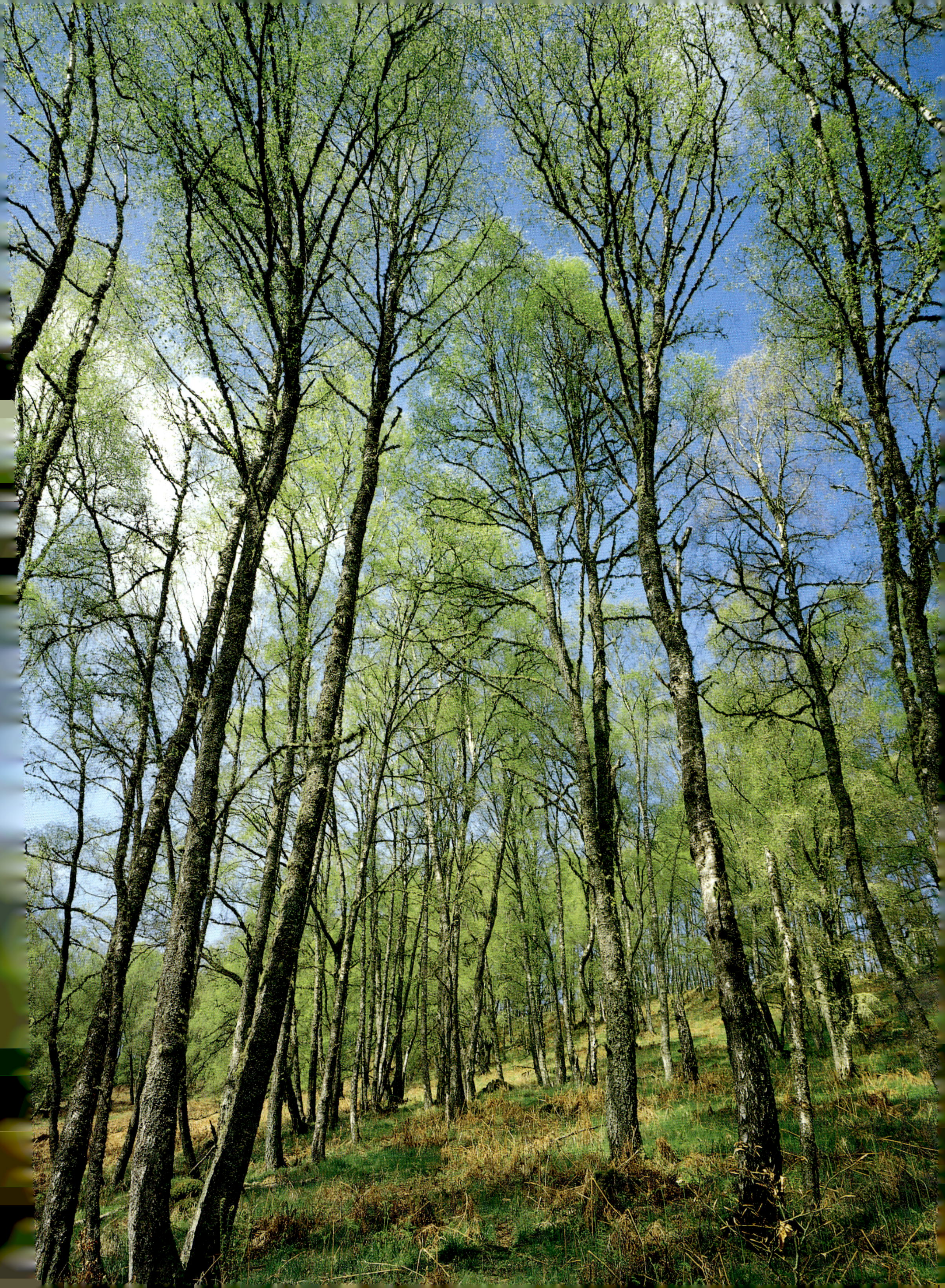

**BELOW**: *A young birch at Lake Siljan, Sweden. Traditional sauna users relax their muscles by gently beating them with boughs of silver birch.*

or May and then dried. Birch leaves also help to relieve the symptoms of gout and rheumatism. The blood-cleansing sap is a general tonic for the whole metabolism. Externally, birch tar oil has been used to treat eczema and psoriasis, and the sap makes an excellent scalp tonic. The young leaves provide a healthy addition to fresh salads.

In classical homeopathy, birch has the same effect that the living tree has in the sombre northern landscape – it brings light to darkness. The tree essence of silver birch enhances the ability to experience beauty and remain calm.

## Culture, Myth and Symbol

Named after the whiteness of its bark, the birch shares its name with the ancient Irish goddess Brigid, both names deriving from the Indo-European word *bher(e)g*, "shining white". Brigid was a benevolent deity, a muse to poets and the patron of crafts, particularly spinning and weaving.

In Norse and Germanic tradition the birch is associated with Freya, the Lady of the Forest, and Frigga, the wife of Odin (who was originally a wind god). In Russian folklore, the birch itself is called Lady of the Forest. The nourishing, caring birch is an image of the White Goddess, and the Germanic rune Berkana, "birch", stands for motherhood, bosom and protection. Furthermore, the actual shape of the rune, which is echoed in our capital letter "B", is derived from the "mother mounds" of the Neolithic. These hills were mostly burial mounds and ceremonial places where the mysteries of death and rebirth were celebrated. Twin hills symbolized the breasts of the Earth Mother. Birth, life and death were all under the dominion of this goddess, and these three aspects of life have created a rich diversity of female deities in different cultures: goddesses of birth and youth, goddesses of mature womanhood, and goddesses of death and winter. During the Bronze Age they took their individual shapes – as did the cultures in which they are worshipped – but they all point back to the ancient Great Goddess of the Paleolithic era who unites all three aspects (and hence is also referred to as the Triple Goddess). Her colours are white, which symbolizes the moon and mothers' milk; red, which represents blood; and black, which depicts the night of the new moon.

There is another aspect to her, too. In early history we meet various manifestations of the battle goddess. However, as the invincible protectoress, she is a defender rather than an attacker. This facet of her is really a part of the maturity phase. Over time, as patriarchal societies prevailed and the social role of woman shrank, there was no longer any room for the wild, unpredictable, dangerous or ecstatic aspects of femininity.

However, vestiges remained in spring and fertility rites. Throughout the Christian Middle Ages, country folk would pair off to the birch groves at the May celebrations. In Scotland, adults were even released from their marriage vows for the one day of Beltane. This practice outraged the Church, so the people simply turned it around: if they were not allowed to go to the birches, they would bring the trees into the villages, and the maypole was created. Carefully chosen and festively adorned, it became the focal point for festivities and merry-making. And many children were born in early February.

**Symbolism:** Renewal and protection

**Divine Associations:** the White Goddess, Brigid (Celtic); Freya and Frigga (Norse); Venus (Roman)

**Astrological Association:** Venus

**Historical Spotlight:** In 1893, the British intelligence officer Captain H. Bower brought back from Turkestan one of the world's oldest birch bark manuscripts, dating from c.350CE.

In the wild, the birch is one of the first trees to colonize new land and prepare the soil for the coming of the forest. This pioneering quality is reflected in its cultural associations. The first versions of the ancient Indian wisdom teachings, the *Vedas*, or "leaves" (of the Tree of Knowledge), were written on birch bark.

According to Irish legend, when the god Ogma brought the magical gift of writing to the early Celts, they learned that *ogam*, the tree alphabet, was first used to warn the sun god Lugh that his wife was about to be captured and taken to the underworld, "… unless she is guarded by birch." Protection again. And in western European tradition, cradles are made from birch wood to protect babies from malignant

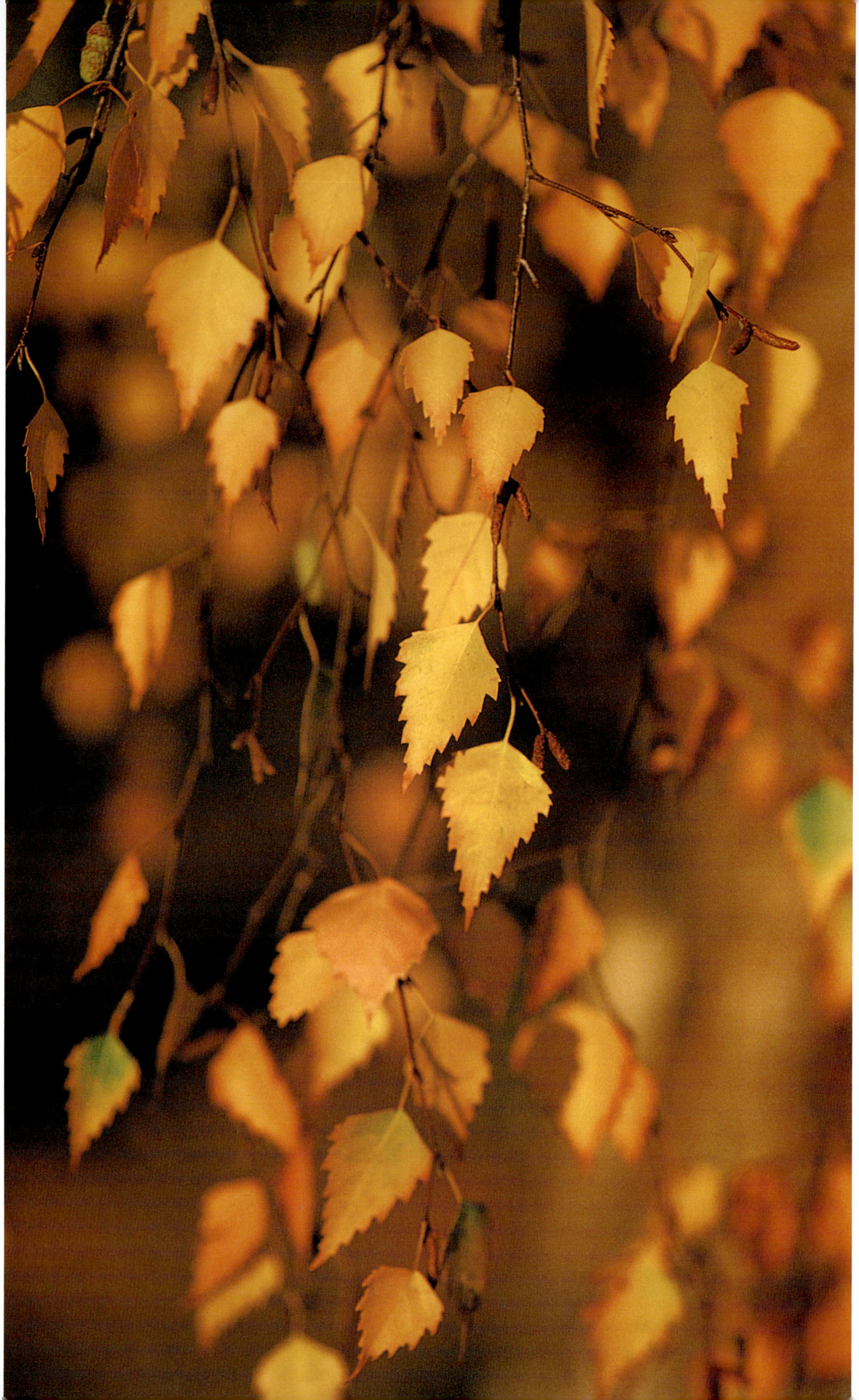

BIRCH 45

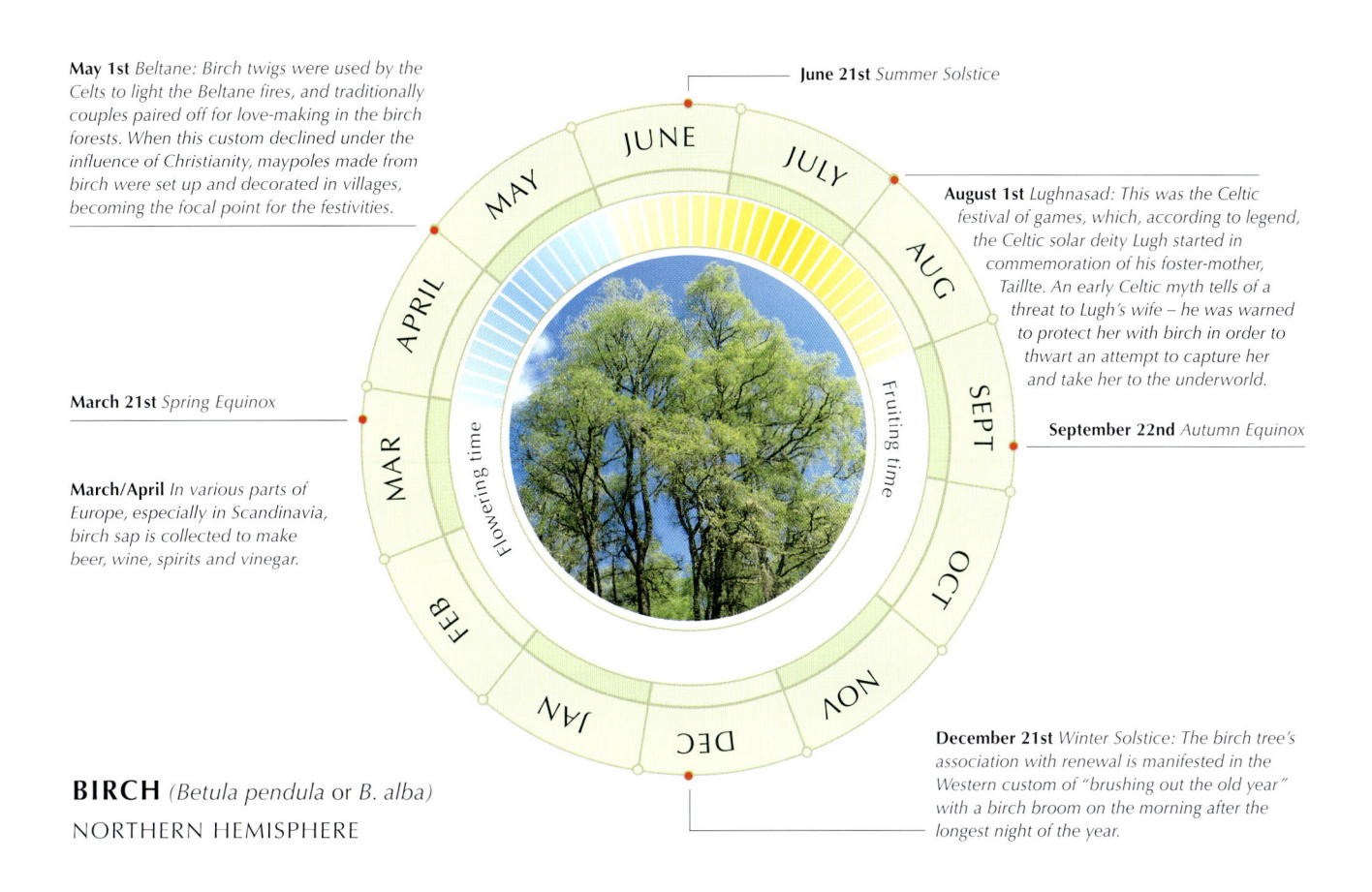

**May 1st** *Beltane:* Birch twigs were used by the Celts to light the Beltane fires, and traditionally couples paired off for love-making in the birch forests. When this custom declined under the influence of Christianity, maypoles made from birch were set up and decorated in villages, becoming the focal point for the festivities.

**March 21st** *Spring Equinox*

**March/April** *In various parts of Europe, especially in Scandinavia, birch sap is collected to make beer, wine, spirits and vinegar.*

**BIRCH** *(Betula pendula* or *B. alba)*
NORTHERN HEMISPHERE

**June 21st** *Summer Solstice*

**August 1st** *Lughnasad:* This was the Celtic festival of games, which, according to legend, the Celtic solar deity Lugh started in commemoration of his foster-mother, Taillte. An early Celtic myth tells of a threat to Lugh's wife – he was warned to protect her with birch in order to thwart an attempt to capture her and take her to the underworld.

**September 22nd** *Autumn Equinox*

**December 21st** *Winter Solstice:* The birch tree's association with renewal is manifested in the Western custom of "brushing out the old year" with a birch broom on the morning after the longest night of the year.

---

forces. The tale of Lugh indicates that the power of the birch tree is stronger than the power of the underworld (death), which will come as no surprise to those who know that rebirth has always been the great gift of the White Goddess.

The full spiritual strength of the birch shines through in Siberian shamanism. Here it is *udesi-burchan*, the "deity of the door" to the spirit world. A birch tree is ceremonially chosen in the forest and brought into a special *yurt* (a tent covered in skins, used by nomadic tribes). Nine notches are carved into it (nine is the number of the Earth Mother) before it is erected as the central pole. In trance the shaman climbs to the top of the pole while his or her spirit journeys up the World Tree to the heavens or down to the underworld. He or she will seek answers from guiding spirits or ancestors, or ask the astral entities of a disease to leave his or her patient. (We will meet the number nine and the World Tree again with Odin and the yew tree: see pp.198–205.)

The aspect of renewal in birch traditions is also emphasized in the Western custom of "brushing out the old year" with a birch broom. This is performed on the morning after the longest night of the winter solstice (December 21 in the northern hemisphere), which marks the true beginning of the new year. This time symbolizes the darkness of the womb, or the dark earth surrounding the seed. The Anglo-Saxons, however, celebrated three "mother nights", or *modraneht*, which brings the rebirth of the sun and the beginning of the new solar year to December 24.

**OPPOSITE**: *The small leaves of the birch produce a soft and pleasant rustle as the tree sways gracefully in the breeze.*

# Hornbeam *Carpinus*

The hornbeams are beautiful trees which thrive easily on clay or chalky soils. They are widely distributed in the northern temperate regions but the majority of the 30-plus species are native to China. The common hornbeam (*C. betulus*) is native to Europe and Asia Minor. It is a medium- to large-sized tree with a characteristic gray, fluted trunk and ovate, serrate, ribbed leaves. It occurs singly, or in hedges where it resembles beech – but grows more slowly. However, the hornbeam is not related to the beech but rather to the hazel, both genera being members of the hazel family (*Corylaceae*).

## Practical Uses

The charcoal of this slow-growing, dense wood burns hot enough to smelt iron. Hornbeam wood is of excellent quality, but so hard that it quickly blunts carpenters' tools, hence its other name – "ironwood". Its durable wood has been the perfect choice for windmill and watermill cogs. Further uses include axles for carts, corn-threshing tools, yokes for farm animals, billiard cues, drumsticks and piano hammers.

---

**Symbolism**: Guardianship

**Divine Association**: Heimdall (Norse)

**Astrological Association**: Saturn

**Historical Spotlight**: The central screws for cider and olive-oil vats, and linen and printing presses, were made from hornbeam wood – that is, until a craftsman from Nuremberg introduced metal screws in *c.*1550. However, it still took about three centuries for the metal screws to catch on.

---

In the USA, among the Chippewa tribe, hornbeam is the traditional wood used for the main supporting posts of the wigwam ridge pole (the wigwam of the woodland tribes is smaller than a tipi, and is covered with tree bark – such as birch – or small hides, rather than buffalo skins).

## Natural Healing

The Tsalagi (Cherokee) used the astringent inner bark of the American hornbeam (*C. caroliniana*) to treat discharges and urinary problems. In Europe, hornbeam leaves have been used traditionally to treat wounds, and distilled water from the leaves, as an eye lotion. The Bach Flower Remedy of the hornbeam counteracts the feeling of being overwhelmed with the day's work. The tree essence clears blocked or stagnant energies and enhances clarity of purpose.

## Culture, Myth and Symbol

The hornbeam is a wonderful tree for hedges, slow-growing but dense once it has established itself. Such hedges once grew around sacred groves north of the Alps. Hornbeam's ancient Germanic name, *hagebuche*, is derived from *hagal*, the all-encompassing World Tree. And the Latin name of the hornbeam, *Carpinus*, is said to derive from the Celtic *carr* (wood), which takes us back to Car, Q'er and Carya, the ancient eastern Mediterranean goddess of wisdom.

The hornbeam guarded the sanctity of the sacred grove, and in this humble service it is akin to Heimdall, the mythical guardian of the rainbow bridge in Norse myth. No god or human speaks much of Heimdall, but without him the gods' abode would have been destroyed by the giants long ago.

---

OPPOSITE, ABOVE: *Autumnal hornbeams in Coldfall Wood, north London. Hornbeam wood was a staple of traditional coppicing.*

OPPOSITE, BELOW: *The rich foliage of hornbeam in full splendour.*

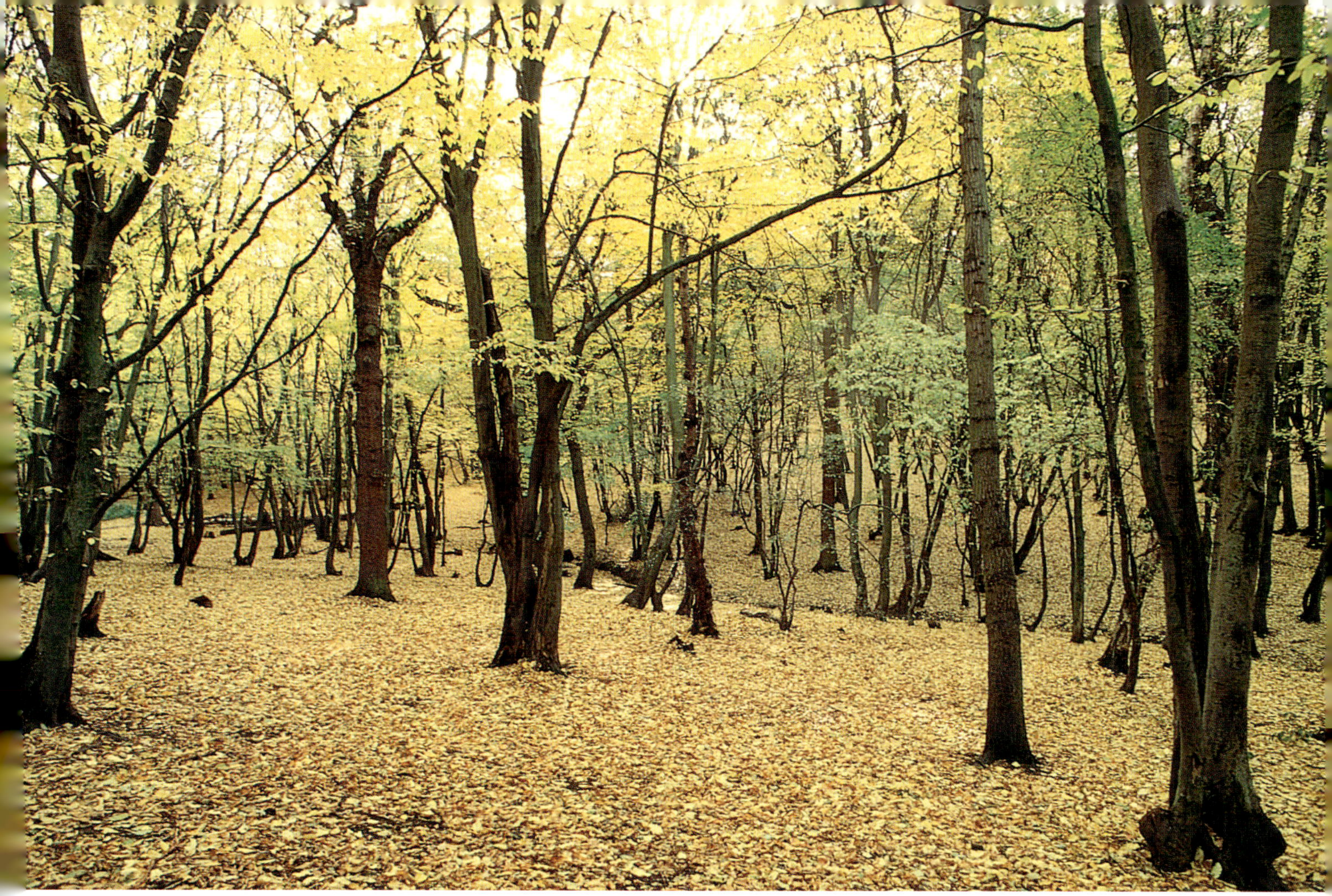
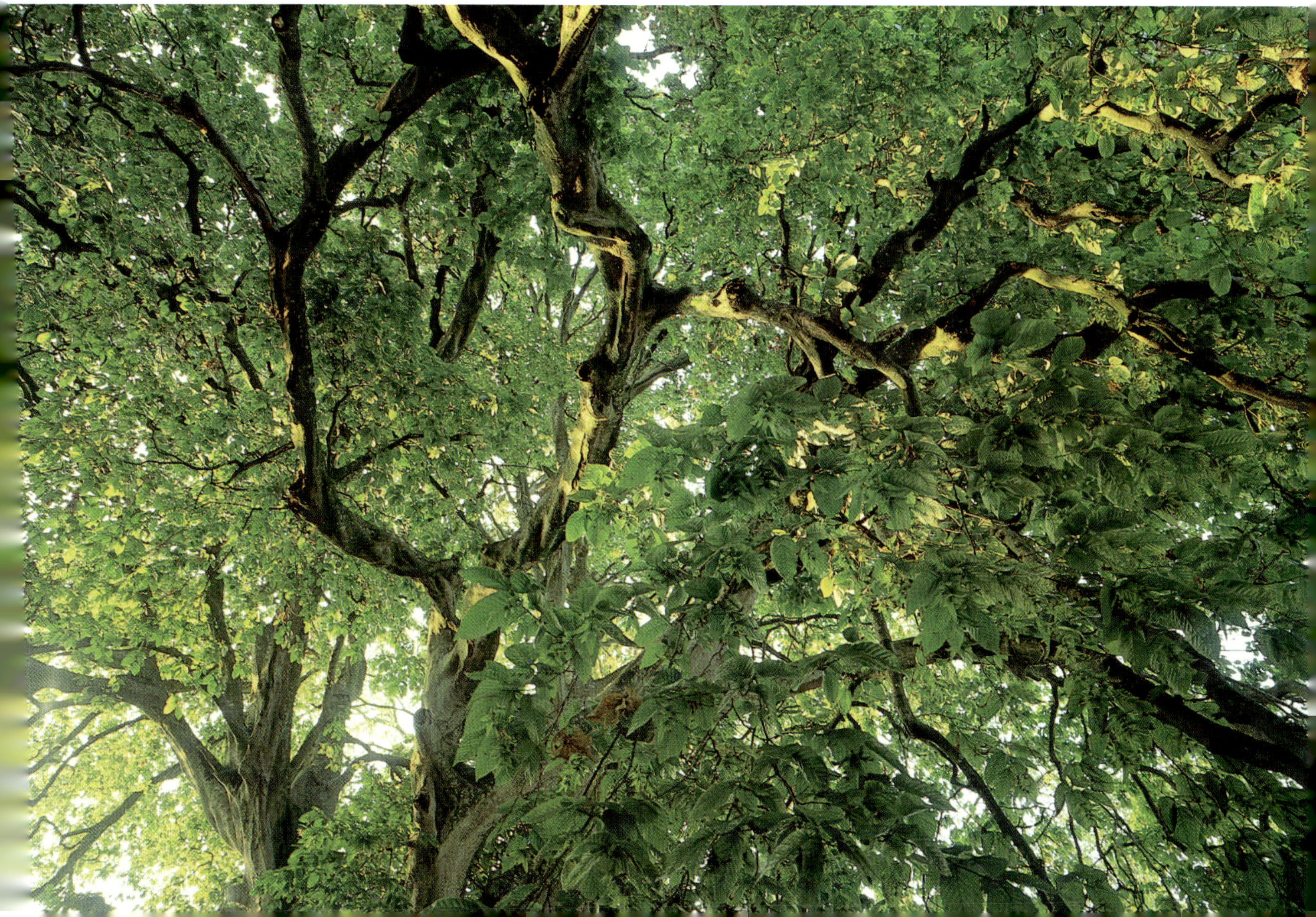

RIGHT: *Sweet chestnut trees can become incredibly stout over time, as this example shows. What might appear to be several trees in close proximity can often be found to share a common root.*

# Sweet chestnut *Castanea sativa*

The chestnuts (*Castanea*) are a genus of about 12 species of deciduous trees and shrubs in the temperate northern hemisphere. All have sharply serrate leaves. The small, yellowish, unisexual flowers are borne on long catkins.

Chestnuts are long-lived, drought-resistant trees that prefer lighter soils. The fast-growing sweet or Spanish chestnut (*C. sativa*) is a native of southern Europe, northern Africa and Asia Minor. Its appearance is particularly ornamental during July, when it is laden with yellowish-green male and female catkins. It is widely cultivated for its nuts, and is naturalized in the warmer parts of the British Isles, such as southern England, where it is believed to have been introduced by the Romans.

## Practical Uses

The Tsalagi (Cherokee) and Iroquois tribes used the nutmeat of the American chestnut (*C. dentata*) in a wide array of dishes, such as cakes, breads, gravies, soups and drinks. In the agricultural areas of central Europe, the twigs were cut for fodder for cattle and sheep. The tree responds well to

ABOVE: *In autumn the nuts fall to the ground and the leaves of the sweet chestnut turn a glorious golden brown.*

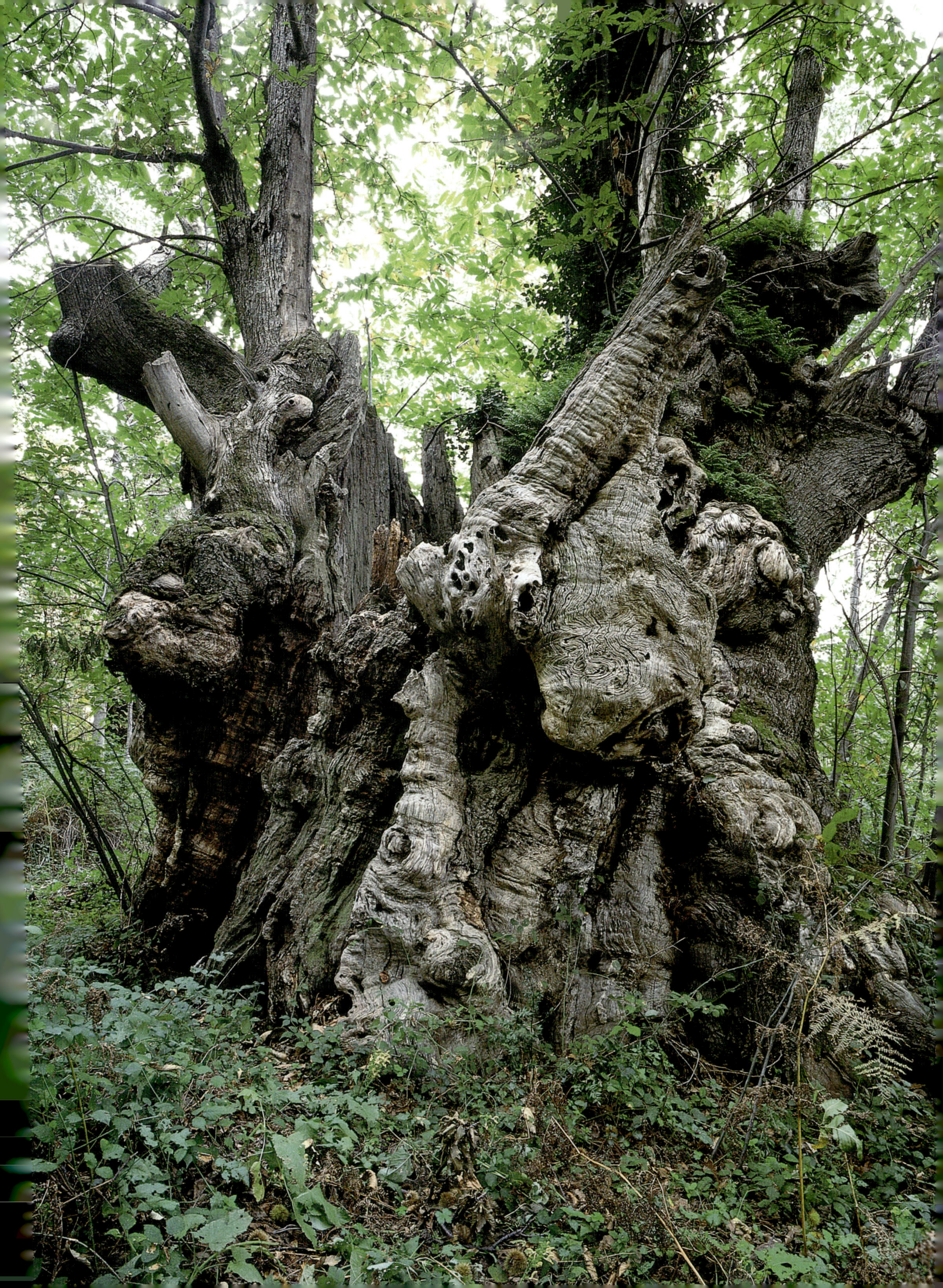

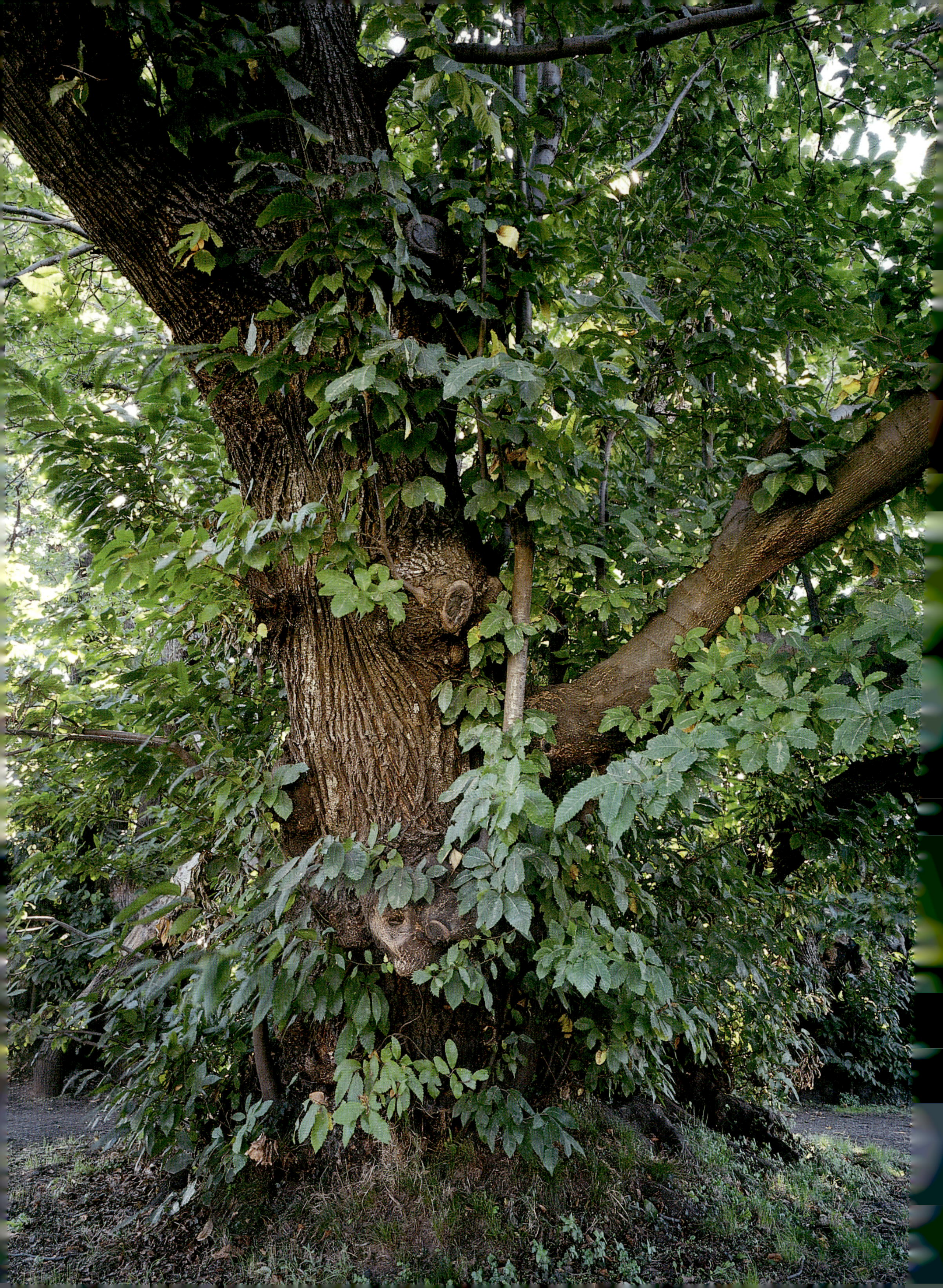

# SWEET CHESTNUT

**OPPOSITE**: *A leaf-clad breakaway limb of Sicily's most famous sweet chestnut, the Castagno dei Cento Cavalli (see box, below right).*

this form of pruning and will grow even more nuts in subsequent years. The wood is of good quality and durable, but the chestnut was rarely grown for timber, because countries where the chestnut grows are naturally rich in oak too.

Sweet chestnut leaves have a long history as a wrapping material for foods, and they regulate the ripening process for soft cheeses.

## Natural Healing

Chestnuts are rich in complex carbohydrates and starch but contain considerably less fat than other nuts, so they are easily digestible. Roasted chestnuts can be incorporated into a variety of dishes, but they can also be ground to a flour and used in bread-making or to make a coffee-like drink. They are rich in vitamins B and C, and minerals such as potassium, calcium, magnesium, phosphorus and iron. The leaves can also be eaten in spring salads, or pickled as an ingredient in potato salad.

Sweet chestnut leaf infusions have been used traditionally for their cough-relieving and antispasmodic effects on whooping cough and bronchitis. The leaves' astringent and antibacterial action makes them useful for treating wounds.

The Bach Flower Remedy is recommended for anguish, despondency and despair. The tree essence helps us to focus and ground ourselves. It also supports the ability to gain a wider perspective on issues.

## Culture, Myth and Symbol

The ancient Greeks revered the sweet chestnut and dedicated it to Zeus. Its name, *castanea*, comes from Castanis, a town in Thessaly (Greece) which cultivated this tree

**ABOVE**: *The sweet chestnut's serrated leaves and its spiky seed husk.*

extensively. However, its ancient Greek name was *Sardis glans* (Sardis acorn), after the capital of Lydia (now in eastern Turkey) where it had come from. Later, in Greece, chestnuts were also called the "acorns of Zeus", as were walnuts.

In Christian symbolism, the sweet chestnut represents goodness, chastity and triumph over temptation. A popular practice in France is to place images of saints in sweet chestnut trees. And in ancient China, these trees were the home of the earth gods of the west.

---

**Symbolism**: Incarnation and nourishment

**Divine Association**: Earth deities

**Astrological Association**: Earth

**Historical Spotlight**: During a storm in 1308, Queen Joan of Aragon and her escort of 100 cavaliers found shelter underneath a colossal sweet chestnut tree in Sicily. By 1770 this tree had grown even more, its recorded girth being about 204ft (68m). Named the Castagno dei Cento Cavalli (Tree of One Hundred Horses), sections are still standing today, even though the tree is now well over 2,000 years old.

# Cedar *Cedrus*

The cedars are large, coniferous, evergreen trees with stiff, needle-shaped leaves borne in clusters. The male cones are ovoid and erect; the female cones are small and have closely overlapping scales, with two winged seeds to a scale. They mature in two to three years. There are only four species of true cedars.

The Atlas cedar (*C. atlantica*) grows to 100ft (30m) or more in height and is native to North Africa. It is distinguishable by its bluish-green leaves which are less than 1in (2.5cm) long. The cones are up to 3in (7.5cm) long. *C. brevifolia* is confined to Cyprus and has shorter cones. The deodar (*C. deodara*), native to the Himalayas, grows up to 150ft (45m) and has drooping branchlets. Its leaves measure up to 2in (5cm) and the cones 5in (12.5cm). The cedar of Lebanon (*C. libani*), which is native to Asia Minor, can reach a stately 100ft (30m) in dense forest, but single trees do not grow as high – instead they have much wider branches and, typically, horizontally-layered crowns. The leaves are about 1in (2.5cm) long and dark or bright green. The cones are up to 4in (10cm) long.

The largest Atlas cedars and deodars have verifiably reached 600 years, but might be older. The most ancient cedars of Lebanon may be 1,000 years of age.

## Practical Uses

Cedar wood has been one of the most sought-after timbers since time immemorial. In antiquity, the best and largest reserves were to be found in the mountain ranges of

**RIGHT**: *For 5,000 years, the cedars of Lebanon have been celebrated – the Lebanese call the best of them "the cedars of the Lord".*

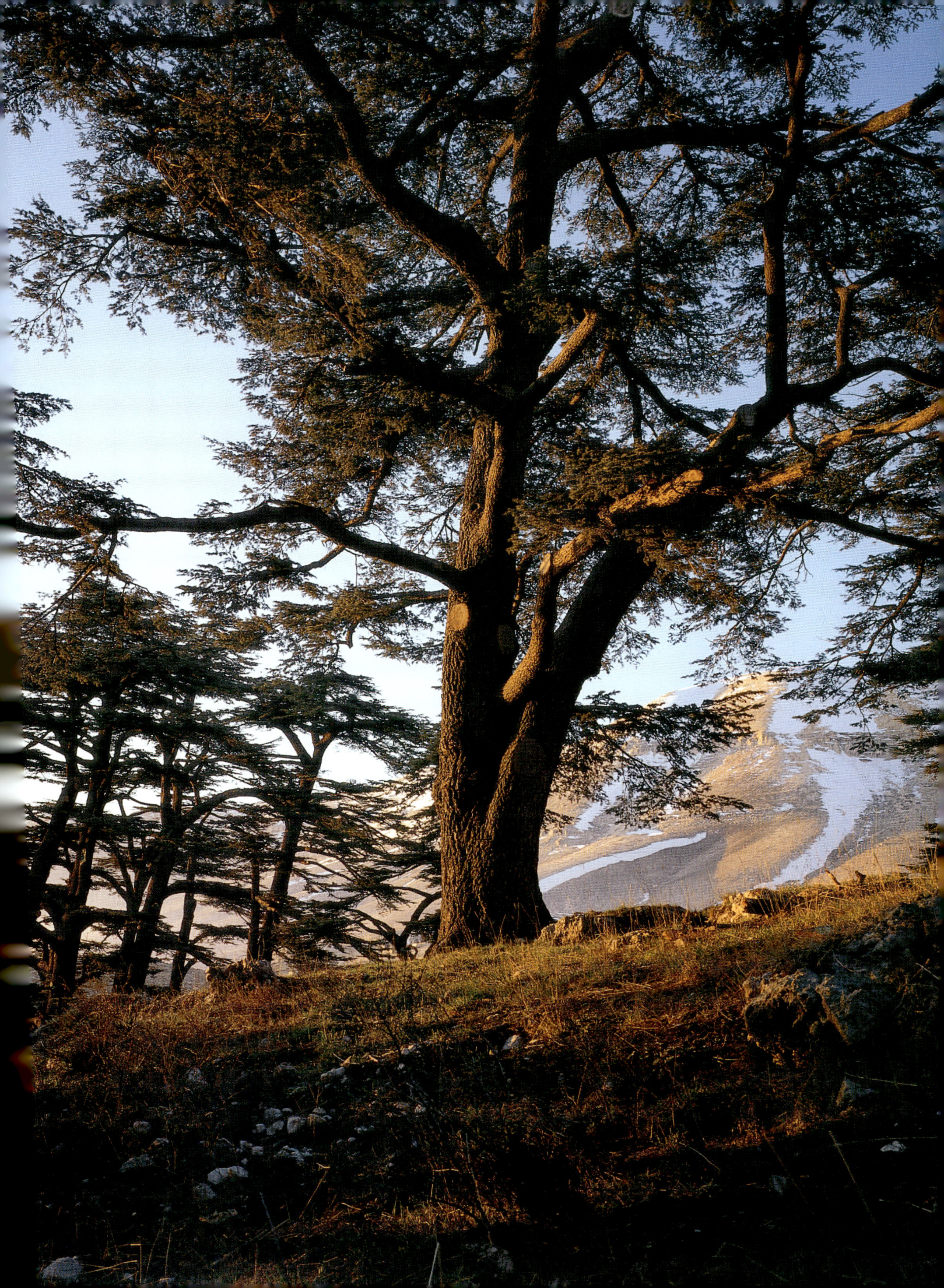

*ABOVE: The Sumerians believed that the mysterious woods of noble cedar trees were home to the god of wisdom and creation.*

Lebanon behind the Phoenician coast; and from the fourth millennium BCE onward, they were exported to all adjoining empires, such as Mesopotamia and Egypt.

Cedar wood was deemed superior to that of other conifers for a variety of reasons. It resists rot and insects, and hence is very durable; it has an attractive aromatic scent; it polishes up beautifully; and it has a close, straight grain which makes it easy to work. Cypress, and juniper, too, have strong scented wood that is reddish-brown in colour. But neither they nor any other tree in the Near East can compare in stature with the cedar. The cedars in parks and gardens today are generally shorter and and have broader crowns (see p.52) because they are not standing in dense forest.

*Being inhabited by Ea, the Sumerian god of wisdom himself, the cedar became an important tree for oracles and prophecy.*

In the Old World, while woods of lesser quality and size were used in everyday life and for the homes of ordinary people, cedar wood was the prime choice for shipbuilding and particularly for the construction of temples and palaces. Snefru, Pharaoh of the fourth dynasty (c.2,600BCE), imported cedar to make the doors of his royal palace. And it continued to be the first choice for monumental doors in the ancient Near East and in Classical Greece and Rome.

King Solomon, too, employed this wood in building the great Temple of Jerusalem: the roof beams were made of cedar, as was the wall panelling of the entire temple, and also the altar in the shrine of the Ark of the Covenant.

Cedar protection occurred early in history – for example in Smyrna (modern Izmir, Turkey) where, in c.200CE, the Greek writer Philostratus described how a very rich man lost a substantial part of his wealth in paying the penalty for having cut down sacred cedars.

## Natural Healing

Oil extracted from the deodar is used in Ayurveda to treat fevers, and pulmonary and urinary disorders. In modern aromatherapy it is used to alleviate the symptoms of dermatitis and nervous tension. The tree essence of the cedar of Lebanon softens resistance to necessary change, clarifies messages from our deeper self and increases the peaceful flow of thoughts.

## Culture, Myth and Symbol

At the very dawn of civilization (about the fifth millennium BCE), in the first city-states of Sumer in southern Mesopotamia, we meet the cedar as the World Tree itself, and as the abode of Ea, the god of wisdom and the principal deity of that culture. Ea, also called Enki, was the Lord of the Earth. He was the creator of the human race and the bestower of all the elements of civilization, such as the laws and moral codes, technology, the arts and healing spells. His name was inscribed in the very core of the sacred tree, whose glyph is translated as "House of wisdom, of strength, of abundance".

Being inhabited by the god of wisdom himself, the cedar naturally became an important tree for oracles and prophecy. Babylonian tablets inform us about initiation rites in which "the Oracle of Heaven and Earth" is delivered under "the cedar-tree, the beloved of the great gods". Later, the Chaldeans (ninth to sixth century BCE) continued to revere this tree: they used some of its green branches in ceremonies and performed magical rites "to restore strength and life to the body".

It is evident that the high priests, kings and pharaohs chose the cedar not only for its physical virtues (size, durability, fragrance, grain quality) but also for its spiritual strength. And these two aspects are not opposites but deeply related: in the eyes of the ancients, the extraordinary

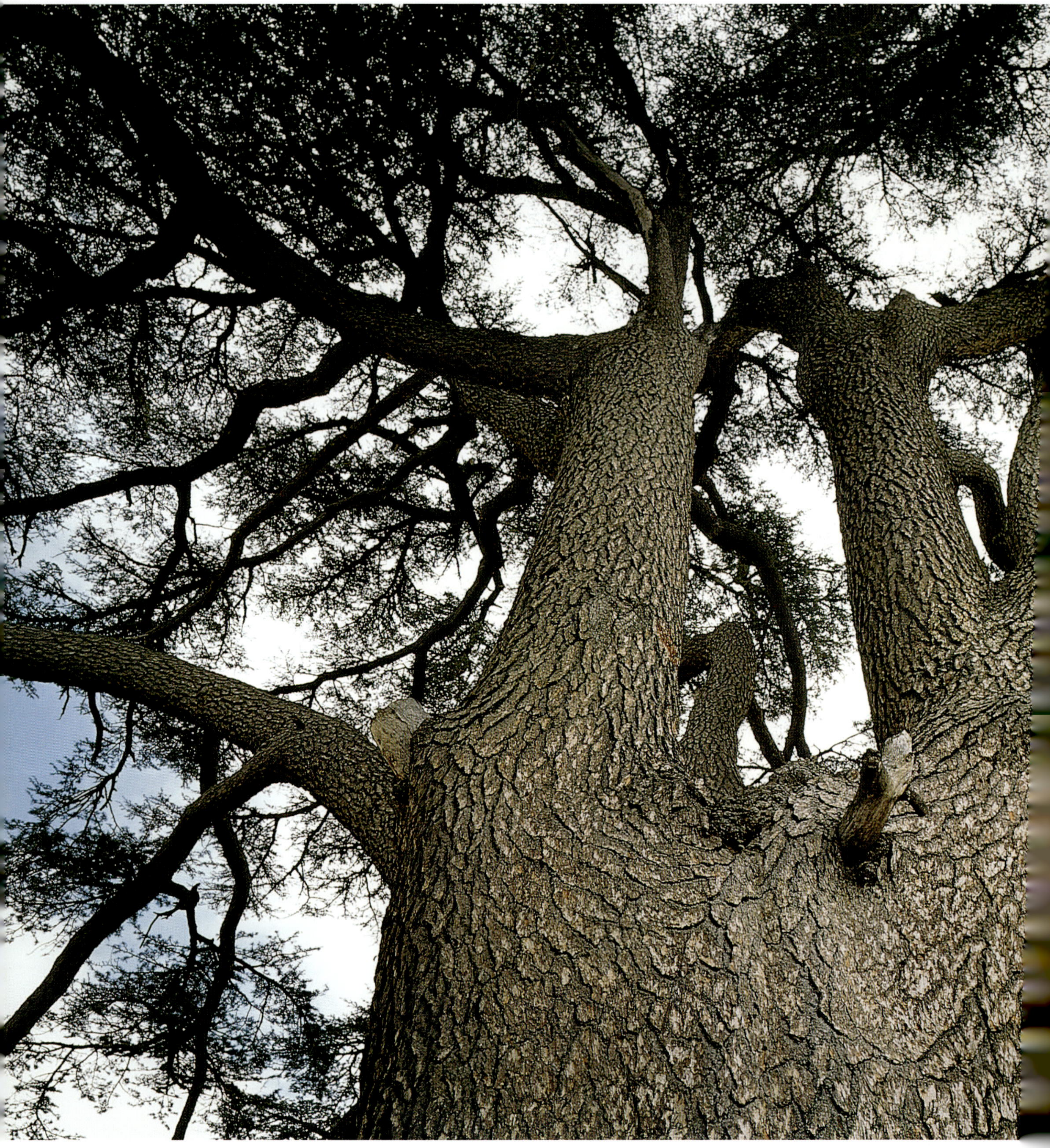

**LEFT**: *A cedar in the oldest grove on the slopes of Mount Makmel, near the town of Bcharré, birthplace of the poet Khalil Gibran.*

physical qualities of the cedar and its wood were reflections of the presence of the divine inside the tree. If the highest god lived in this cedar, it was most appropriate to ask these trees to give their bodies for the panelling in the temple so that the innermost shrine resembled the inside of the sacred tree. And it was deeply meaningful to have the doors to the throne room made from this wood, because the tree was a gate to the divine, and the king or pharaoh in the throne room was the god's representative.

In ancient times, all peoples in the Near East acknowledged the land beneath their feet as being imbued with spirit and they called it "God's land", which was Baal's Land, in both Semitic and Arabic languages. Baal was the "Lord of the Land"; or if the land was feminine, the spirit was called Baalath. In Phoenicia, the mightiest of the *baalim* (gods) were said to live in the cedars of Lebanon with the highest, densest crowns. The trees' glory spread far, and in Mesopotamia they inspired the *Epic of Gilgamesh*:

> "They stood still and gazed at the forest,
> They looked at the height of the cedars,
> They looked at the entrance to the forest …
> They beheld the cedar mountain, abode of the god,
> Throne-seat of Irnini.
> From the face of the mountain
> The cedars raise aloft their luxuriance.
> Good is their shade, full of delight."

The story of Gilgamesh was the most popular and widespread tale throughout the ancient Near East. It relates how a man named Gilgamesh visits a cedar forest in a quest for timber and, falling prey to his own greed and desire for

ABOVE: *The slow-growing cedar's distinctive, egg-shaped cone, which sits upright on the horizontal boughs. It takes approximately four decades for the cedar to produce fertile seeds.*

fame and eternal life, destroys the forest and its spirit guardian, the giant Humbaba. But the consequences are dire, for he finds himself also responsible for the death of his dear companion, Enkidu, and in bitterness and despair loses his own life as well as his afterlife. The ecological moral in this legend is obvious, and, interestingly, it is the oldest written text humankind possesses. Fragments of this text have survived in Sumerian, Akkadian, Hittite and Hurrian, indicating its wide distribution. And, indeed, its ecological message must have had the effect of encouraging people to respect the forest and natural resources, for how else could the relatively small mountain chains of the Lebanon have met the demands of the entire Near East for cedar timber for over three millennia?

The cedar does not grow in Israel and Judea, but nonetheless it was equally celebrated there. Under its Hebrew name, *erez*, it occurs over 70 times in the Bible. For example, the beauty of the cedar is celebrated in Isaiah 60:13:

> "The glory of Lebanon [the cedar] shall come to you,
> the cypress, the plane and the pine,
> to beautify the place of my sanctuary,
> and I will glorify where my feet rest."

Thus speaks Yahweh the Lord in a time when living trees were still an indispensable part of temples and sanctuaries. The proud height of the cedar was second only to the Tree of Life itself, as it stood in the Garden of Eden: "No cedar in God's garden eclipsed it." (Ezekiel 31:2).

Cedar wood was also employed in the Hebrew *Para Adumma*, the Ritual of the Red Heifer. This ceremony was held to restore ritual purity after contact with the dead. Our word *cedar* stems from the Hebrew *qatar*, meaning "to smudge", which indicates that the wood was used in purification rituals and smoke offerings.

In the USA (as well as in Japan), many sacred trees used for smudging and cleansing and in other ceremonial activities are called cedars, but botanically these trees belong to the cypress family (see Cypress pp.72–7).

OPPOSITE: *The small, often isolated, pockets of cedar groves that remain in Lebanon are a tiny fraction of the once vast forests.*

---

**Symbolism:** Wisdom and strength

**Divine Associations:** Ea, Enki (ancient Mesopotamian)

**Astrological Association:** Sun

**Historical Spotlight::** When Lebanon gained independence from France on September 1st 1920, the nation chose the *tricolore* with a green cedar on a white strip as their national flag. However, sadly, only a few small remnants of the ancient forests have survived.

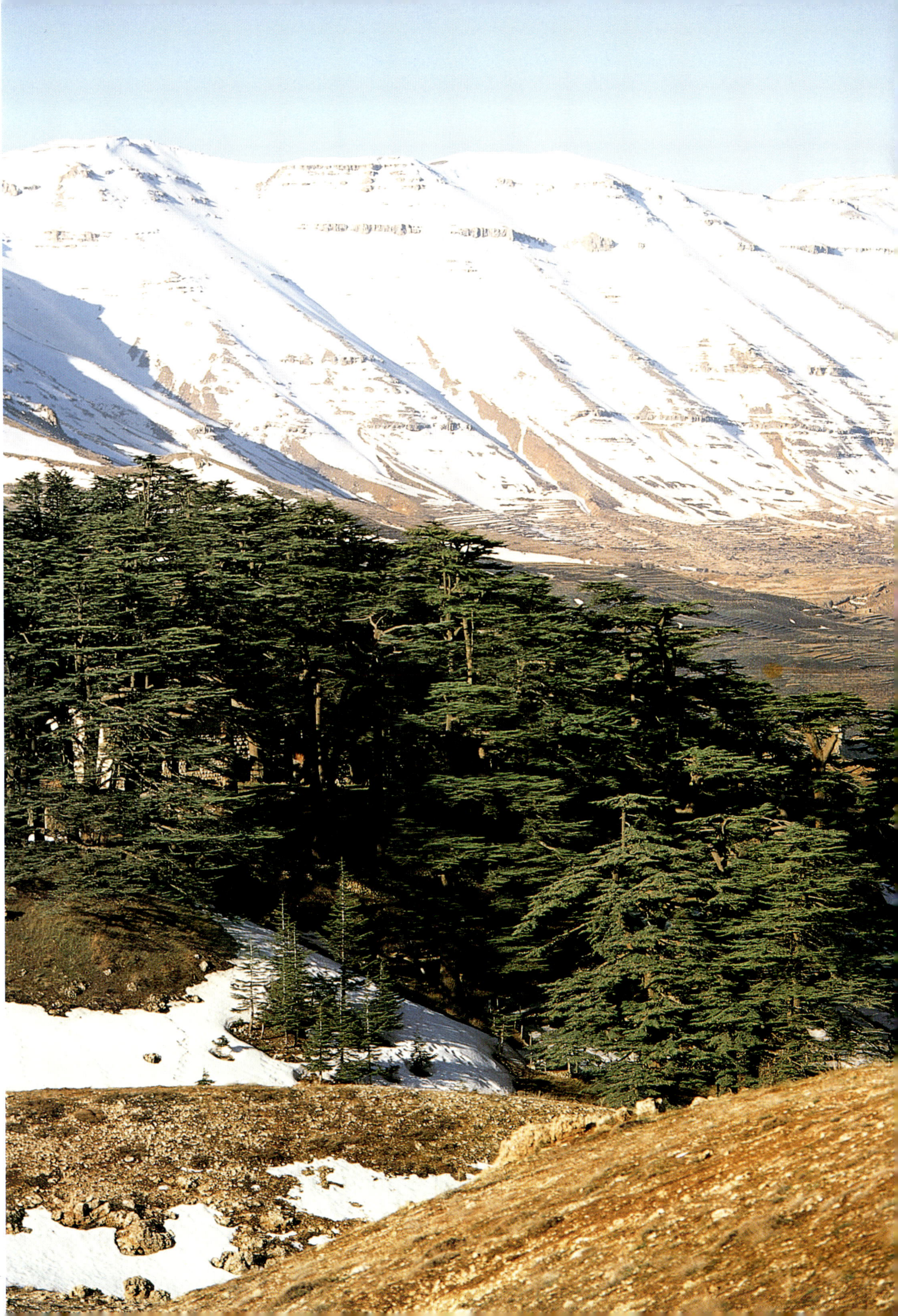

# Orange  *Citrus sinensis*

A genus comprising about 15 species of semi-evergreen spiny shrubs or small to medium-sized trees, the citrus was originally native to southeast Asia. The species soon spread throughout the subtropical and warmer temperate regions of the world. These trees are of great economic importance for their fruits. The genus includes lemon, grapefruit, mandarin and lime trees. The alternate leaves are thick, leathery and dotted with glands. The solitary flowers are white or purplish and usually fragrant. They are mostly bisexual and usually have five petals and 20 to 60 stamens which occur in bundles. The fruits are large, aromatic, leathery-skinned berries which have eight to 15 internal segments containing juicy pulp.

## Practical Uses

The orange tree (*C. sinensis*) is cultivated for its refreshing and nutritious fruits. Native to northeast India, the orange spread to China, where its occurrence can be traced back to *c.*500BCE. From China, this popular tree made its way to the Near East. The Arabs were the first people to mention it in writing, adopting its Sanskrit name, *nagarunga*. The Moors used the orange both medicinally and in religious ceremonies, and brought it to Spain; and from here it made its way to the New World. Although the orange was known in Sicily in 1002, the Portuguese picked it up in the early 16th century in the Far East. Then, the Italians temporarily called it *portogallo* after the Portuguese, as did the Greeks, the Arabs and the Kurds.

RIGHT: *An orange orchard near Papantla in Veracruz, Mexico. Sweet varieties of the fruit were introduced 500 years ago by the Spanish.*

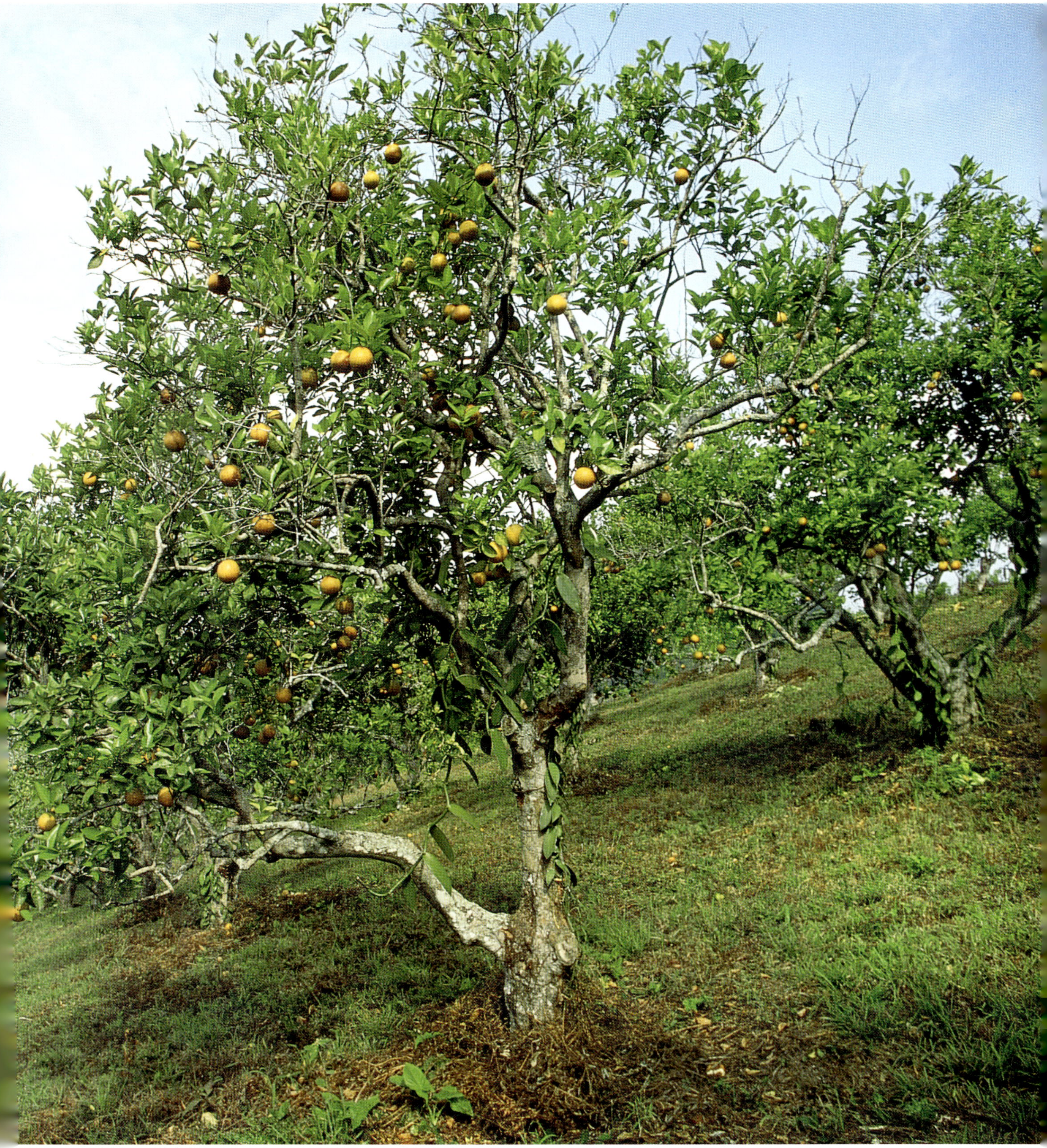

*ABOVE: A fruit of the orange tree shining like a miniature sun amid its dark green foliage.*

The cultivation of the orange spread throughout Europe from Portugal, while the Germans obtained their first orange trees from Italy. They called the fruit *Apfelsine*, the "Chinese apple", while the famous German physician Paracelsus named it *pomerancia*, blending one of the Latin words for apple, *pomum*, with its later Italian name *arancia* (orange).

The cooler countries showed more enthusiasm for the orange than their weather allowed and soon invented the *orangerie*, a special conservatory or greenhouse in which oranges could be grown. Already celebrated as a fruit epitomizing the sun by France's Roi Soleil ("the Sun King"), Louis XIV, the orange became the cult tree of the Baroque period. Its fruits appeared in paintings, jewelry and garden sculpture, and in objects made from wax, metal and glass. Cities and aristocratic estates vied to have the best orangeries. The oldest German one, in Stuttgart, dates from 1568. The orange was seen as a symbol of abundance and good luck, but this was nothing new – the Roman poet Virgil (70–19BCE) had already called the fruit *malum felix*, the "lucky apple".

Marmalade and other orange preserves are exclusively made from bitter or Seville oranges (*C. aurantium*). Pectin, the essential setting agent for preserves and jams, is extracted from the peel of lemons, limes, oranges and grapefruits, and also from apples.

### Natural Healing

Oranges are a good source of vitamin C and potassium, as well as other vitamins and minerals. But, depending on their origin, oranges can contain up to 60mg of vitamin C, or none at all. In naturopathy, the fruits are seen as challenging because they can cause a strong release of toxins from cells into the blood stream.

In Traditional Chinese Medicine oranges are considered to create internal heat, aggravating skin conditions, such as eczema. The Chinese advise pregnant women to abstain

RIGHT: *Less well known than its fruits are the orange tree's fragrant flowers – its name in Persia,* narang, *means perfume.*

from eating this fruit because it causes hyperactivity in the baby. Interestingly, oranges have also been identified as a trigger food for hyperactivity in children in the West.

In ayurvedic medicine oranges are used to dispel internal heat – for example, toxicity manifesting as diarrhea or nose bleeds.

## Culture, Myth and Symbol

A Christian legend from Andalusia (Spain) tells how Mary and Joseph, travelling with the child Jesus, came upon an orange tree guarded by an eagle. Mary begged the tree to give her one of its fruits, whereupon the eagle fell asleep. She then received three oranges, one for each member of the Holy Family.

Initially not so lucky is the girl in "The Magic Orange Tree", a tale from Haiti. She finds three oranges on the table of the family home and, because her cruel stepmother rarely feeds her properly, devours them all with delight. When her stepmother arrives, she is irate and threatens the girl, who runs away and cries all night at the grave of her real mother.

In the morning the sun wakes her, and when she gets up the girl notices an orange seed falling from her skirt. It starts to sprout and grow the moment it touches the ground. Somehow the girl has magical powers over the tree and by singing she is able to make it blossom and bear fruit. She takes home an armful of oranges to pacify her stepmother. But the greedy woman is not satisfied and wants more, so she forces the girl to lead her to the tree. As the evil stepmother climbs up the trunk to reach the oranges, the girl sings to the tree to grow high into the sky and then break. This kills both the tree and her stepmother, but the girl finds a new seed. The second tree grows like the first one and gives her plenty of oranges, which she takes to sell in the market. She lives happily ever after.

In both the Andalusian legend and the Haitian story, the orange, like the sun, shines its light on everyone and offers its fruits unconditionally.

**Symbolism**: Fairness and justice

**Astrological Association**: Sun

**Historical Spotlight**: In c.100BCE, Wuti, a Chinese emperor of the Han dynasty, introduced the government position of "Orange Minister". The incumbent was responsible for the supply of oranges to the palace.

# Myrrh
## *Commiphora myrrha*

Trees of the *Commiphora* genus are found in the drier parts of tropical Africa, Arabia, Madagascar and India. The myrrh of the Old World is a gnarled shrub or small tree (*C. myrrha* or *C. abyssinica*) endemic to the narrow coastal region of the southern coast of the Arabian peninsula (modern Yemen and Oman). When injured, the trunk exudes a white "wound milk", which gums up the mouths of attacking insects and protects the wound from bacterial infection. In the open air it soon crystalizes to a golden-yellow resin.

### Practical Uses
The use of myrrh resin for smoke offerings goes back to Neolithic times. When the resin was harvested (around July) each tree received 10 to 30 gashes to release the milky liquid, which was collected afterwards.

The growing demand resulted in the expansion of plantations in southern Arabia. With the domestication of the camel in the second millennium BCE, large caravans could cross the vast Arabian desert, and after a 2,300-mile (3,700 km) journey they could sell their goods in Babylon or at the Mediterranean ports of Israel and Phoenicia. From here the myrrh was shipped all over the ancient world.

The demand increased even more at around the time of Christ. Then, a kilo of myrrh cost the monthly income of a working man. In around 50CE, Rome alone imported spices and incense worth 100 million sesterces annually (an amount which, at the time, could have bought 1.6 million litres – over 2 million bottles – of wine at the wholesale price). With the spread of Christianity and Islam, the myrrh trade shrank, finally collapsing at the end of World War II.

### Natural Healing
Diodorus Siculus (a Greek historian who lived during the first century BCE) called myrrh resin a vital medicament needed by all physicians. Throughout history it has been valued for its antibacterial, anti-inflammatory, analgesic, anti-congestive and cancer-inhibiting qualities. Recent research indicates that myrrh also contains substances that lower blood lipids, including cholesterol.

### Culture, Myth and Symbol
Whether among the ancient Egyptians, Phoenicians, Greeks or Romans, and whether celebrating deities, spirits or ancestors, there was hardly a religious practice that did not employ this fragrant resin. Myrrh has even been found in Celtic tombs in Germany (second century BCE). In ancient Egypt it was used to anoint the dead. In the process of mummification it disinfected, reduced decay and smelled sweet.

OPPOSITE: *The trunk of the myrrh tree contains a milk-white sap that was once traded in large quantities around the Mediterranean region.*

The arrival of a caravan of more than 400 camels, each packed with up to 440lbs (200kg) of Oriental treasures such as myrrh, spices and agate, and emanating exotic scents such as cinnamon and sandalwood, must have been an enchanting experience. But nobody knew where they came from, and the Arabian traders kept their secrets well. All this only added to the mystique surrounding myrrh.

In Greek legend, the god Adonis, the lover of Aphrodite, was born from a myrrh tree. Ovid describes how Adonis' mother, Smyrna, was transformed from a remorseful woman into this tree: "Although along with her shape she has also lost her emotion, she cries, and hot tears flow from the tree. The tears, too, have their honour – the myrrh which drops from the wood carries the name of this lady, and she will always be remembered." However, Adonis is the Phoenician name of the Syrian Attis, the son of the Great Goddess. The Babylonians burnt myrrh to her, as did the Hebrews in the desert. Ultimately, the myrrh tree is a manifestation of Astarte, the Queen of Heaven and Great Mother, and its beneficial "milk" fits in with this symbolism perfectly.

In Exodus (30:22–9), Yahweh the Lord tells Moses how to make sacred anointing oil from myrrh, cinnamon, olive oil and other ingredients. Then Moses is instructed to anoint with it the Ark of the Covenant and the altar, and also the priests. Ever after, the kings of Judea and Israel were anointed with the same formula.

According to Flavius Josephus (Jewish priest and historian, c.37–100CE), Jericho and its beautiful gardens housed the myrrh trees which the Queen of Sheba (whose kingdom controlled the myrrh trade) had presented to King Solomon on her visit in the tenth century BCE.

In the New Testament, the "Wise Men from the East" bring gold, frankincense and myrrh to the stable in Bethlehem where Jesus was born. Thus, the myrrh offering comes full circle – from the divine mother and back to her. And given the ancient tradition of using myrrh oil to anoint the dead, the gift of myrrh here symbolizes Christ's humanity. This is later echoed when Nicodemus brings "a mixture of myrrh and aloes" with which to prepare Jesus' body for burial (John 19:39). Together with Joseph of Arimathea, he wraps the body with the spices in linen cloth according to Jewish custom.

Mary in Hebrew is *Myryam* or *Maryam*, which originated in the Sumerian *Ma-ri-enna*, the High, Fertile Mother of Heaven. In Egypt she was known as Isis, the Mother of the Universe, and from her Christianity borrowed Mary's deep blue cloak sprinkled with stars. Other names of the mother goddess from the Near East include Myrtea (myrtle tree), and Myrrha (myrrh tree).

**Symbolism**: Devotion and mediation

**Divine Associations**: The Great Mother: Isis (ancient Egyptian), Ishtar (Mesopotamian), Astarte (Phoenician), Mary (Christian)

**Astrological Association**: Neptune

**Historical Spotlight**: In 1470BCE Queen Hatshepsut of Egypt, intrigued by the mystery surrounding the origin of myrrh resin, sent an expedition to the land of Punt. The ships returned laden with Oriental delights, including heaps of myrrh resin and 31 living trees. This is the earliest-known foreign tree transplantation in recorded history.

*OPPOSITE: Many myths are associated with the hazel tree and its large, downy leaves are a popular food among wild deer.*

# Hazel *Corylus*

*Corylus* is a genus of about ten species of deciduous, monoecious shrubs and small trees native to the northern temperate zone. The alternating leaves are generally ovate and double-toothed. The unisexual flowers develop before the leaves and the male flowers are drooping catkins. The fruits are nuts with a leafy involucre clustering at the ends of the branches. The American hazel (*C. americana*), native to the eastern part of North America, and the European hazel (*C. avellana*) are both widely grown for their edible nuts and as ornamentals.

## Practical Uses

Native North Americans have many traditional uses for the hazel, both in medicine and as food. It was also used in basket making, and the Chippewa and Ojibwa tribes use hazel twigs for drumsticks. In Europe, it used to be an important coppice tree, providing leaf fodder as well as flexible poles and sticks for basketry and fencing, and for wattle-and-daub walls. Water diviners use forked twigs of hazel for their divining rods. And, of course, hazelnuts are a popular food.

## Natural Healing

Hazel leaves have an astringent action largely thanks to their tannin content, hence their traditional use against diarrhea. Hazelnuts are a good source of protein, vitamin E, calcium, magnesium and potassium. They contain at least 50 percent oil, which is rich and nourishing and can be eaten as part of a salad dressing, or used externally as an ingredient in massage oils for dry skin.

## Culture, Myth and Symbol

The hazel's original Latin name, *sylvestris*, recalls the ancient Latin forest god, the mischievous Silvanus. The *Dinnshenchas*, an early Irish topographical treatise, speaks of the "poet's music-haunted hazel", and of the "nine hazels of Crimall the sage", which "stand by the power of magic spells". The hazels of poetic art are a recurring theme in Irish Celtic tradition; and, like poetry, these magic trees produce flowers and fruits (beauty and wisdom) at the same time.

In Welsh myth, King Arthur and his companions search for the divine child, Mabon ap Modron, the "Son of the Great Mother". After a long journey, a magic salmon eventually takes them to the mythical well where they find the boy under a hazel tree. The Celts considered the hazel to be a "tree of knowledge". This myth demonstrates that the wisdom of the hazel is not the wisdom of great age and experience, but that of simplicity and innocence.

---

**Symbolism**: Playfulness and enchantment

**Divine Associations**: Silvanus (Roman), Mabon (Welsh)

**Astrological Association**: Mercury

**Superstition**: In 19th-century Germany, it was thought that there were witches beneath the bark of hazel trees – hence only the peeled branches were allowed in churches.

**Historical Spotlight**: In 1463, Pope Pius II praised the hazels in the Via Appia (near Rome) and in the forests of the Albanian mountains. He said that they provided ideal walks for poets, as well as a home for the Muses and nymphs, and perhaps even Diana herself. No wonder – Pius' real name was Silvio!

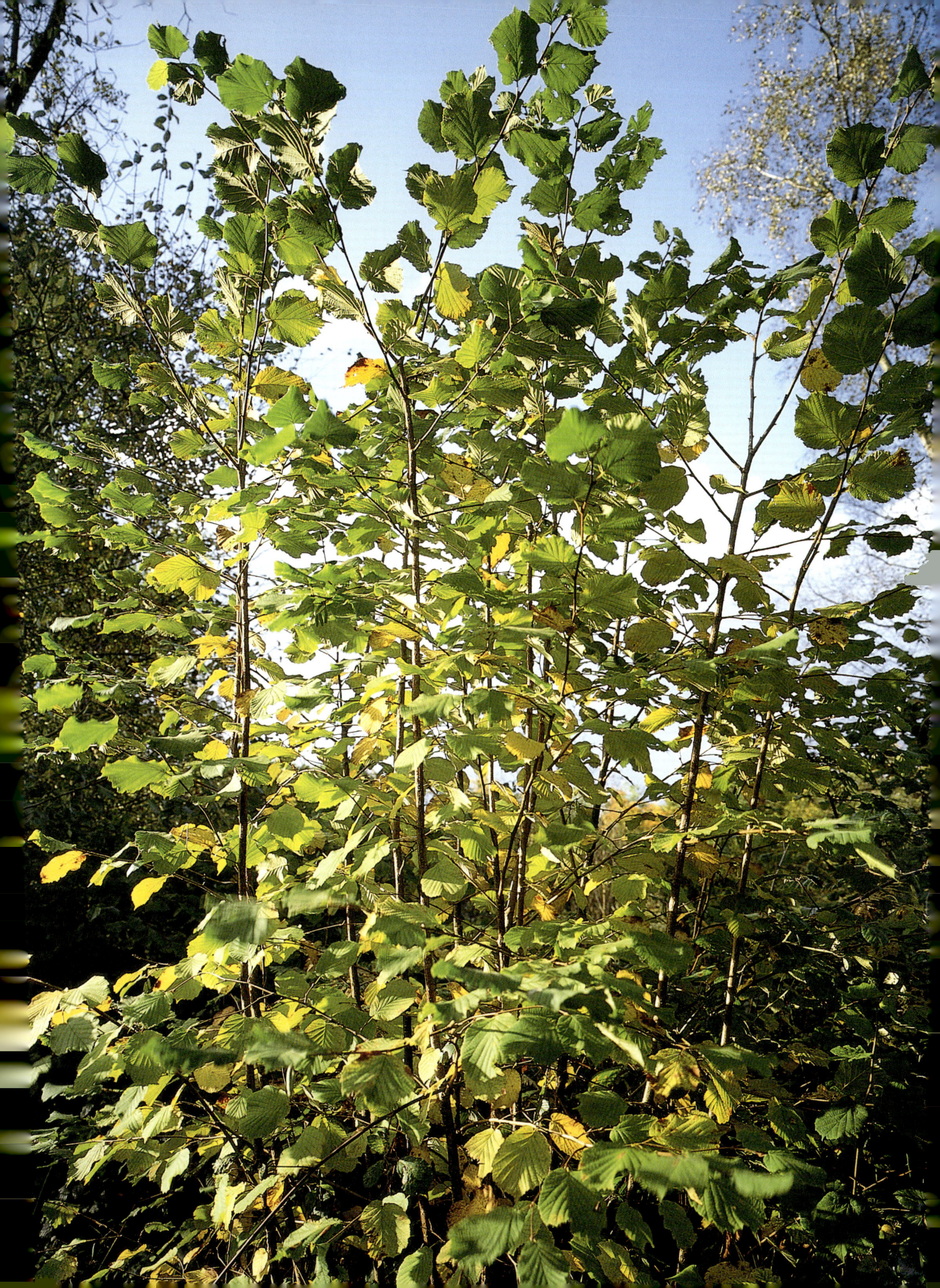

# Hawthorn
## *Crataegus*

More than 1,000 species of *Crataegus* have been described, but the vast majority are hybrids. The thorns are among the hardiest and most adaptable trees, tolerant of strong winds and dryness as well as excessive moisture. Most are thorny, deciduous shrubs or small trees, with white flowers that open in May and June, and red fruits. They are native to the northern temperate zones. The common hawthorn (*C. monogyna*) or maythorn is popular in Europe, often seen in hedgerows. Its flowers are white and fragrant. The "Glastonbury thorn" belongs to the subspecies *biflora*, which produces leaves earlier than normal and occasionally an early but smaller crop of flowers in winter.

**Practical Uses**

Hawthorn has a long history of use as a boundary marker and in forming hedges. In the Anglo-Saxon charters it is by far the most frequently named tree. In Britain, during the Parliament Enclosures between 1750 and 1850, an estimated 200,000 miles (320,000km) of hedges were planted, mostly with hawthorn. The wood is fine-grained, even, hard and tough, and it is used for fine work, such as veneers and cabinet making. Hawthorn berries and flowers have been used to make jellies, wines and liqueurs.

**Natural Healing**

Hawthorn is an important herbal remedy for heart disorders. Both the blossom and the berries normalize blood pressure.

RIGHT: *During the autumn bright red hawthorn berries, or "haws", provide a feast for blackbirds, thrushes, waxwings and other birds.*

*The Welsh goddess of the hawthorn once walked the empty universe and her white track of hawthorn petals became the Milky Way.*

strating how much its protective force was valued. This protection is based on spiritual cleansing, as expressed in various sacred Hittite texts from c.1500BCE, which ask the tree to "pluck any evil, impurity or wrath of the gods from this initiate, who walks through the gate [of your hedge]". These references to the "gate" indicate that hawthorn-enclosed sanctuaries existed in ancient Anatolia (modern Turkey) too.

The physical, moral and spiritual purity which humans struggle for is symbolized in the overflowing abundance of the white flowers of the hawthorn (and they are also why it is sometimes called the whitethorn). They have played a part in spring celebrations, fertility rites and marriages for millennia. The hawthorn has always been seen as a herald of summer. It is also a tree of the White Goddess. Hence the legend that the Welsh goddess, Olwen, "She of the White Track", once walked the empty universe and her white track of hawthorn petals became the Milky Way.

This tree was also dedicated to Cardea, the Roman goddess of childbirth, and to Hera, Zeus' wife, who conceived Ares and his twin sister Eris when she touched its blossoms. The fact that Hera gives birth to a twin brother and sister points to the balance of male and female as a theme strongly associated with the hawthorn – whose blossoms are hermaphrodite as well. The babies who were protected by Cardea were regarded as the Heaven-given result of the sacred union of male and female creative energies. Similarly the Welsh legend of Culhwych and Olwen echoes early Celtic traditions of the sacred marriage of a mortal king with an immortal queen or the sovereignty of the land. This is a deeply mystical union which ensures fertility and good harvests for the year, as well as a respectful, loving attitude toward nature by humans – put in modern terms, a strong economy and a healthy ecology.

The Glastonbury thorn acquired its fame from the legend that it grew from the staff of Joseph of Arimathea, who is said to have travelled from Jerusalem to Britain shortly after the crucifixion of Jesus. However, there is no (written) connection between Joseph and the thorn before the 16th century. The cult status of the Glastonbury thorn simply continues the ancient theme of purity in a Christian context.

**Symbolism**: Purification, sacred marriage and male-female unity

**Divine Associations**: Olwen (Welsh), Cardea (Roman), Hera (Greek)

**Astrological Associations**: Mars and Venus

**Superstition**: In Christian Wales and parts of southwest England, people believed that to take a blossoming hawthorn branch inside their house would cause their mother to die.

**Historical Spotlight**: The maythorn used to flower around 1st May (the Celtic festival of Beltane) until the calendar revision in 1752 catapulted the blossoming time forward to mid-May.

OPPOSITE: *The cypress is a famous feature of the landscape of Tuscany. In Italian there is a distinction between an upright masculine cypress (cipresso) and a rounded feminine (cipressa) one.*

# Cypress *Cupressaceae*

The cypress family (*Cupressaceae*) comprises about 21 genera (and 140 species) of resinous, coniferous, usually evergreen trees and shrubs. The genera include *Cupressus*, *Chamaecyparis* and *Thuja*. The various species of the true cypress genus (*Cupressus*) are native to North America, Europe and Asia. They are monoecious trees with small, scale-like leaves. The female cones are globose and have woody scales, with many seeds to each scale. The Italian cypress (*Cupressus sempervirens*) reaches up to 80ft (24m) and is distributed across southern Europe and western Asia. Its subspecies 'Stricta' supplies the slender columns typical of the Mediterranean landscape.

The species known as the Lawson false cypress or Port Orford cedar (*Chamaecyparis lawsoniana*), a native of Oregon and California, is botanically neither a true cypress (in other words, it does not belong to the genus *Cupressus*), nor is it a cedar, but it is a member of the cypress family (*Cupressaceae*). Confusingly, many species of this family are referred to colloquially as "cedars".

**Symbolism**: Heaven's calling (universal)

**Divine Association**: the Great Spirit

**Astrological Association**: Sun

**Historical Spotlight**: On 17 June 379CE, King Theodosius of Syria renewed the tree protection law for the sacred grove of Daphne (Phoenicia). The *Codex Theodosianus* (X 1, 12) commits the police prefect of Antiochia to planting new cypress trees in the grove. At that time, the penalty for stealing a tree from a sacred grove was five pounds of gold.

## Practical Uses

Together with the cedar, the cypress could be called one of the pillars of the early high civilizations of the eastern Mediterranean and Asia Minor. As construction timber it is second only to cedar, but was more widely distributed in the former region. However, the tall species of juniper (another member of this family, see pp.116–9) are of equal quality, and these three tall-growing genera provided the necessary lengths of timbers for the roof beams of palaces and temples. The wood's durability and aromatic scent added to their noble image.

## Natural Healing

The essential oil of cypress is distilled from the cones. It can be used as an astringent component in oil blends, with the particular property of supporting the venous system. Used diluted, it is helpful for treating piles and varicose veins, while it also has a reputation for use externally in painful and heavy periods. Navajo women take an infusion of cypress branches to regain their strength after childbirth.

The tree essence of the Lawson false cypress helps us to identify our true needs and to initiate appropriate change.

## Culture, Myth and Symbol

For Native North Americans various species of the cypress family are important in ceremony and ritual. This is particularly true of the Lawson false cypress. For example, after smudging the ceremonial area with sage to cleanse and purify it – as well as the sacred tools and the participants – the smoke of the Lawson false cypress ( or "cedar") is used to "call in the spirits".

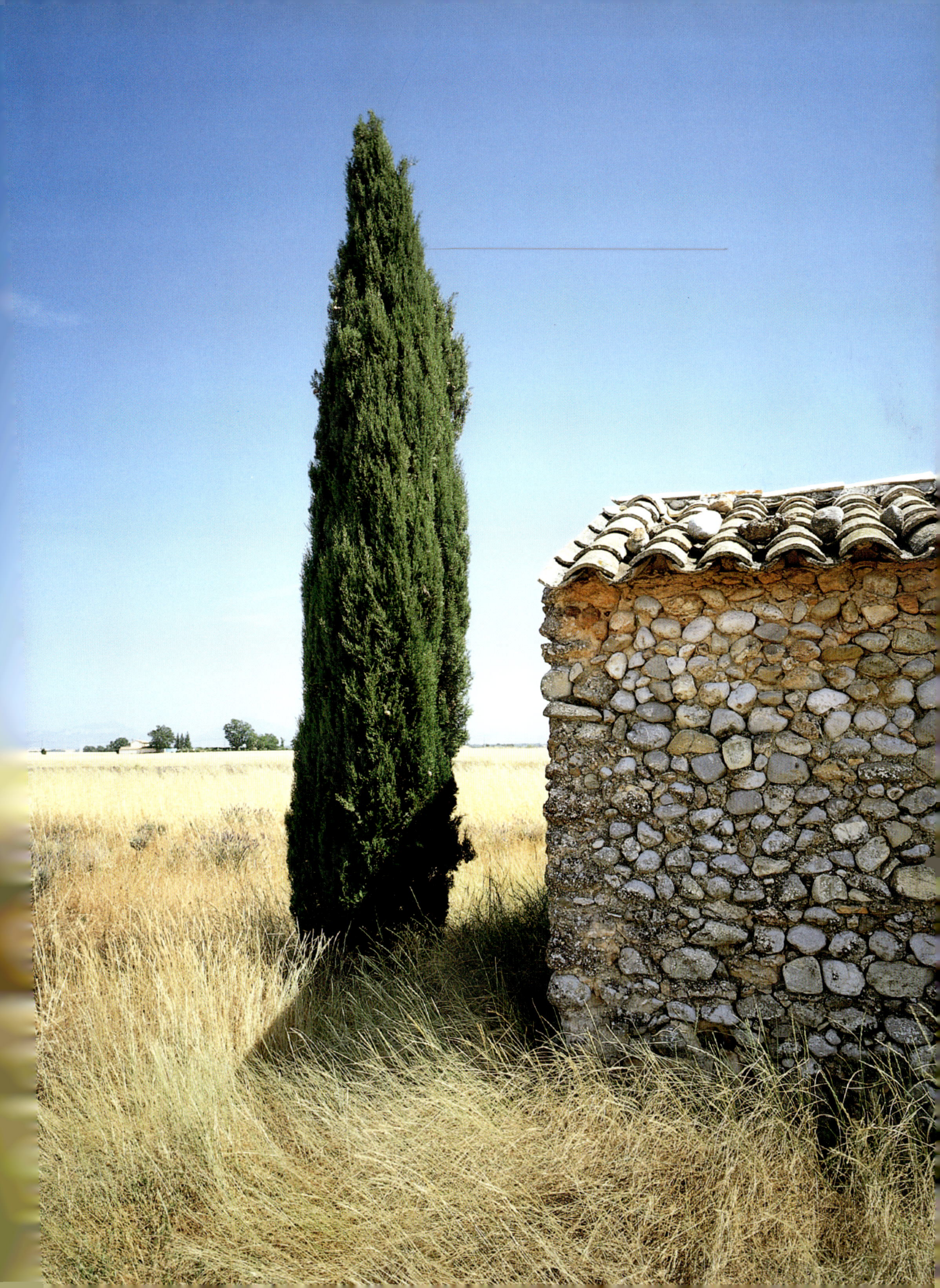

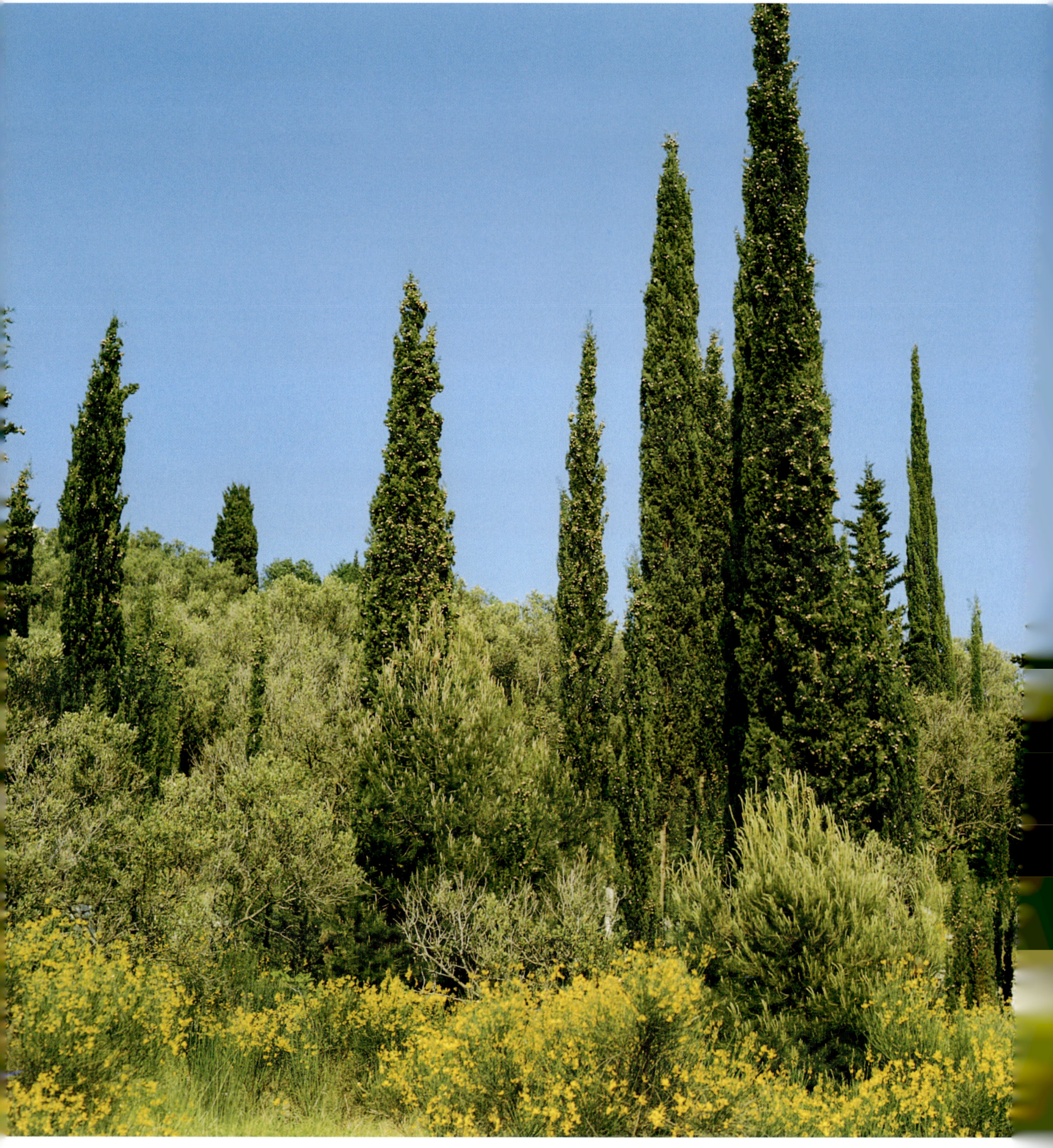

**LEFT**: *Young cypress trees rising from the low* maquis *vegetation is a typical and well-loved element of Mediterranean scenery.*

*After the ceremonial cleansing with sage smudge, the smoke of the sacred cypress ("cedar") "calls in the spirits".*

Among the indigenous peoples of eastern Canada, the sacred tree from which their totem poles are made is the Western red cedar (*Thuja plicata*), another member of the cypress family. "The Legend of the Flute" from the Brule and Lakota Sioux tribes associates the "cedar" with the gift of music. In a dream, a young hunter was shown a hollow branch by a red-headed woodpecker. The wind sang hauntingly through the holes made by the bird, and so the flute came to humans. A Navajo tradition celebrates the cypress by making necklaces of its dried fruits.

In the Old World, the cypress was regarded as a "tree of light". Its extensive use in funeral customs and as a graveyard tree came about because of its associations with divine light and the heavens, not because it is an "underworld" tree. Today, it is still found in many graveyards (its evergreen leaves are symbolic of belief in resurrection) in the Christian Mediterranean and also in Islamic countries.

A cypress grove at Titane in the Peleponnese peninsula was dedicated to Aesclepius, the ancient Greek god of healing. Serpents sacred to him were kept there and roamed freely among the trees. And the cypress grove at Phlius, like

ABOVE: *A Tuscan rural idyll, seemingly unchanged for centuries, but during the 1970s many cypress trees were lost due to fungal attack.*

countless other sacred groves in ancient Greece, is reported to have been a place in which people sought political and judicial asylum. Refugees in such sanctuaries were protected, and, in some places, a twig from the grove would even secure them free passage to the border or the next harbour. Much later the tradition of offering asylum in a sacred place was carried on by the Christian church.

The ancient Persian, Egyptian and Assyrian kings introduced many trees and plants to their homelands, and commissioned large palace gardens and arboretums. They planted cypresses, cedars, palms, and many others, and enjoyed

BELOW: *The cypress family offers the best-known examples of trees with scale-like leaves, as contrasted with the needle-shaped leaves possessed by the majority of conifers.*

botanical variety – which also represented the geographical extent of their empires. The Persian word for temple garden, *pairi daeza*, became the Greek *paradeisos*, "paradise".

*The Book of Kings*, the national epic of Persia written c.1000CE, relates how the prophet Zoroaster himself planted a cypress at his Fire Sanctuary at Keshmar (Chorasan, in modern Iran). The seed which he had brought from Paradise grew into twin trees. These cypresses are believed to be the "Sun Tree" and the "Moon Tree" that were encountered by Alexander the Great. According to another, medieval source, when Alexander was proceeding with his army through Persia, he was approached by a mysterious old man who led him to a sacred mountain. After a long ascent, Alexander eventually arrived at a tree sanctuary: a male cypress named Mithra, "[Tree of the] Sun", and a female cypress named Mao, "[Tree of the] Moon". He kissed both, made an offering, and asked the trees his future. The oracle of the trees told him that he would successfully conquer India, but die soon after his return to Babylon. And this is, of course, exactly what happened. Caliph Mutawakkil of Samarra (modern Iraq) had one of the 1,450-year-old trees felled in 846CE, a deed for which he was himself murdered.

According to Chinese Taoist tradition, some of the immense life force of cypress can be absorbed if we chew the resin. The earth spirits of the East dwell in cypress trees, and cypress wood is used for coffins.

In Japan, the *sugi* is a highly venerated tree. It is usually translated as Japanese cedar, but it is actually a false cypress (*Cryptomeria japonica*). The national tree of Japan, it is often found around Buddhist temples and Shinto shrines. An old tale, "Orosu", tells of the sacred *sugi* tree that whispers in the wind, and when the air is still asks the birds to deliver its messages. It is the king of the forest, and when it is harmed all the other trees assemble at night to heal its wounds.

An old tradition in Japan (and Korea) is *shinrinyoku*, "forest bathing". This does not involve bathing in water, but rather in the fresh and healing air of the forest. The two trees that are particularly praised for making the air beneficial and fragrant are the *sugi* and a relative of the Lawson false cypress, the *hinoki* (*Chamaecyprus obtusa*), which is commonly (though incorrectly) called the Japanese cypress or white cedar. *Shinrinyoku* became even more popular when it was discovered that many plants, particularly conifers, produce "phytoncides" – natural anti-bacterial substances.

In seventh-century Japan, the Shogun burial site of Nikko (Tochigi Prefecture) was connected with the royal residence of Edo (now Tokyo) by an avenue of *sugi* trees. About 13,000 trees still protect visitors from the sun along the 22-mile (35.41km) route. It is the world's longest tree-lined avenue. However, the most impressive *sugis* of Japan are in the national park of Yakushima, on Yaku island, off Kyushu.

# Quince *Cydonia*

*Cydonia* is a monotypic genus of the rose family (*Rosaceae*). The common quince (*C. oblonga* or *C. vulgaris*, sometimes *Pyrus cydonia*) is a native of northern Iran and Turkestan. It is a small tree which can reach 20ft (6m) in height. The fragrant, solitary flowers have five white to rose-pink petals, and the fruit is a golden-yellow colour. The leaves often turn a rich, mellow yellow before falling. The botanical name, *Cydonia*, refers to a town (modern Khania) on the Greek island of Crete, which was once famous for its quince exports.

### Practical Uses
Since ancient times the quince has been widely cultivated for its fruits. As they are hard and acidic when raw, they are eaten stewed, or used to make jam or jelly.

### Natural Healing
The English herbalist John Gerard (1545–1612) says in *Herball* (1597), "The boiled seeds from the fruit exude a soft, mucilaginous substance that is very soothing to hot inflamed surfaces". Quince is an excellent anti-inflammatory remedy for the digestive tract, and it can be used also for sore mouths, throats and nipples. Traditionally a broth from the fruit has also been used to treat vaginal infections and rectal inflammations. A decoction of the seeds can be used to soothe the digestive tract, as an eye lotion, and as an ingredient in skin lotions and creams.

RIGHT: *A quince orchard in bloom. The fruit is not eaten raw but used as an ingredient to make other foods. The word marmalade originally meant quince jam, from* marmelo *("quince" in Portuguese).*

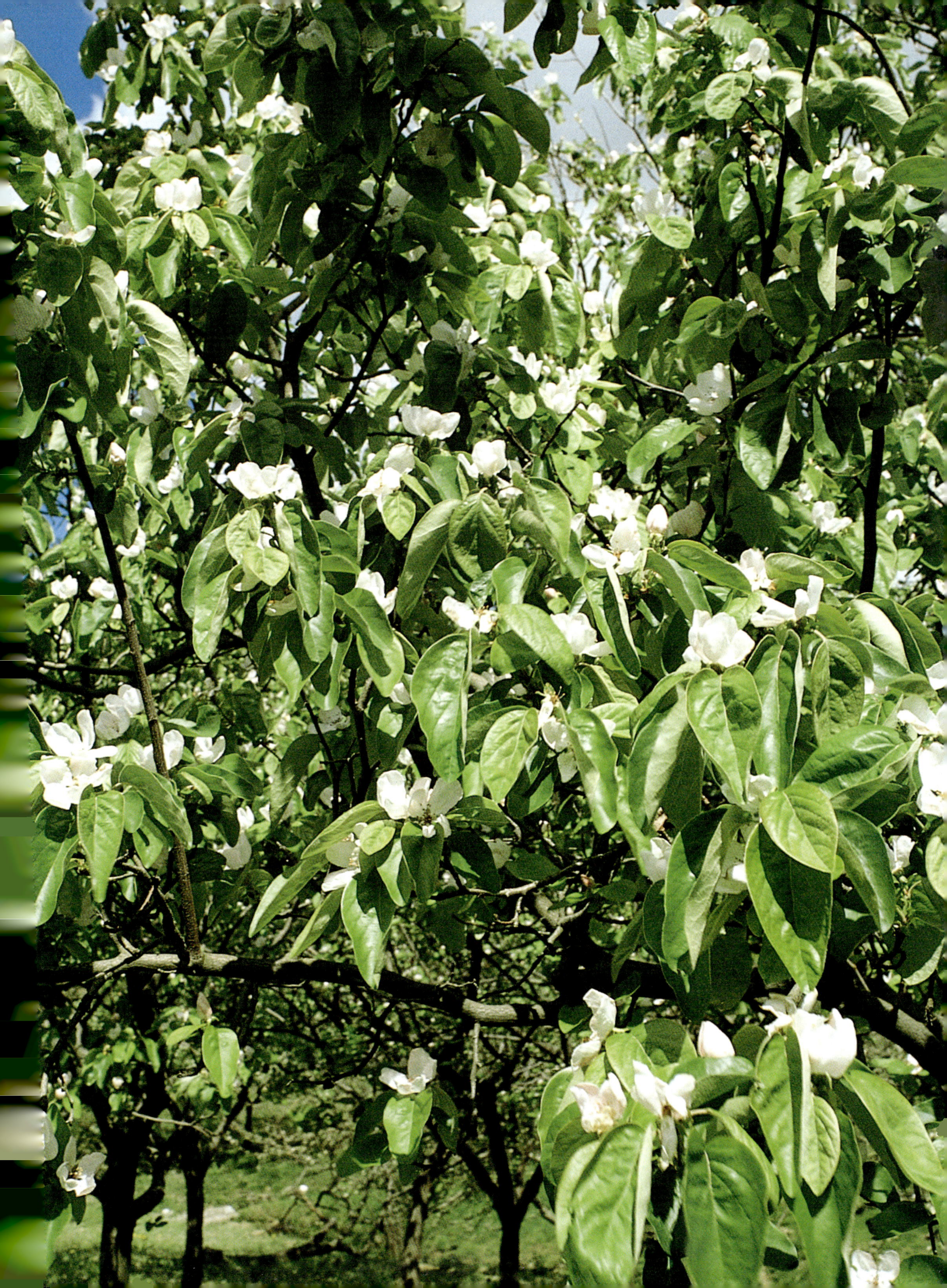

# QUINCE

BELOW: *Fallen quince, a large and hard fruit – not dissimilar to a pear or apple. The ancient Greeks called them "golden apples" and it may well be that these were the paradisial fruit Heracles stole.*

In Traditional Chinese Medicine the fruits are regarded as a warm food with a sour taste, stimulating secretions from the gall bladder and the pancreas, and lowering the acidity in the intestines.

## Culture, Myth and Symbol

The Pelasgian (pre-Greek) sea goddess Marian, whom the Greeks named Aphrodite, held a quince in her hand as a love gift. The quince remained sacred to her, and a symbol of love and fertility. Following ancient customs, young Greek and Roman couples shared a quince at their wedding banquet, to symbolize their loving union.

The ancient Greeks called this tree *chrysomelon*, "golden apple", and the mythical golden apples of the Hesperides were, in all probability, quinces, not apples. In the myth of the 11th labour of Heracles, Mother Earth gives Hera a special "golden apple" tree at her wedding to Zeus. Hera plants it in her sacred garden on the slopes of Mount Atlas, where the chariot horses of the sun complete their daily journey. Atlas, the mighty shepherd, builds a wall around the orchard, and the tree is guarded by his three daughters, the Hesperides, and the ever-watchful dragon, Ladon. It is Heracles' task to steal some of these fruits. He finally succeeds, but in the end Hera's rightful property is given back to her.

The motif of the sacred garden with the tree at the centre, guarded by the dragon, is reminiscent of the World Tree. And this is further enhanced by ancient Greek art, which depicts the Tree of the Hesperides carrying stars as its fruit.

In the times of the Temple at Jerusalem, the worshippers at the Feast of the Tabernacles carried an *ethrog* in their right hand, and a *lulab* in their left. Until recently, the *ethrog* was believed to have been some sort of citrus fruit, but as we know now that citrus trees had not yet been introduced from India at that time, the golden-yellow fruit must have been a quince. The *lulab*, on the other hand, is a bundle of intertwined boughs from the palm, the willow and the myrtle. As all these trees were expressly connected with the female aspect of God – the Goddess – the English scholar Robert Graves (1895–1985) surmised that the ritual use of *ethrog* and *lulab* in the Feast of the Tabernacles was originally taken over from the Canaanites by the Hebrews, along with other rites dedicated to the moon goddess. However, because of its erotic connotations the quince was replaced with the citrus during the Babylonian exile, or as part of the great cultural reform in 621 BCE ascribed to King Josiah.

The connection between the ancient Mediterranean love goddess, Marian, and the quince has survived in a Christian custom on the Balearic island of Mallorca. In the middle of the 20th century, Robert Graves witnessed the Feast of the Blessed Name of the Virgin Mary, which is held on the first Sunday after September 12th (corresponding with the autumn equinox on September 23rd). The villagers of Bonanova, near Palma, would perambulate a hill, carrying boughs of quince and sorb apple (*Sorbus domestica*).

**Symbolism**: Fertility and love

**Divine Associations**: Hera, Aphrodite (Greek), Marian (Pelasgian), Venus (Roman)

**Astrological Association**: Venus

OPPOSITE: *The fast-growing eucalyptus produces some of the tallest trees on earth. This mature tree is in Mortolo, northern Italy.*

# Eucalyptus *Eucalyptus*

The genus *Eucalyptus* comprises more than 400 species of fast-growing, evergreen trees (or sometimes shrubs). They are mainly native to Australia, where they have conquered the tropical north, the temperate south, the moist east and the dry west alike. Eucalyptus trees are not found wild in New Zealand. Also known as "gum" trees, they grow in a wide range of soils and conditions. They have lush foliage, unusual multi-stamened flowers and attractive, peeling bark. The seeds are contained in woody (and sometimes hard) capsules, which protect them from potential hazards such as forest fires and insects.

## Practical Uses

The eucalyptus accounts for more than 90 percent of the trees in the forests of Australia. The hard wood has been used for a multitude of purposes. Some species also furnish essential oils and tannins. Most species are very ornamental, and hence some 200 of them – but mainly the Tasmanian blue gum (*E. globulus*) – have been introduced to other temperate regions.

However, outside the parks and suburban gardens, there is a danger that eucalyptus trees can take over and push out many local species. Preferred by the paper industry, they grow very quickly (up to 100 ft/30m in only ten years) and hardly need any attention. They have also been "enhanced" by geneticists to make them super-resistant to disease, which has resulted in some eucalyptus plantations posing ecological problems in areas far away from their native ecotope of Australia. Micro-organisms cannot break down the fallen leaves, the phenoles of the leaves act like a poison to other plants, and no humus builds up on the ground. Hence the eucalyptus plantations offer no habitat for undergrowth, bees or birds – just a strange silence.

The thirsty eucalypti can also lower the ground water table, which is disastrous for neighbouring fields or woodlands. Farmers in Spain and Portugal demonstrate against having such plantations because big landowners sacrifice many cork, oak and olive trees to make room for them.

## Natural Healing

Two species of eucalyptus, the Tasmanian blue gum and the gully gum or Blackbutt peppermint (*E. smithii*), are most frequently used in healing practices.

Eucalyptus is a key ingredient in inhalants that have a powerful action in relieving blocked sinuses and clearing congestion from the head and the lungs. Both the Tasmanian blue gum and the gully gum have these properties, though the oils of the gully gum are gentler and more suitable for children. Modern research has confirmed that the oils have

*Eucalyptus oil is well known as a key ingredient in inhalants that have a powerful action in relieving blocked sinuses and clearing congestion from the head and the lungs.*

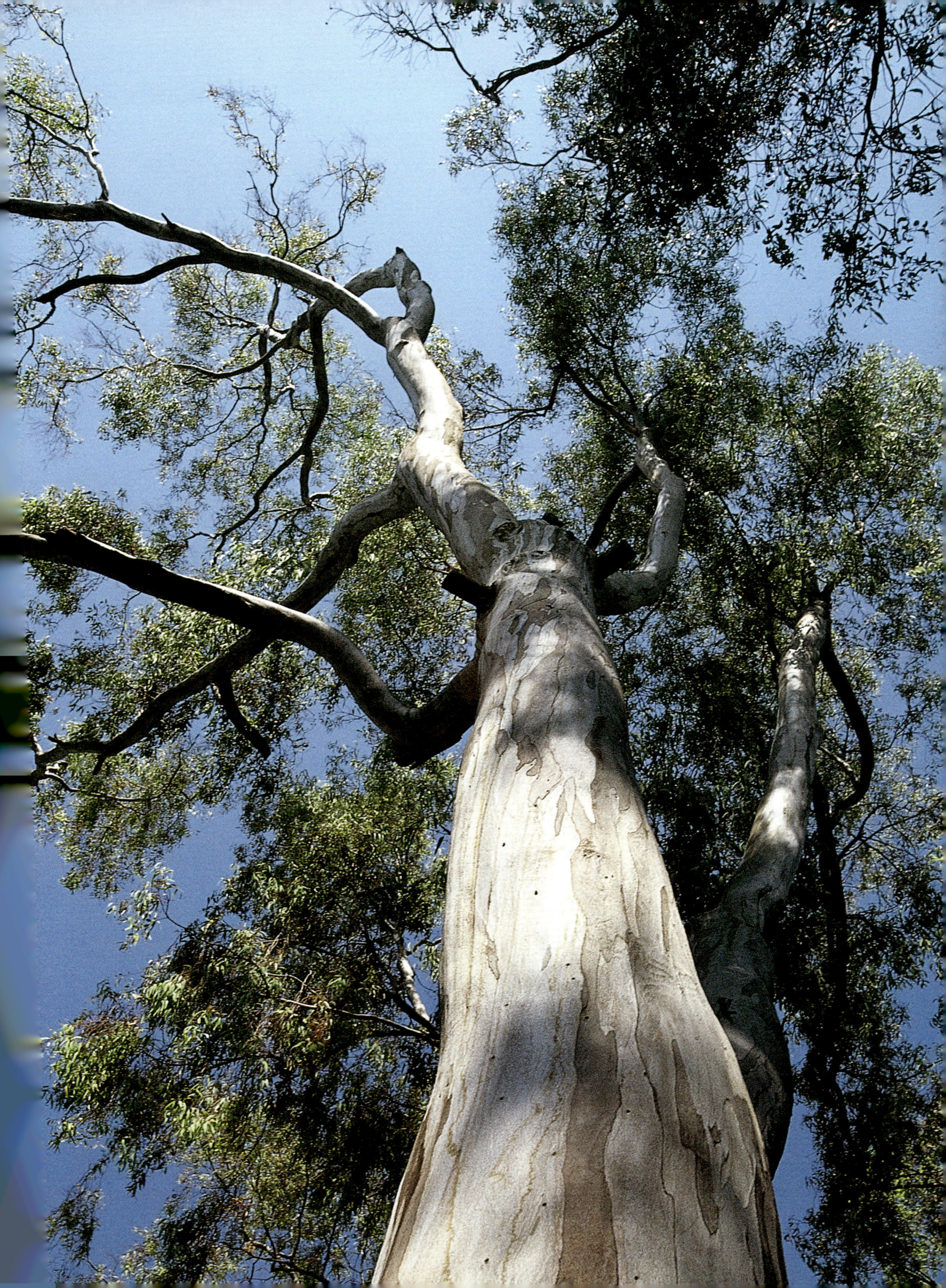

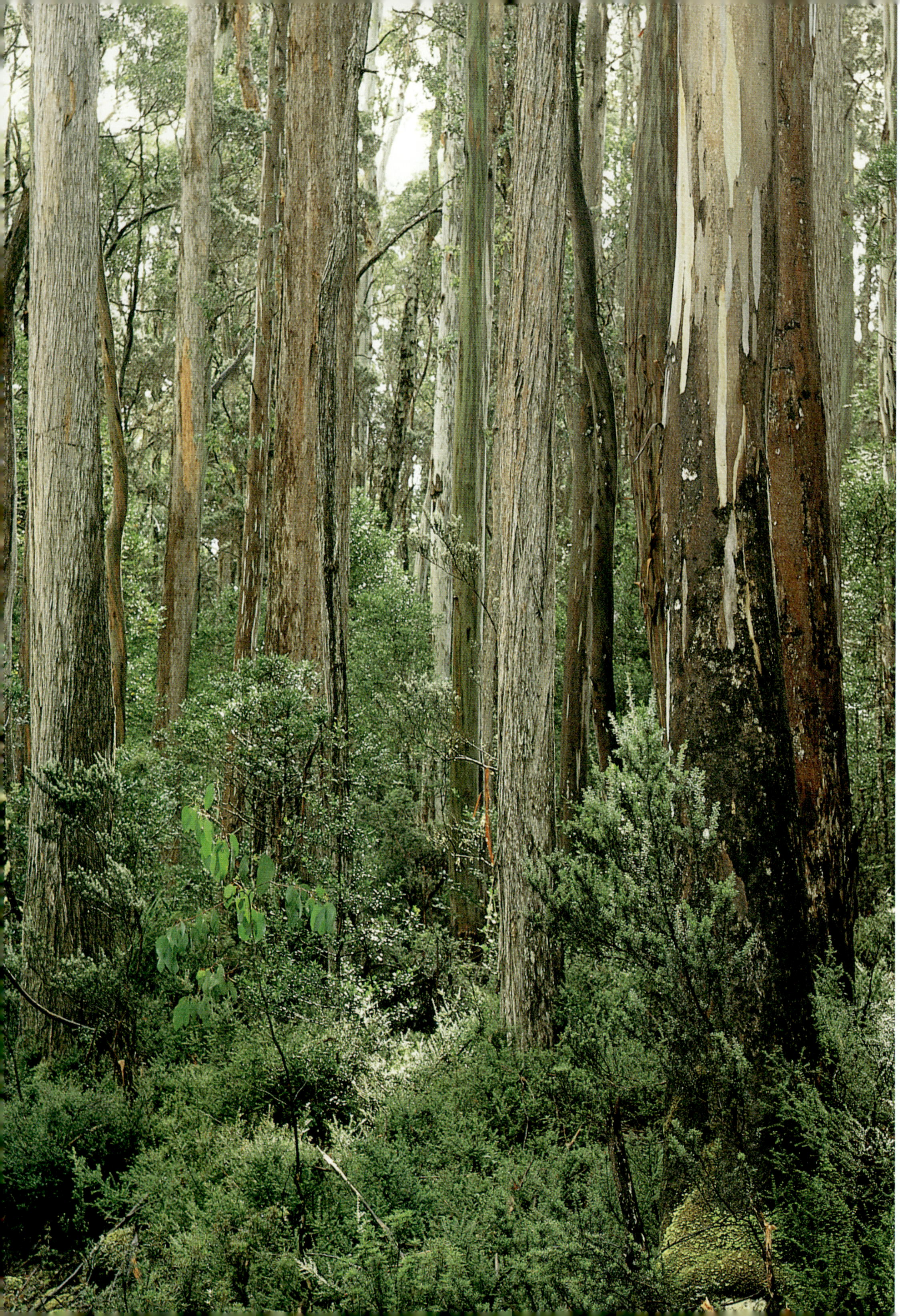

EUCALYPTUS

**OPPOSITE**: *The eucalyptus trees of the rainforests of northern Australia are a powerful presence in the "dreamtime" stories of Aborigine traditions.*

**LEFT**: *Many species of* Eucalyptus *can twist their leaves away from direct sunlight in order to decrease water transpiration.*

an antibacterial action. Applied in an oil blend, eucalyptus makes a fine massage oil for arthritis and tense muscles.

## Culture, Myth and Symbol

There is, of course, an abundance of native Australian customs and legends concerning eucalyptus trees. They are among the most sacred trees for many Aboriginal tribes, but without the tribes' permission this subject cannot be written about. Like many extant tribal nations, Aborigine groups keep an ancient *oral* tradition and do not permit the reproduction of sacred – and for a good part still *secret* – knowledge in any media. Profound wisdom about a special tree would be "initiation knowledge", passed on from an elder only to a chosen initiate who would have to come from the correct clan and background. Our lesson here is respect.

However, one sacred use of the eucalyptus that most Westerners are familiar with is the didgeridoo. Originally, this ancient ceremonial instrument was formed from a eucalyptus branch hollowed out by termites. Playing the didgeridoo creates an intense and distinctive droning sound, which is the result of the unique "circular breathing" technique employed by the player. However, it is much more than a mere hum, for traditionally among the forest tribes of northern Australia a myriad of variations, overlays and sound effects can be created by the didgeridoo user, often simulating the natural noises made by birds and animals.

The huge worldwide interest in the didgeridoo from modern musicians and New Age "shamans" alike is threatening some of the Australian eucalyptus stands (with the natural work of the termites now being replicated by that of woodworkers). Of course, the sale of a "didge" might contribute to the livelihood of an indigenous family in the short term, but most of the profits usually go to the tradespeople. If you wish to purchase a didgeridoo it might be more ethical – unless you have personal connections with the Australian "outback" – to have one made in your own locality, using *local* wood.

**Symbolism**: Restoring balance; increasing vitality

**Astrological Association**: Mercury

**Historical Spotlight**: The tallest tree ever recorded was not a redwood (as we might have expected), but a eucalyptus (*E. regnans*). Standing at Watts River, Victoria (Australia), in 1872, it was measured at 435ft (132.6m) tall, and is thought to have been previously even taller at over 500ft (152m).

OPPOSITE: *A stunning mature beech whose copper-brown buds are just bursting open to release young, vibrantly green foliage.*

# Beech *Fagus*

Beech is a small genus with about ten species of large, deciduous, monoecious trees in the northern temperate regions, easily recognized by their smooth, silver-gray bark. The alternating leaves are toothed, the male flowers occur in drooping heads. The fruits are three-angled nuts enclosed in a prickly involucre.

The common or European beech (*F. sylvatica*) reaches its maximum size of about 80ft (24m) in the deep, well-drained soils of the British Isles. Beech trees usually live for about 250 to 300 years, and a specimen occasionally reaches 500 years of age or more. Often they fall prey to core rot during their second century because of the absence of tannic acid (which is present in oaks) or resin (present in conifers). Nonetheless, the European beech is a very successful species, which, after the last Ice Age, spread over wide areas in temperate Europe.

The European beech has ovate, toothed leaves up to 4in (10cm) long, with five to nine pairs of veins. They are shiny green above, distinctively acid-green in spring, and in the autumn turn copper-brown. A popular cultivar is the copper beech (var. *purpurea*), whose leaves appear purple from below.

The American beech (*F. americana* or *F. grandifolia*) has leaves up to 5in long (12.5cm), with nine to 15 pairs of veins. The Oriental beech (*F. orientalis* or *F. macrophylla*) grows up to 100ft (32m) high and has silky, hairy twigs.

## Practical Uses

Up until the Iron Age, the beech made an essential contribution to human nutrition. It is no coincidence that the ancient Greek name for this tree, *phegos*, is related to their word for "to eat", *phagein*. The leaf buds and spring leaves are a healthy addition to vegetable salads or soups.

Shelled beech nuts can be roasted and used in bread and pastries, and also made into a coffee-like beverage. In the Alpine regions and north of the Alps, where no olive trees grow, beech nuts were once an important local source of cooking oil. They comprise up to 50 percent oil, which can be extracted by pressing. And beech oil contains up to 23 percent protein, making it a rich source of this essential dietary component.

Among Native North American tribes too, beech nuts have been widely used as food. The Tsalagi even seek out and raid the beech-nut stores of chipmunks, which saves them the labour entailed in gathering and hulling the nuts themselves, and also ensures that any bad nuts have already been discarded.

However, in more recent history the sustenance provided by the beech has been mainly for livestock. Cattle, goats and sheep thrive when leaf fodder is part of their diet, because the leaves are rich in minerals, starch and protein. This ancient agricultural practice only changed in the 20th century, when artificial fodder supplements were introduced. You can sometimes still observe cows and horses today chewing away at wooden fences because these contain the carbohydrates missing from their modern diet.

What makes the beech tree so important is its highly nutritious nuts, or "mast", which traditionally were fed to pigs. Cultivating pig mast in the autumnal oak and beech forests was a widely accepted practice in many parts of Europe (see "Oak", pp.172–7) right up until the Middle Ages. In fact, the three trees that provide the most nutrient-packed

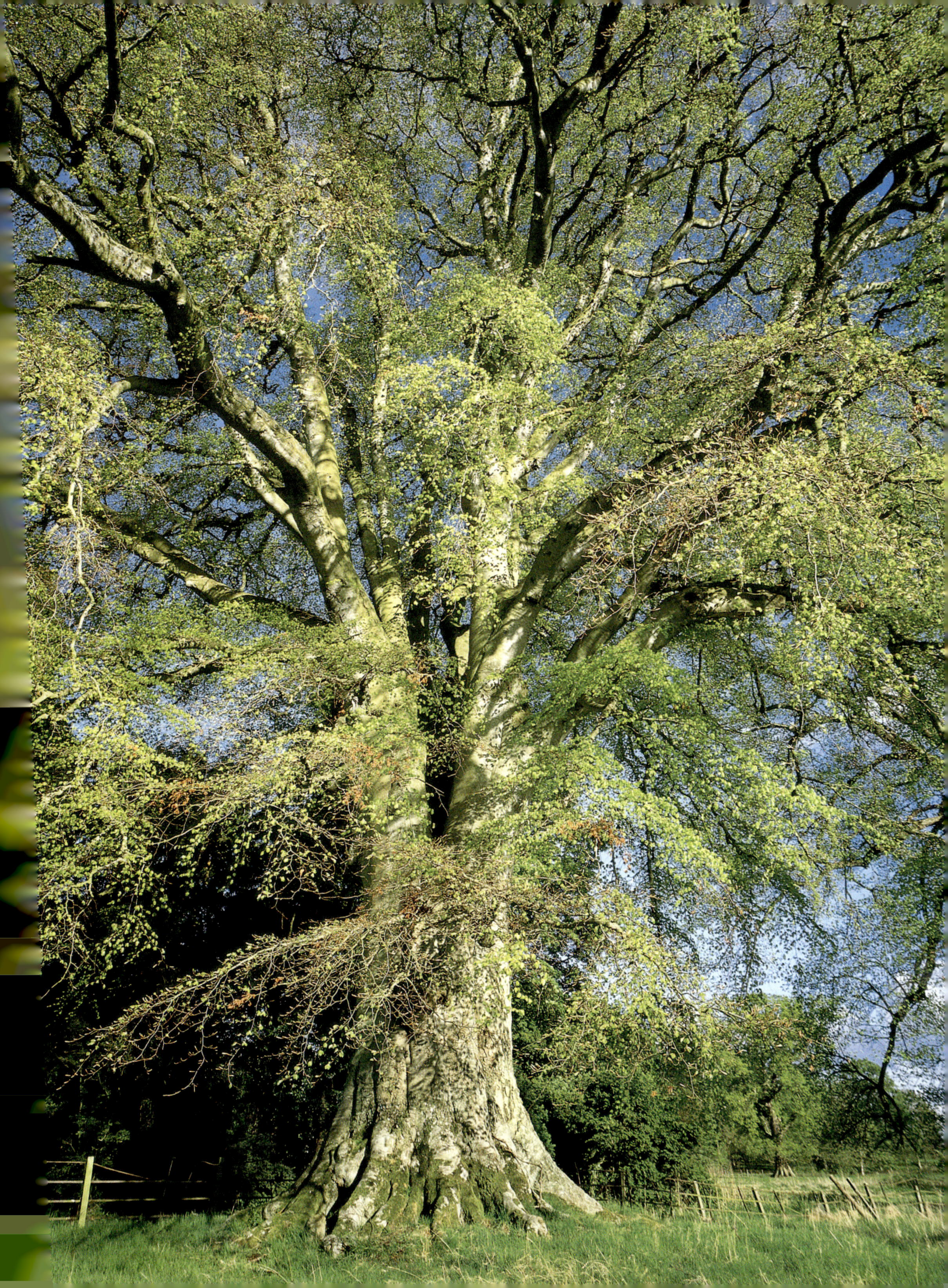

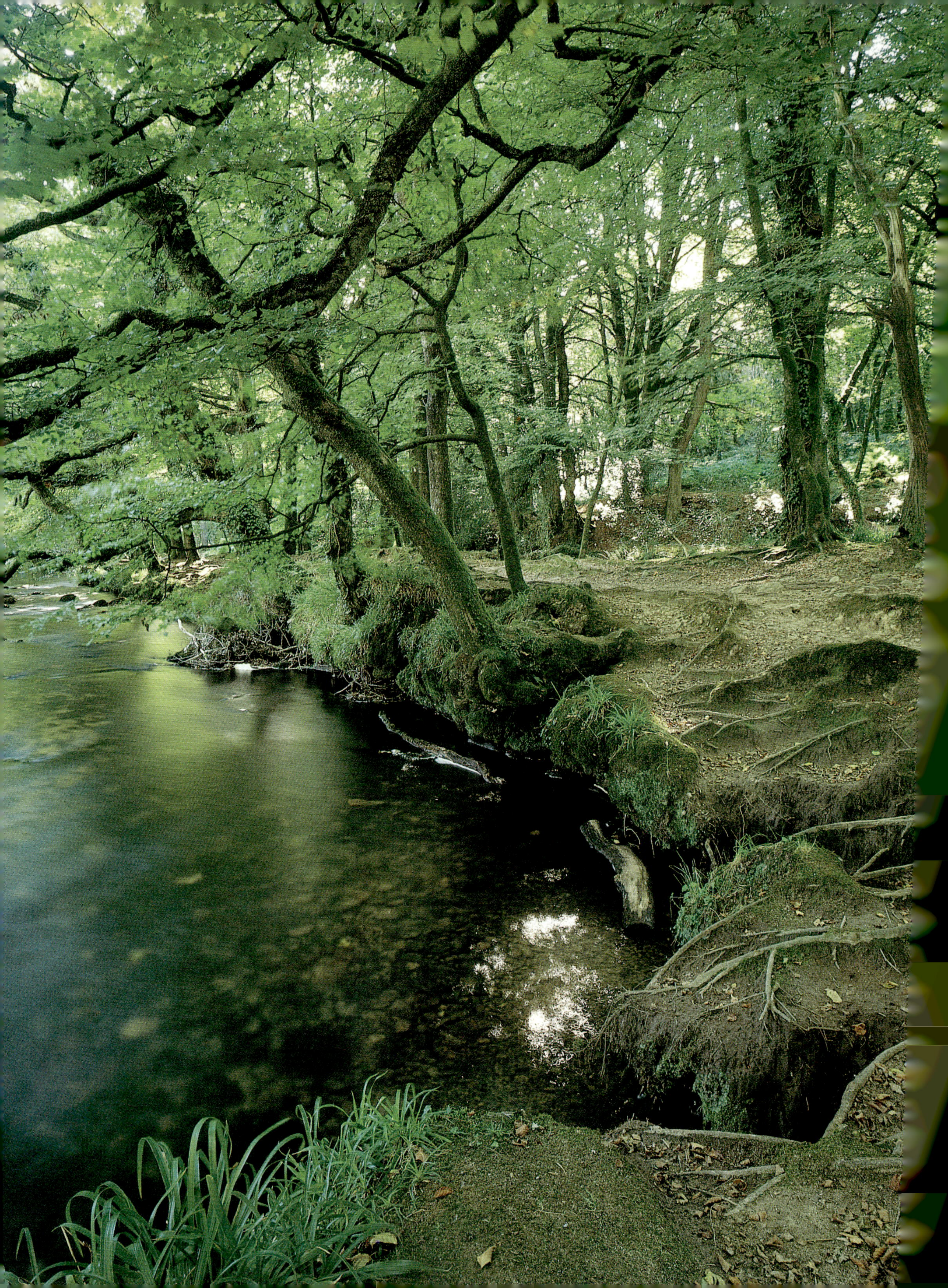

OPPOSITE: *A river runs through the beechwood on Bodmin Moor, an expanse of historic common land in Cornwall, southwestern England.*

fruit – the oak, the beech and the sweet chestnut – are all members of the beech family (*Fagaceae*).

Because beech wood is heavy and hard (but not very durable) it has also been used widely in many cultures to make objects such as furniture, tool handles and bowls.

## Natural Healing

In both Native North American and European traditions, the astringent, antiseptic and disinfectant properties of the beech have been used medicinally. Beech is generally cooling, and a bark preparation was an old remedy for fever. However, it is no longer used in herbal medicine. The Bach Flower Remedy of beech enhances sympathy and tolerance. The tree essence brings confidence in self-expression.

## Culture, Myth and Symbol

In the French Pyrenees, various ancient Celtic altars have been found dedicated to the god Fagus, or "beech tree". While in Rome, Jupiter – who, like Zeus, was generally regarded as the god of the oak tree – was also worshipped in a beech sanctuary on the Esquiline (one of the seven hills of Rome), under the name of Jupiter Fagutalis. Another sacred beech grove, at Tusculum, was dedicated to Diana, the goddess of the wild woods.

During the Iron Age, Germanic tribes practised divination by means of writing runes on wooden sticks or tiny tablets. Although most of the runic talismans that have come down to us today are made from yew wood, various trees were used depending on the local ecology, the preference of the rune-reader and the nature of the questions to be asked. Beech wood was one of them. And parallel to the transition from magical alphabet (which the original runes were considered to be) to ordinary alphabet in the eighth century or before, the once sacred symbols became known as *letters* (from the Latin *littera*). In German the word for letters is *Buchstaben*, which translates as "beech sticks". Thin tablets of beech were bound together to create an alternative to scrolls and a novel way in which to accumulate and preserve knowledge: the book. Hence many words for "book" are derived from the name of the beech – for example, the Anglo-Saxon *bok* (beech) and *bec* (book), the modern German *Buche* (beech) and *Buch* (book); and the Swedish *bok* (beech) and *bok* (book).

As we have seen, the beech has not only offered humans physical food, but also intellectual sustenance through its association in Europe with the development of writing. Writing gave humankind greater access to knowledge. Hence the beech can be said to bring together the traditions of the Tree of Life and the Tree of Knowledge.

**Symbolism**: Understanding, sustenance and preservation

**Divine Association**: Jupiter Fagutalis (Celtic and Roman)

**Astrological Association**: Saturn

**Superstition**: In Westphalia, Germany, in the 18th century, it was believed that babies were picked out of a hollow beech tree, rather than delivered by the stork.

**Historical Spotlight**: Johannes Gutenberg invented the printing press in about 1450. A curious tale relates that he first had the idea when a letter he carved from beech bark made an imprint in the paper it was wrapped in.

# Common fig *Ficus carica*

Figs are a vast genus of over 800 species of trees, shrubs and woody vines with milky sap, found throughout the tropical and subtropical regions. Figs thrive in warm climates but can tolerate frost. The leaves are lobed, thick and usually large. The many seeds are contained in a globose, oblong or pear-shaped, fleshy fruit which has a small opening at its tip. Not all figs have edible fruits.

The common fig (*F. carica*) is a broad, irregular, deciduous tree that can grow up to 30ft (9m) in height. The thick, deeply-lobed leaves are rough above and downy underneath. In the strict botanical sense, the figs are not fruits but hollow fleshy receptacles which contain the many true fruits that we call "seeds".

The fig has a most unusual way of reproduction. It occurs in two forms: the "wild" bisexual tree, the caprifig (*F. capriticus*), and the cultivated, female tree. The latter has female flowers only, while the wild form has bisexual flowers inside hollow receptacles. In the early ripening stage there is an opening at the tip of the "wild" caprifig that gives access to a special insect – a gall wasp (*Blastophaga psenes*) – which deposits its eggs in the ovaries of the flowers inside and turns them to galls. This prevents the flower from fruiting, but the young wasps will be dusted with pollen before leaving the caprifig. They then visit the female figs on the cultivated tree and fertilize it. Its fruit production is totally dependent on these insects.

## Practical Uses

Figs have been a principal part of human sustenance since times immemorial. Archeologists found 7,000-year-old dried figs at the Neolithic settlement at Gezer in Israel. The common fig has been cultivated since the earliest times for its delicious and nourishing fruits. In hot climates fig trees also provide welcome shade.

## Natural Healing

Figs are rich in calcium, potassium, phosphorus and iron. The syrup is a well-known, safe and gentle laxative with some soothing expectorant effects that are useful for relieving dry, irritating coughs. The milky latex is effective when applied directly to warts (but avoid getting it on the surrounding skin, because fig latex is an irritant and can provoke dermatitis). An infusion of fig leaves has traditionally been used effectively in the treatment of diabetes – a use that has been supported by recent research that indicates it can have a hypoglycemic effect on patients with insulin-dependent diabetes.

In Chinese Traditional Medicine the fruits of the fig tree are considered to be sweet and of neutral temperature. They act as a tonic for the essential energy of the body, as well as the blood. This is important because in Traditional Chinese Medicine the blood is also the house of the mind and provides the physical root of our consciousness – it grounds thoughts and emotions within the body. Figs help to regulate the heart and to remove toxins from the body. One or two eaten at bedtime can relieve constipation.

In ayurvedic medicine, figs are considered to be sweet, astringent and cooling. They increase *kapha* and relieve *vata* and *pitta*.

The tree essence of figs is regarded as a soul food that combats feelings of emptiness while at the same time boosting energy to aid achievement.

# COMMON FIG

**BELOW**: *A young fig requires an uncrowded location if its fruit is to benefit from ample levels of sun to help it to ripen.*

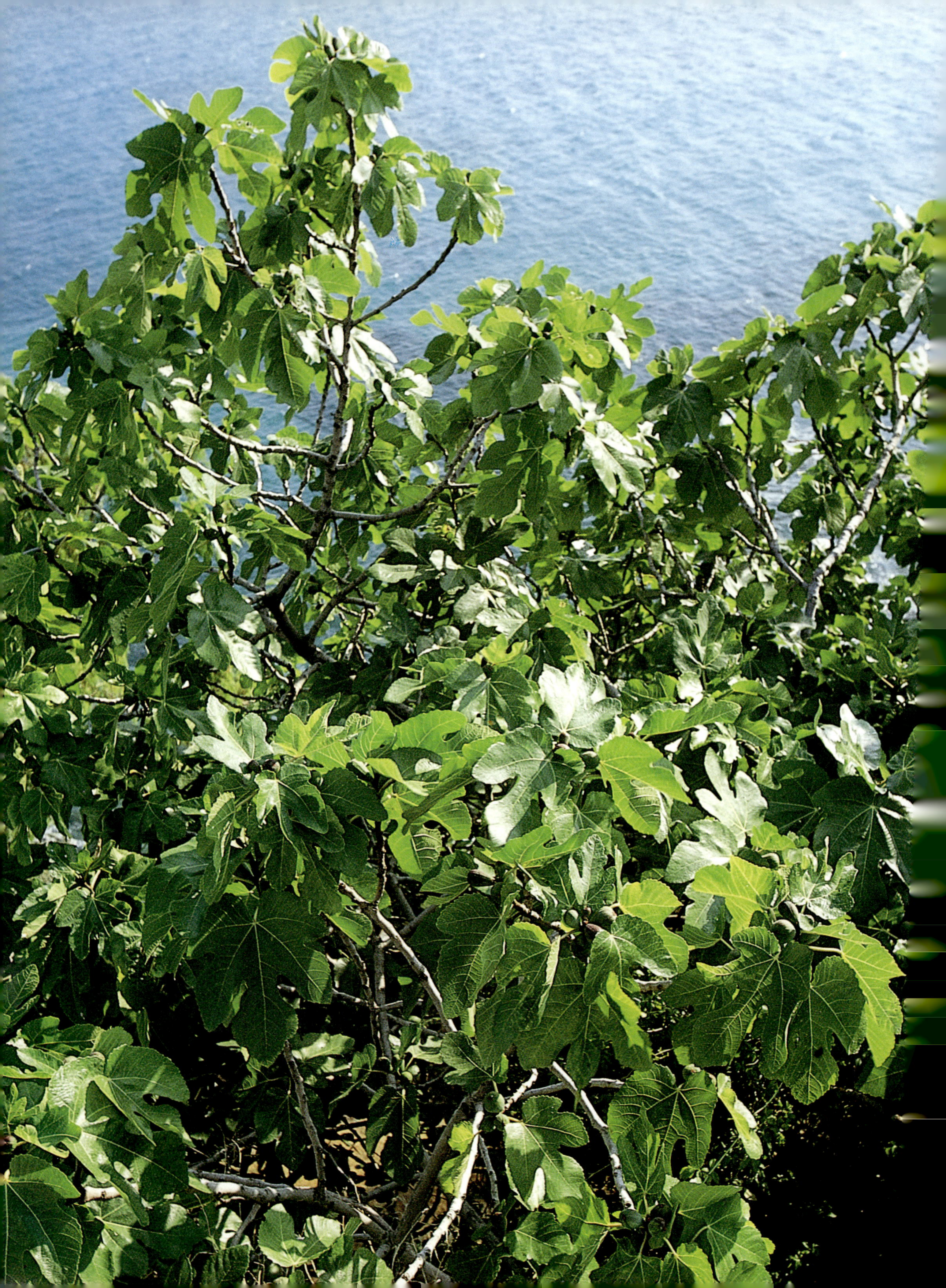

**LEFT**: *Fig trees fare best in Mediterranean and tropical climates, but they are able to tolerate a degree of frost.*

**RIGHT**: *Figs are beautiful as well as delicious, changing their colour from green through to pink, red, scarlet and deep purplish black as they ripen.*

## Culture, Myth and Symbol

The fig tree is mentioned 37 times in the Old Testament, and it is the very first plant named in the Bible – after eating the forbidden fruit, Adam and Eve "knew that they were naked; so they stitched fig leaves together and made themselves loincloths" (Genesis 3:7). And, ever since, scholars have wondered time and again whether the fig tree – standing so close by – could have been the Tree of Knowledge itself. Interestingly, in Greek Orthodox iconography, the fig is the fruit of temptation. But the original Hebrew text only mentions a "fruit" (not an apple or a fig). So the fig tree is not the culprit; rather, it helps Adam and Eve in providing their first clothing for their new lives outside Eden.

In many ways, this fruit is associated with fertility. In the ancient Mediterranean, figs were a symbol of sexuality, and used as an aphrodisiac. Noteworthy is the fig's similarity in appearance to human testicles – in ancient Greek the plural for figs was also the word for testicles. And the fig was sacred to Dionysus, the god of ecstasy. In Attica (the fertile peninsula on which Athens is located), Dionysus was called *Philosykos*, "friend of the fig", and statues of him were made of its wood. At the annual festival of Dionysus, a giant phallus made from fig wood was carried around in procession.

The Spartans, too, had a cult which gave thanks to Dionysus for giving this tree to humankind. Because the ancient gift of the fig marked the important cultural transition from nomadic, hunter-gatherer society to a sedentary population of farmers, the fig was carried at the very front of the Greek *plynteria* meaning "procession," and called *hegetria*, "(female) leader". In Athens there was a consecrated place, named *Hiera Syke*, or "sacred fig", where the first fig tree was said to have grown. This fig was sacred to Demeter, the grain goddess, who also had a sacred fig grove near the major sanctuary of Eleusis.

In Rome, on the western slope of the Palatine hill, stood the consecrated "Ruminal Fig", protected by a fence. At the time of Augustus (63BCE–14CE), this was said to be the place where Romulus and Remus, the mythical founders of Rome, had been washed ashore by the Tiber river. They sheltered by the tree, underneath which they were suckled by a wolf. The name of the *Ruminal* fig is derived from *ruma*, "mother's breast", an association that was passed on in the names of Romulus, and Rome itself, where henceforward the fig was regarded as a bringer of good luck.

---

**Symbolism**: Fertility and good fortune

**Divine Associations:** Dionysus and Demeter (ancient Greek)

**Astrological Association**: Venus

**Historical Spotlight**: The Athenians were so proud of their figs that exporting them was forbidden by law. When the Persian King Xerxes invaded Greece in 480BCE, raiding Athens on September 21st, he celebrated by having figs as one of the courses at dinner.

# Sycomore fig *Ficus sycomorus*

A species of the vast *Ficus* genus, the sycomore fig (*F. sycomorus*) is a handsome tree that reaches up to 60ft (18m) in height. Native to northern Africa and Asia Minor, it is much larger than the common fig. Its leaves are oval to heart-shaped, and up to 6in (15cm) long. The ovoid to globular figs are 1in (2.5cm) in diameter, and are borne in panicles on leafless twigs from the trunk and older branches.

Like the common fig (see p.90), the sycomore fig co-operates with its own special insect, *Sycophaga sycomori*, a tiny wasp that enters the fig through a small opening in the apex, and carries out the complicated fertilization process. However, unlike the common fig, all sycomore trees have figs containing both sexes of flowers.

Before the advent of modern agriculture, with its extensive irrigation systems and plant imports, these majestic, shady trees must have been a stunning sight. Then, they were the largest and sometimes the only trees in the desert – flourishing as if by magic in the driest of environments with no visible water source. They survived, of course, because they drew from hidden subterranean watercourses.

## Practical Uses

The sycomore fig was of outstanding importance in ancient Egypt, where it was one of the most sacred trees. But despite its revered status, people were permitted to eat its fruit. Certain trees were ceremonially chosen for their timber, to be used for coffins.

In Palestine, the sycomore fig (Hebrew *shikmim* or *shikmoth*) was common in the lowlands, and its fruits, which were inferior in taste and sugar content to those of the common fig, were eaten by the poor. Here, the tree was valued mainly for its lightweight wood. The sycomore fig is still cultivated in South Africa, Egypt and the Lebanon.

## Culture, Myth and Symbol

In ancient Egypt, various principalities took their names from sacred trees – for example, the "Principality of the Terebinth". The area around Memphis was known as the "Land of the Sycomore Fig". Here, the most famous specimen was the "Sycomore Fig of the South". Like all sycomore fig trees, it was regarded as the living body of Hathor, who is the important goddess of the sky. Hathor was also called the "Mistress of the Sacred Tree".

Another famous sycomore fig, the "Tree of the Virgin", stood at Metairieh. Others were sacred to Nuit (an alternative form of the sky goddess), Selket (Isis' sister, who protected the dead), and the ancient creator goddess, Neith. All these trees were worshipped enthusiastically and presented with regular offerings of produce from the land, especially cucumbers, figs and grapes. Water jars stood next to the sacred trees so that passers-by could recite a prayer and pour some of the precious liquid over the roots.

Even more significant was the blessing that the goddess of the sycomore fig offered for the rite of passage into the afterlife. When the soul of the deceased started its journey

---

**Symbolism**: Nourishment and ultimate blessing

**Divine Associations**: Hathor, Nuit, Selket, Neith (all ancient Egyptian)

**Astrological Association**: Pluto

*ABOVE: A group of sycomore fig trees growing in South Africa's Kruger National Park.*

through the dangerous realms of the underworld, it soon came to the eternal sycomore fig. Out of its crown Hathor or Nuit would appear and offer otherworldly figs and the water of life to the deceased. This encounter would bestow the soul with the highest prize of all: eternal life. The following invocation in the Egyptian *Book of the Dead* asks the goddess of the tree for the breath of immortality.

> O, Sycomore of the Goddess Nuit,
> let there be given to me
> the air which is in Thee.

Being of utmost importance in the realm of the dead, sycomore fig trees also enjoyed first-class treatment in the land of the living. Indeed, the sacred trees of ancient Egypt – the sycomore fig, the persea, the acacia, the tamarisk and the willow – are all prime examples of the positive effects that religion can have on ecology. Unfortunately, the persea is now extinct in Egypt (although a few specimens survive in Ethiopia.) The others have had more luck and still grow in Egypt today. But the status of the sycomore fig has sunk from that of master to slave – where once it was worshipped and brought offerings, it is now regarded merely as an ordinary plant that is useful for commercial fruit production.

# Banyan
## *Ficus bengalensis*

A member of the vast *Ficus* genus, the banyan (*F. bengalensis*) is one of the wonders of the plant world. Its ability to form and send down aerial roots to make additional trunks to support the canopy enables a single tree to spread over several acres. A single individual banyan in the Calcutta Botanical Gardens in India took only about 200 years to grow into one of the world's largest-canopied trees. Its crown has an average diameter of more than 430ft (131m), and is supported by more than 1,775 prop-roots. This tree can shelter more than 20,000 people. However, there are a number of banyan trees that are considerably older, and other specimens of even greater dimensions.

Banyan leaves are leathery, ovate to elliptic, and up to 8in (20cm) long. The globose, orange-red, downy figs are up to ½in (1.3cm) in diameter and appear in axillary pairs.

The Krishna-bor (*F. bengalensis* var. *Krishnae*) is a unique variety with curiously cup-shaped leaves, hence its other name, "Krishna's buttercup". A related species is the Chinese banyan (*F. infectoria*) – a huge specimen was described by the English botanist Ernest H. Wilson in 1913 as measuring 70ft (21m) in height, with a girth of 47ft (14m).

### Practical Uses

The banyan is sacred to many peoples in India, Pakistan, China and southeast Asia. Although sacred trees by their very nature don't yield "practical" products (such as timber or leaf fodder), they are valuable in other ways.

RIGHT: *In south and east Asia, banyans are considered to be the home of tree spirits.*

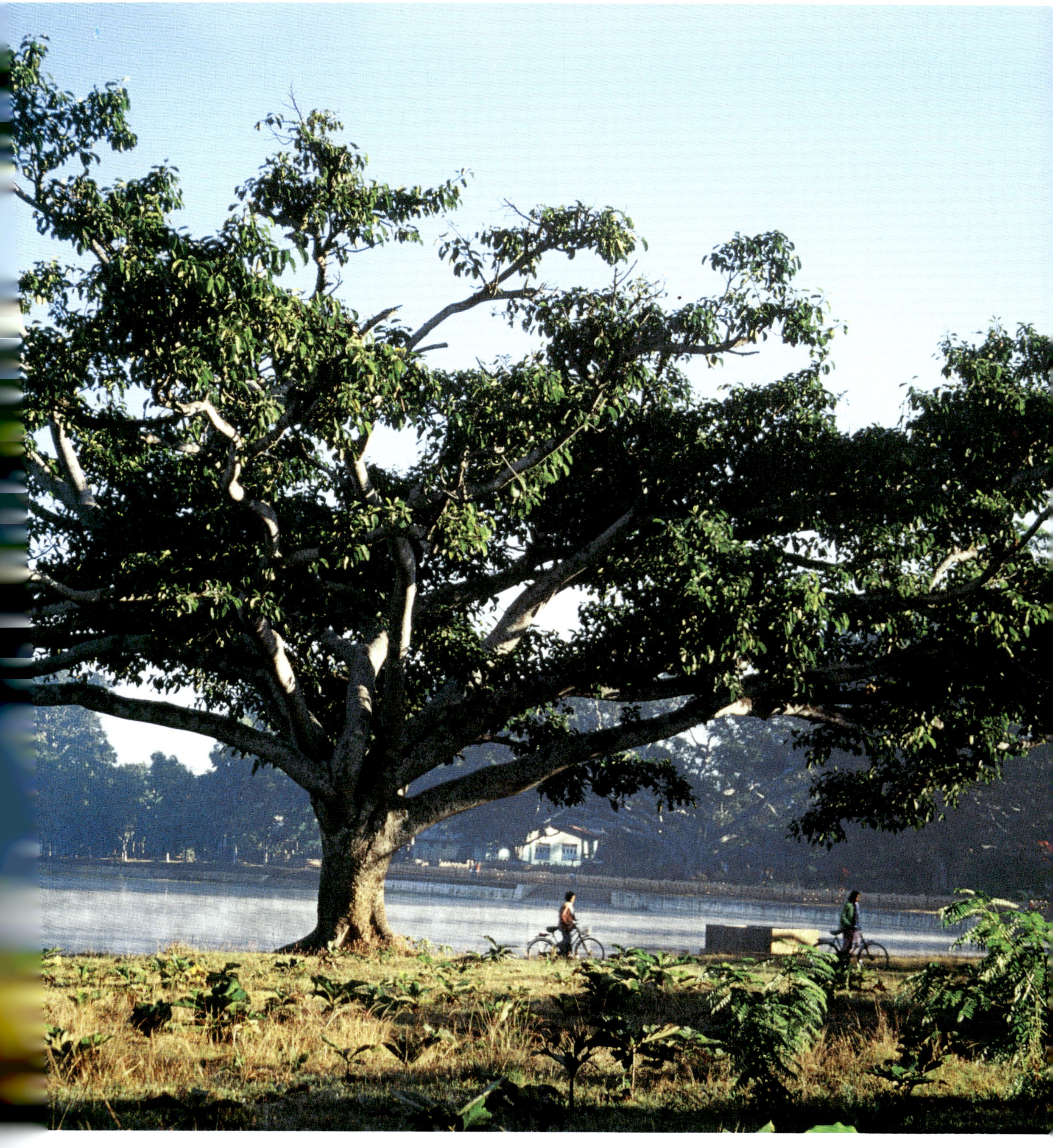

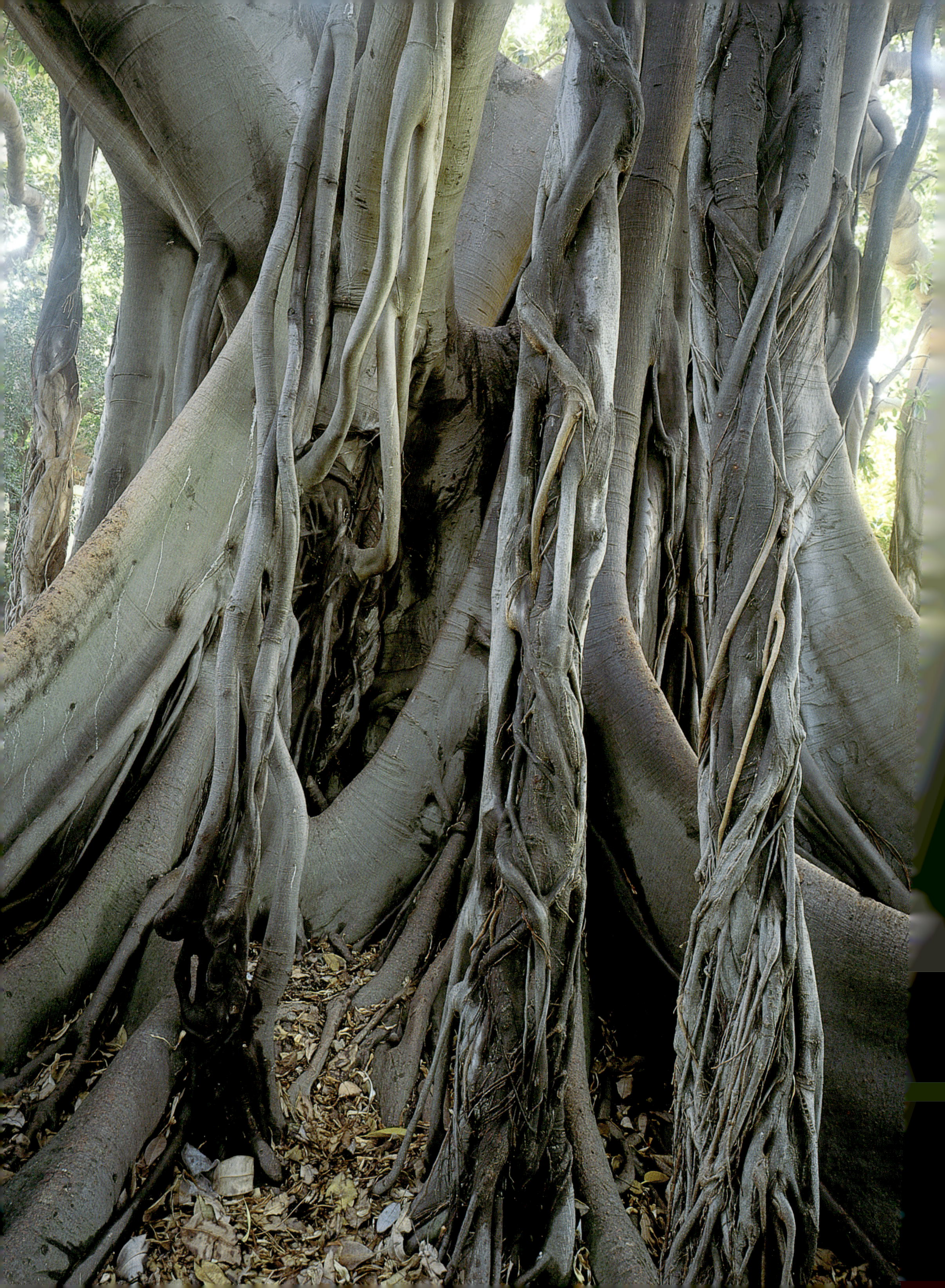

**OPPOSITE**: *Old banyans spread out laterally with the help of aerial roots, which can develop to form entire groves.*

A sacred tree is a part of the biosphere that is safe from human harm and often provides a habitat for other rare species of plants, as well as for animals, birds and insects. It also gives shelter to humans, and offers peace for the mind or the soul as a place for contemplation or worship.

## Natural Healing

The bark and leaf buds have been used in ayurvedic tradition to stop wounds bleeding. Banyan bark is taken internally as an infusion for its astringent effect on the bowels, which helps in conditions such as dysentery and diarrhea.

## Culture, Myth and Symbol

The banyan has been one of the most sacred trees of eastern Asia. According to Indian anthropologist Dr Alka Pande, ancient traditions state that "at the time of the deluge [flood], the eternal power had transformed itself into the banyan tree". In Hinduism, the tree maintained its ancient role as the abode of divine presence. The earliest Indian scriptures, the *Vedas* and the *Upanishads*, link trees, and in particular the banyan, with Brahma itself – the immortal, innermost spirit of the universe. The *Katha Upanishad* says, "This universe is a tree existing eternally, its root aloft, its branches below. The pure root of the tree is Brahman, the immortal … ."

The tree also features in the *Bhagavad Gita*, which states "There is a banyan tree which has its roots upward and its branches down, and whose leaves are the Vedic hymns. One who knows this tree is the knower of the *Vedas*." The sacred scriptures themselves are regarded as the leaves of the Universal Tree. This makes it the Tree of Knowledge as well as the Tree of Life.

The motif of an upside-down tree also appears in Jewish mysticism, in the Kabbalah. The tree denotes that the root of the world is the ("upper") spirit world, the forces of which emanate to form the worlds of lower vibrations, right down to the physical plane.

During the centuries following the enlightenment of Gautama Siddhartha (the Buddha) under the pipal tree (see pp.100–101), there were others who achieved the Buddha state. Seven are celebrated in the famous Stupa of Barhut, which dates from 184–72BCE, and one of its reliefs depicts the banyan as the Bodhi tree of Kasyapa, a bodhisattva.

One of the most sacred mountains in China is Mount Omei or Omei Shan. In 1913, the botanist E.H. Wilson described the path to its peak as lined with more than 70 Buddhist temples and monasteries. A number of "truly magnificent" and enormous banyan trees sheltered the old temples. Wilson measured the largest one as 80ft (24m) tall, with a girth of 48ft (14.6m) at 5ft (1.5m) above ground.

**Symbolism**: The World Tree

**Divine Association:** Brahma (Hindu)

**Astrological Association**: The universe

**Historical Spotlight**: Legend has it that on his India campaign in 326BCE, Alexander the Great and his entire army found shelter under one single banyan tree. This tree is said to be the one on the banks of the Nebudda River, east of Mumbai, which in 1999 reportedly had a crown of 637ft (194m) in diameter, supported by about 320 main trunks and more than 3,000 smaller ones – huge indeed.

OPPOSITE: *The bodhi tree at Bodh Gaya – a sanctuary that attracts pilgrims from all over the world – is a descendant of the tree under which Buddha attained enlightenment.*

# Pipal or Bo *Ficus religiosa*

The pipal or bo (*F. religiosa*), another member of the vast *Ficus* genus, is a large, deciduous, fast-growing tree that starts its life as an epiphyte (a plant growing on another plant, but not deriving nourishment from it). Its round-ovate leaves have a unique, narrow, terminal projection half as long as the main leaf body. The sessile, dark purple figs are up to ½in (1.3cm) in diameter. Native to India and southeast Asia, this tree is now widely planted in the tropics.

## Practical Uses

Sacred to Hindus and Buddhists, the pipal has always been revered by the indigenous peoples of India. Only the vessels containing the sacred soma drink (said to confer immortality) and the fire-drills (used to start sacred fires) in the temple were made from pipal wood.

## Natural Healing

In India the pipal has a rich heritage of traditional medicinal uses. The juice from the leaves (extracted by holding them near a fire) was dripped into the ear as a remedy for earache. The powdered bark has been used on wounds, applied directly as a powder or made up into a paste. In Ayurveda, decoctions of powdered bark are used externally as an astringent and antiseptic – for example, for wounds and ulcers, and to treat infections of the uterus and the vagina.

**Symbolism:** Enlightenment

**Divine Association:** Buddha

**Astrological Association:** The universe

## Culture, Myth and Symbol

The pipal is one of the most sacred trees not only in India but also in Sri Lanka and Nepal. More than 2,600 years ago, the Indian Prince Siddhartha Gautama, weary of the profane life at court and looking for deeper truth, came to the tree sanctuary of Bodh Gaya in the province of Bihar, in northeast India, and its huge pipal tree. At this time, the pipal was the sacred tree of Vishnu, the eternal divine being, and it was, by Brahma's word, the appointed ruler over all trees.

Siddhartha chose this tree under which to seek the knowledge that might release all beings from suffering. He found the ideal position under the tree – this physical place under the World Tree being symbolic of the perfect point of balance in the mind. From this point of stillness and non-attachment, he could see the wheel of the world spin. The sacred tree became his all-supporting mid-point, and the pairs of opposites all around came together in the centre, like the spokes of a wheel radiating from the hub.

After he had succeeded in finding the "ultimate and unconditioned truth" (*bodhi*), Siddhartha became *Buddha*, "the Enlightened One", and the tree that had given him shelter and strength was called the *bo* or *bodhi* tree – the "tree of awakening". Many devotional images and statues have since been created, portraying Buddha under the bodhi tree, fighting his inner battles against demonic assaults and temptations. However, during the first centuries of Buddhism, the Enlightened One was not depicted as a human sitting under a bodhi tree, but as a bodhi tree with an empty seat or throne at the base of its trunk. This was to symbolize that enlightenment is not about the human being, but about transcending the boundaries of the human condition, and in a deep, mystical way becoming one with the universe, which is represented by the World Tree. In this sense, the Great Awakener was not Buddha, but the bodhi tree.

Buddha's sacred pipal at Bodh Gaya was still thriving in the seventh century CE, when the Chinese traveller Hiuen Tsiang (603–664) described the sanctuary. The pipal was 40–50ft (12–15m) high, and its roots were bathed with scented water and perfumed milk at an annual festival. The sounds of music and the fragrance of flowers and incense filled the air, while tens of thousands of pilgrims joined in the ceremonies. Buddha himself had encouraged the worship of the pipal. He had asked his disciple Ananda to take a branch from the pipal tree under which he had found enlightenment, and to plant it in the court of Vihara at Sravasti. According to the Indian anthropologist Randhawa, Buddha said that "he who worships it [the pipal tree] will receive the same reward as if he worshipped me in person."

In the third century BCE, King Ashoka (268–232BCE) took a cutting (some sources say a fig) from Buddha's pipal and sent it as a gift to King Tissa of Sri Lanka. It was planted in Anuradhapura by the king himself, who prophesied that it would thrive forever. It is still standing today and many sacred bodhi trees in temple gardens throughout Sri Lanka are believed to be cuttings from this pipal.

BELOW: *An old but still thriving ash coppice near Aberfeldy, Scotland. Ash coppices particularly well, producing good wood for centuries.*

# Ash *Fraxinus*

*Fraxinus* is one of about 29 genera of the olive family (*Oleaceae*). It comprises about 65 species of mainly hardy, fast-growing trees, mostly native to the northern temperate zone with a few extending towards the tropics. They thrive in almost any soil, and are tolerant of windswept and even air-polluted conditions.

The leaves are opposite, in most species pinnate and usually deciduous. The small flowers appear in panicles in early spring, in some species before the leaves. The small flower is four-lobed or irregularly cut; the two to six petals are separate or united in pairs at the base. The fruits, known as "keys", each contain one seed and are winged.

The common ash (*F. excelsior*) is native to Europe and the Caucasus, and reaches a height of up to 140ft (42m). It has distinctive black winter buds. The leaves have seven to 11 leaflets, each up to 5in (12.5cm) long. In eastern North America, the white ash (*F. americana*) is a noble shade tree and one of the fastest-growing hardwoods, while the medium-sized black ash (*F. nigra* M.) grows much better in the wild than in cultivation.

BELOW: *An ash silhouetted in late spring. The common ash is among the latest of deciduous trees to come into leaf.*

## Practical Uses

In Europe, many warriors of the Bronze and Iron Ages (including Celtic and Germanic tribes, as well as the Greeks and their neighbours) used straight, strong and tough ash wood to make their spears and shield handles. In legend, Achilles kills Hector with an ash spear. In peaceful times, too, the wood has many uses. For example, it is used to make tool handles, oars, gates and sports equipment. The ash is one of the prime trees for coppicing, and hence has provided humans with sticks and poles since Neolithic times.

However, perhaps the ash's greatest significance is in its function as a living tree that contributes to farmyard and forest economies. In and north of the Alps, its leaves are second only to elm foliage as leaf fodder, as they are rich in nutrients and soft for cattle, sheep, goats and deer to chew. The lopping of ash trees on the farm was a vital, traditional practice until the agricultural industry developed artificial supplements for stockfood and bred cows that thrived on such food. Today in the Alps, an increasing number of farmers have begun to question such practices (which are often compulsory by legislation) and they are searching for ways to return to traditional methods and cattle breeds.

## Natural Healing

In Europe, the ash has been praised in herbal medicine texts since the fourth century BCE, when the Greek physician Hippocrates (c.460–377BCE) used it as an infusion for gout and rheumatism. Tea made from ash leaves collected in spring or early summer and dried has a laxative and diuretic effect. It increases the flow of urine and the excretion of uric acid and also stimulates sluggish bowels, thus helping the

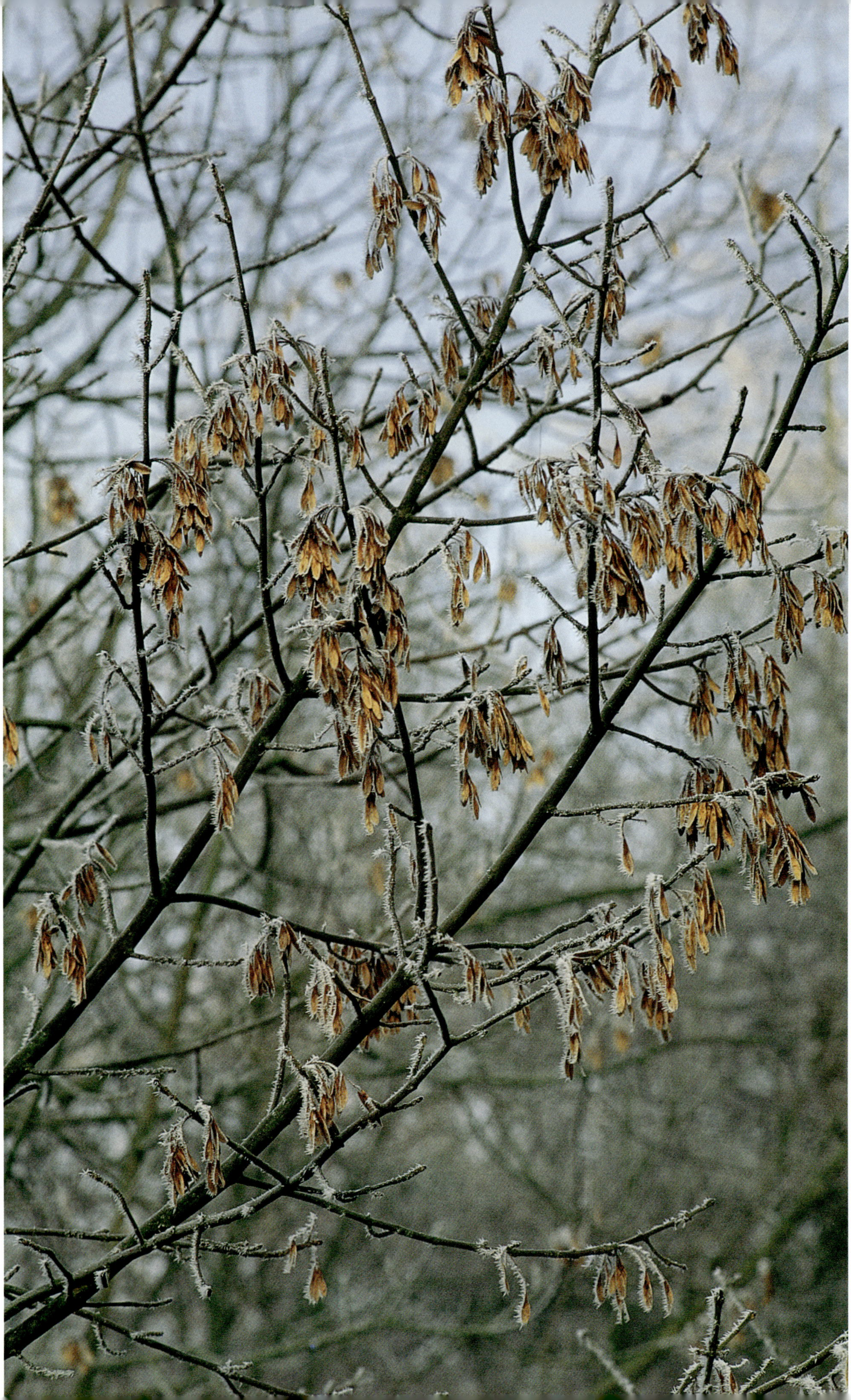

OPPOSITE: *Dry ash keys can last on the tree well into winter and even beyond. Traditionally, ripe ones were prized by herbal physicians.*

body to detoxify. Ash keys make a delicious addition to spring salads.

In classical homeopathy, too, the ash remedy helps with gout and rheumatism. The tree essence enhances a sense of strength and flexibility.

**Culture, Myth and Symbol**

In ancient Greece, the nymphs of the ash, the Meliae, were said to be the daughters of the cloud and sea spirits. Later, in Classical times, the ash was sacred to Poseidon, the god of the ocean, and pieces of its wood were taken aboard ships as good luck charms on sea crossings. Interestingly, thousands of years later in the 19th century, and at the other end of Europe, many of the Irish migrants did exactly the same when they crossed the Atlantic to America. The ash's ancient Irish name, *nion*, connects it intimately with the Irish god Nuadu, and its British equivalent Nodens or Nodons, who had a huge temple of healing on the shores of the Severn river until the fifth century CE. The name of both is translated as "cloud-maker", an obvious parallel with Greek tradition, where ash twigs were used in rain-making ceremonies.

There is a stronger association between the ash and Gwydion of Welsh myth. Gwydion is the master druid, who has been taught by old Math, the wisest person in the land, and reveals more magical skills than anyone else in Welsh legend. The link between the ash and druidry was confirmed with the finding on the isle of Anglesey of a first-century druid staff made from ash, decorated with a solar spiral.

The ash carries some of the power of the sun, hence its rule over water (ocean charms, rain-making rituals). Humankind's era of intense sun worship coincides roughly with the Bronze Age. This was when warriors changed from the yew hunting weapons of the Paleolithic to the ash spears made for mortal combat. Greek tradition reflects this when Hesiod says that the "third and brazen race of men" was the "fruit of the ash". Similarly, the Icelandic *Eddas* (the main collections of Norse myth) report that the first man was made of ash wood (and the first woman of elm). Neither refers to the "first" human (as in the biblical Book of Genesis), but to the first wave of Aryan invaders of Neolithic Europe, at some time in the second millennium BCE. A new age of worldly power struggles arrived with the ash spear.

Despite all this, the ash had nothing to do with the Norse World Tree, Yggdrasil, as has been commonly believed. The *Eddas* describe this poetically as the "evergreen needle-ash", which is a metaphor for a conifer, the yew tree (see pp.198–205). The ash is neither evergreen nor has it needles. The myth of a "World-ash" is a 19th-century misconception that, unfortunately, lingers on. However, the ash is perhaps the most majestic deciduous tree in the maritime climate of northwestern Europe.

**Symbolism**: Mastership and power

**Divine Associations**: Gwydion (Welsh), Nuadu (Irish), Nodens/Nodons (Celtic British)

**Astrological Association**: Sun

**Superstition**: In 19th-century England and France, the finger- and toe-nail clippings of a person who had a fever or who was suffering from toothache were buried under an ash tree in the belief that this would cure their affliction.

# Ginkgo  *Ginkgo biloba*

The maidenhair or ginkgo (*Ginkgo biloba*) is the sole species in the single genus of the Ginkgo family (*Ginkgoaceae*). It evolved separately from the conifers, but subsequently became classed as a conifer. This ancient tree is the only survivor of a family that once occurred in many parts of the world, including Europe, about 160 million years ago. Long thought to be extinct in the wild, it survived in Zheijang and Guizhou provinces in eastern China.

The ginkgo is a deciduous, resinous, dioecious tree that generally grows to 120ft (36m), although in cooler climates it reaches only half that height. Its alternate or clustered leaves are fan-shaped, long-stalked and cut or divided in the middle. The male flowers are catkin-like. The female flowers consist of rarely more than two ovules on a long stalk, and usually only one of these matures into the plum-like fruit, which has a fleshy rind enclosing an edible, white nut.

**ABOVE**: *The ancient Chinese name for ginkgo was* ya chio *("duck foot"), because of the curious shape of its leaves.*

### Practical Uses
The kernels or "ginkgo nuts" are commonly eaten in Asia, but the seeds should be handled with caution as they contain an oil that causes dermatitis in some people.

### Natural Healing
The medicinal use of gingko seeds is mentioned in *Pen Tsao Kang Mu*, the "Great Herbal" by Li Shih-chen (1578), which is still used today in Traditional Chinese Medicine. They are recommended for treating asthma, coughs and bladder problems. The seeds are used raw to treat cancer, and cooked to promote digestion. In the West, ginkgo is now a popular remedy on account of the potent effects of the leaves on the circulatory system. It is useful where sluggish circulation occurs in conjunction with poor memory and concentration, in some types of migraines and in Alzheimer's disease.

### Culture, Myth and Symbol
The ginkgo is a sacred tree in eastern Asia, where it is often planted near Taoist and Buddhist temples.

A food source since at least the second century BCE, the ginkgo was always rare, and its roasted nuts were a precious delicacy. The royal palace of China received them as tribute from the southeastern provinces, until Prince Li Wen-ho (who lived during the first half of the 11th century) had some ginkgo trees transplanted near to his residence. He had to wait most of his life for the first fruits to ripen – they were then presented to the old king in a golden bowl.

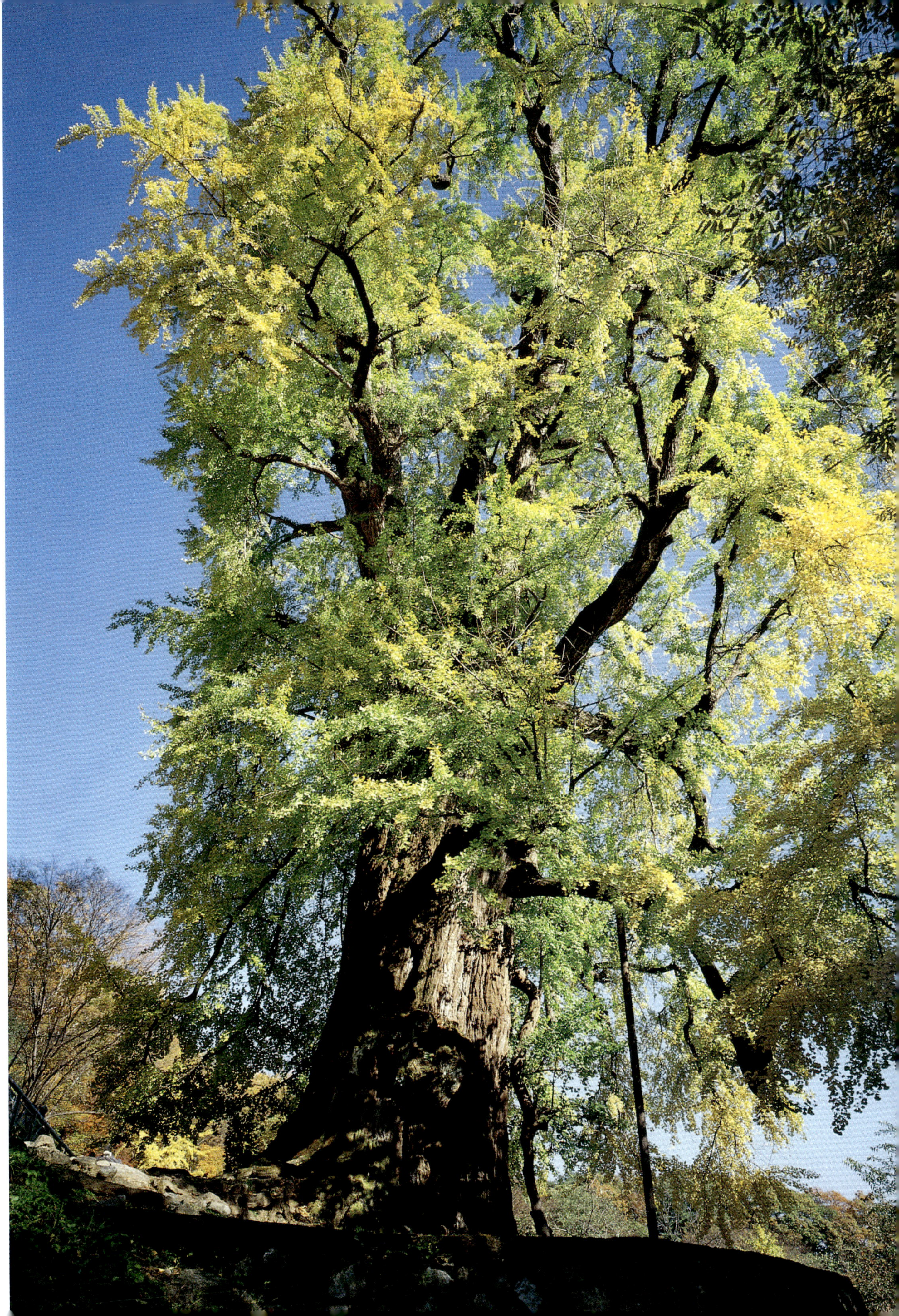

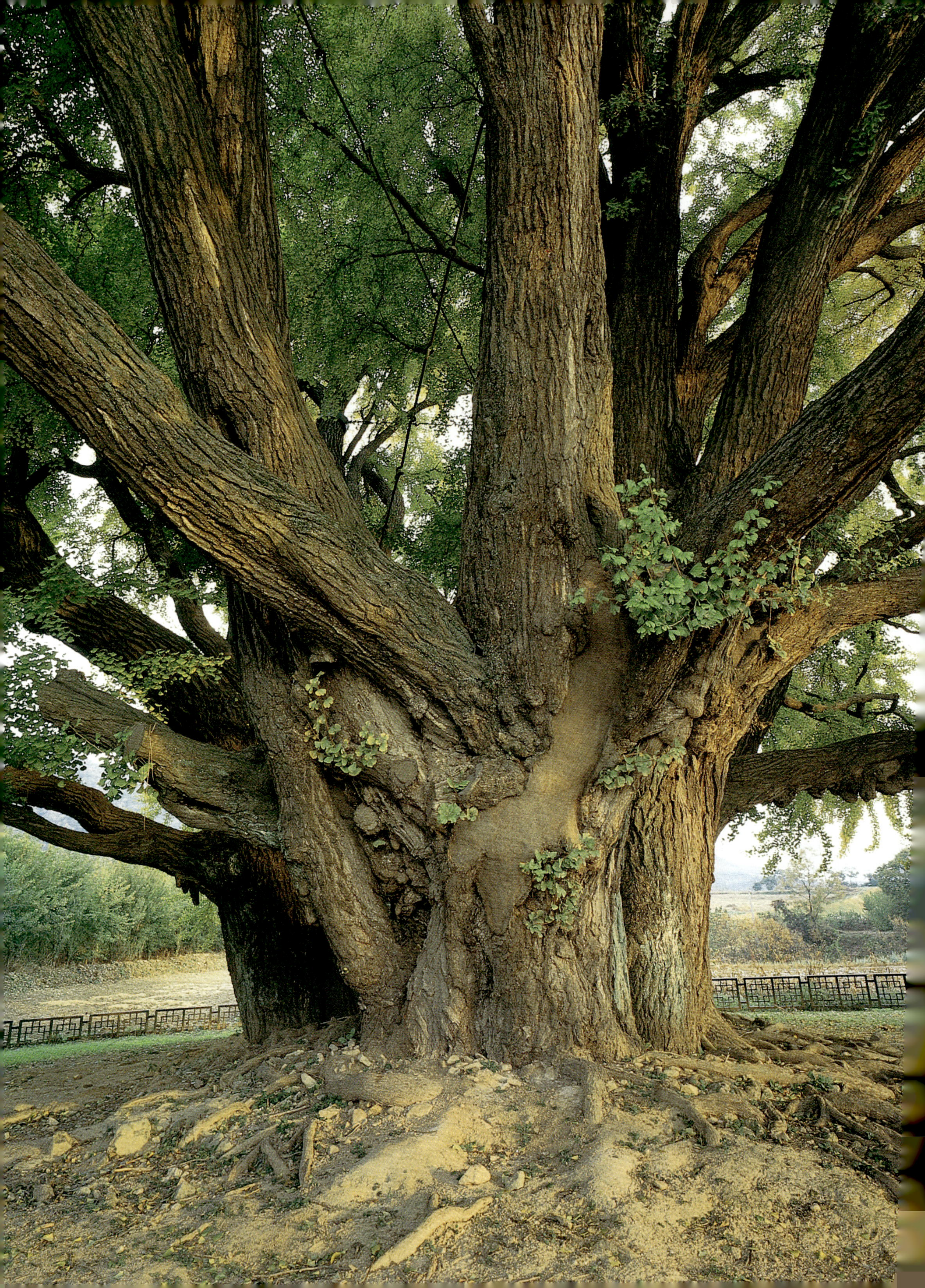

**OPPOSITE**: *The bole of an ancient ginkgo known as the "Snake Tree" near Seoul, South Korea.*

*As the ginkgo takes three generations to mature, it became known as the "Grandfather–Grandchild Tree".*

In the 11th century the ginkgo was called Yin Hsing (Xing), the "Silver Apricot". As the tree takes three human generations to mature, it also became known as *kung sun shu*, the "Grandfather–Grandchild Tree". After the Yuan dynasty (c.1279–1368), the ginkgo tree was widely cultivated throughout China, particularly in temple grounds, which preserved venerable specimens.

Buddhist monks introduced the ginkgo tree to Korea and Japan. We do not know exactly when, but many of the magnificent ginkgo trees in Japan today are estimated to be well over 1,000 years old. Ginkgo nuts are documented as having been used in the tea ceremony as a dessert from 1492. And since the 18th century, the nuts have been served as a side dish to accompany *sake* (rice wine).

In 1712, the German physician Engelbert Kampfer "discovered" the ginkgo tree in Japan, (it was thought to be extinct in the West) and he sent some seeds to Europe. In around 1815, the great German poet and mystic Johann Wolfgang von Goethe plucked a ginkgo biloba leaf in his garden and wrote the following poem:

> This leaf from a tree in the East,
> Which has been entrusted to my garden,
> Reveals a secret meaning,
> Which pleases those who know.
>
> Is it one living creature
> Which has divided itself?

> Or are these two, which have decided,
> That they should be as one?
>
> To reply to such a question, I found the right answer:
> Don't you feel in my songs and verses
> That I am One and Two?

In the wake of the atom bomb dropped in 1945 on Hiroshima in Japan, every living thing around the epicentre of the blast was destroyed. An exception was provided by four remarkable ginkgo trees that survived, and which by the following spring had even started to blossom again. The closest, at Hosen-Ji, was only 0.7 miles (1,130m) from the epicentre of the explosion. All four trees are still thriving today. Ever since, in Japan the ginkgo has been regarded as the "bearer of hope". Today there are plaques near some of these trees bearing prayers for world peace.

**Symbolism**: Primeval life-force

**Divine Association**: Oneness

**Astrological Associations**: Moon, Pluto

**Historical Spotlight**: In 1796, an English botanist, now only known to us as Smith, disputed the ginkgo's scientific name as " uncouth and barbarous". He proposed to call it *Salisburia adiantifolia*, a name which was politely ignored by the rest of the scientific community.

OPPOSITE: *The holly is a welcome evergreen in churchyards, and through the symbolism of its spiky, red-fruited foliage some associate it with Christ's Passion and the bloody crown.*

# Holly *Ilex*

*Ilex* is a large genus of about 400 species of evergreen and deciduous trees and shrubs in the temperate and tropical zones of both the northern and southern hemispheres. Hollies are dioecious or polygamodioecious. The alternate, short-stalked leaves are often thick, leathery blades with toothed or spinescent margins. The white or greenish flowers appear solitary or in dense clusters or cymes.

The common holly (*I. aquifolium*) is usually a small tree or bush but can reach 50ft (15m) or more. It is native to western and southern Europe, northern Africa and western Asia. In central and eastern Europe, where it lacks the maritime climate, its growth is stunted by the winter cold. The leaves are up to 2in (5cm) long; the small white flowers are fragrant and the globose fruits are bright red.

## Practical Uses

Holly has long been cultivated for its hedges, and birds eat the fruits in winter. In Europe and western Asia, the wood has been used for carving, veneers and inlays. In North America, the Seminole tribe make arrows from the wood.

---

**Symbolism:** The sword of truth

**Divine Association:** The Green Man (Pagan), Jesus (Christian)

**Astrological Association:** Mars

**Superstition:** In a 19th-century Swiss legend, the palm trees, whose fronds had been used to welcome Christ to Jerusalem, turned into spiny hollies when the crowd shouted "Crucify Him!" Therefore, in a French tradition also collected in the 19th century, holly is a creation of the devil.

---

## Natural Healing

The dried leaves of some hollies provide a tea-like beverage. Those of *I. paraquariensis* supply *maté*, the popular South American drink. In North America, the Iroquois tribe widely use decoctions of the bark of the gray holly, *I. verticillata*, for healing, and as an emetic (to cause vomiting) and for treating psychological problems. The Tsalagi use a leaf infusion as an emetic, and also as a sacred hallucinogenic, to "evoke ecstasies". The berries are poisonous, emetic and purgative. Holly should never be used without professional advice.

The Bach Flower Remedy of holly dissipates anger and releases jealousy and envy. The tree essence, too, calms these symptoms, bringing a peace of mind that does not exclude assertiveness.

## Culture, Myth and Symbol

In Welsh myth, the beautiful, fair-haired goddess Creiddylad represents the sun, and the knights of the waxing and the waning year fight over her. From midwinter to midsummer, when the days get longer, the sky god rules. His symbol of power is the deciduous oak. From midsummer to midwinter, when the days grow shorter, the god of the earth and the underworld reclaims the sun. His tree is the holly, which is linked to the spirit of vegetation, the Green Man.

In medieval Christianity, John the Baptist was associated with the oak tree, and Jesus with the holly. The word "holly", derived from the Anglo-Saxon *holegn* and Old High German *hulis*, means "holy". Hence, holly made its way into church ceremonies, both as a substitute for palms on Palm Sunday, and as a Christmas decoration, particularly in Britain where it is one of the few native evergreens.

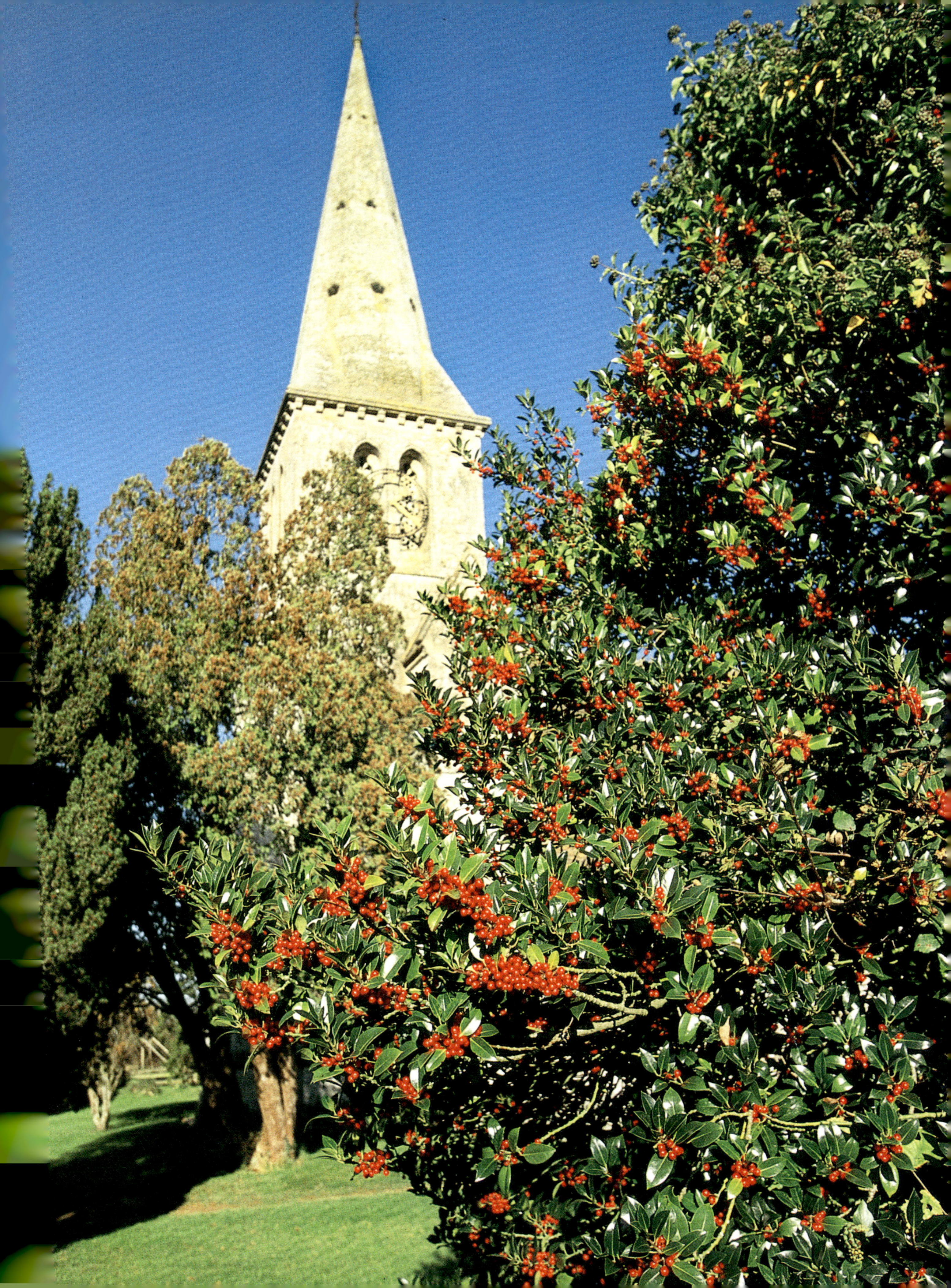

OPPOSITE: *Mature walnut trees in a traditional farm walnut grove in Dorset, England. Although the tree's nuts are of value, its beautiful wood is more prized for furniture, veneer, and even gun stocks.*

# Walnut *Juglans*

*Juglans* is a genus of some 20 species of deciduous, mostly fast-growing trees native to North and South America, southeast Europe and southeast Asia. Walnut leaves are aromatic, pinnate, and in some species rather large. The male flowers appear in catkins drooping from the twigs of the previous year, while the female flowers are borne on the wood of the current year.

The common walnut (*J. regia*), which is native to Iran or China but long cultivated in the Mediterranean, is a slow-growing tree that reaches up to 100ft (30m) high, and can attain a thousand years of age. It has a silvery-gray bark and a characteristic rounded crown. It usually has seven to nine oblong leaflets up to 5in (12.5cm) long. The wrinkly nut is enclosed within a hard shell, and this in turn is found within a thick, fleshy but inedible husk.

## Practical Uses

As well as being a food, walnuts were used by the Romans to make a wine known as *carynium*, and to make hair dye. A cloth dye was also extracted from unripe walnut shells.

*Through the walnut's connection with the nature goddess Artemis, it became associated with fertility and love, and found its way into marriage customs.*

The timber of many walnut species is highly prized and very valuable – hence it is used in cabinet-making. Many Native North American tribes, too, have used walnut wood, as well as the wood from trees in the walnut family (*Juglandaceae*) and hickory trees (*Carya*) to make furniture. The Apache use walnut for the construction of their dome-shaped lodges, while the Tsalagi make decorative carvings from it. The nut husks also yield a dye that is used by many tribes. The Kiowa boiled the roots to make a blue-black dye for buffalo hides.

## Natural Healing

Walnuts are a good source of potassium and folic acid. They contain about 15 percent protein and 50 percent or more of their weight is oil, including alpha linoleic acid (Omega 3), which enhances the immune system and has a beneficial effect on the heart and circulation. Externally, walnut oil is a nourishing and anti-wrinkle ingredient in cosmetic skin creams and moisturizers.

In Traditional Chinese Medicine, walnuts affect the energy of the kidney meridian, which is connected with the blood sugar level and our vital energy. They are considered warm and sweet, and act to balance yin and yang in the body. Because they counteract cold energy and remove phlegm, they are good for coughs, constipation, kidney and bladder stones, and impotence. Chewing 3¼oz (90 grams) of walnuts slowly each day is recommended to relieve sore throats, hoarseness, constipation and gastric ulcers.

Walnuts are sweet and astringent in Ayurveda. Their heat increases *pitta* and *kapha*, decreasing *vata*. According to herbal medicine, walnut leaves stimulate the liver, and

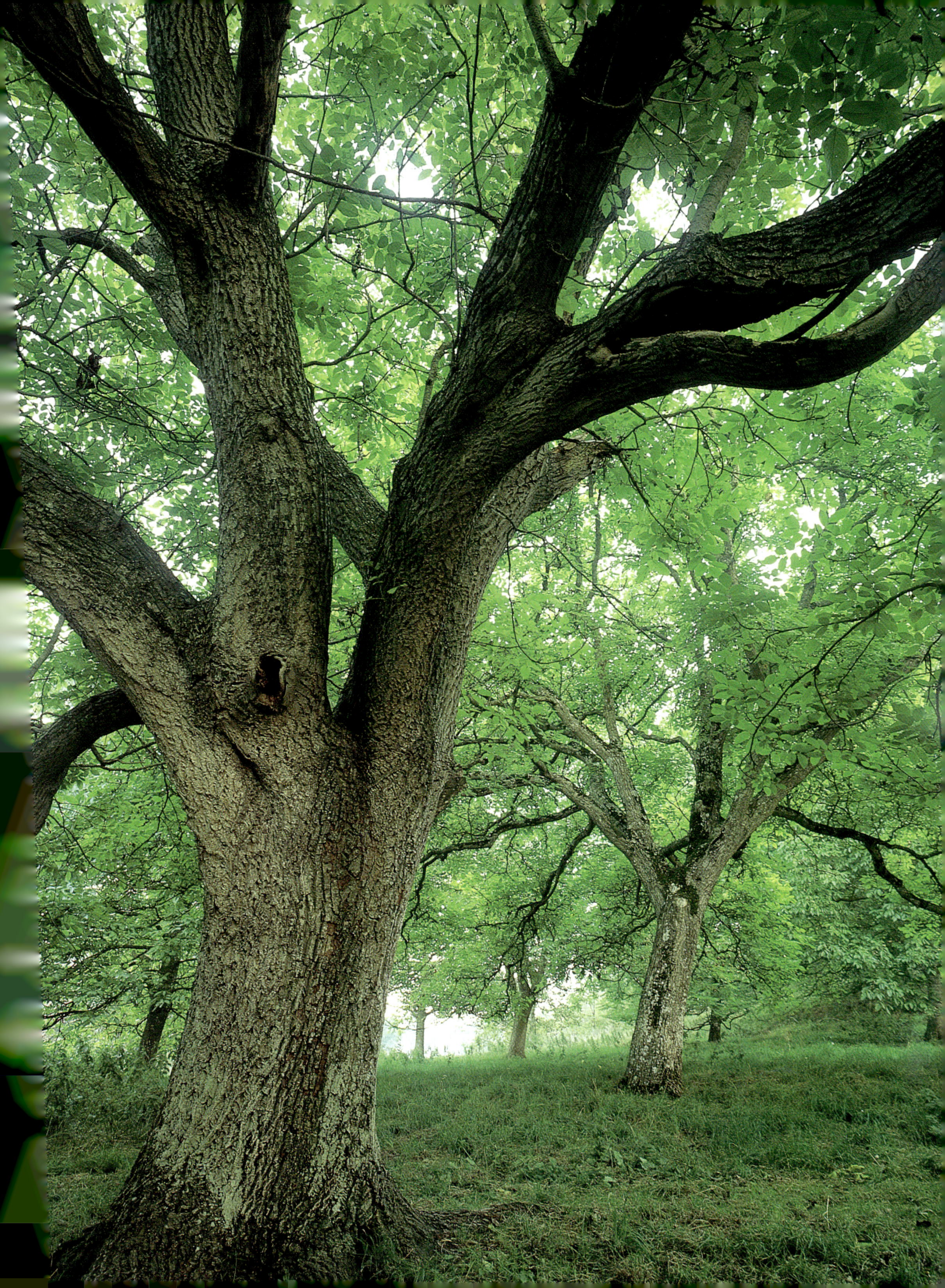

ABOVE: *Leaves and fruits on the walnut tree. The leading commercial producers of walnuts are the United States, Turkey, China and Iran.*

can be used to treat skin problems, such as acne, as well as swollen glands and lymphatic congestion.

The Bach Flower Remedy of walnut is excellent for helping us to "move on" – to break links with the past and adjust to changes in life. The tree essence brings liberation and purification.

### Culture, Myth and Symbol

The original Greek name for the fruit of this tree, *caryon*, is related to *cara*, which means both "head" and "tree top", and stems from the ancient Pelasgian goddess Car or Cer, who also gave her name to the mountains of Caria in Asia Minor. The tree itself (as well as its nymph) was called Carya. In Greek legend, Carya is one of the three daughters of Dion, a Laconian king. Apollo grants the king's wish of bestowing the gift of prophecy on his daughters. When Carya dies, the god Dionysus changes her into a walnut tree. Hence, the tree's status as an oracular tree in Greece.

The sad news of Carya's death was announced by the goddess Artemis, and a temple was dedicated to Artemis Caryatis. The walnut columns in this temple were carved into female statues, and named caryatids, after the nymphs of this tree. Through the walnut's connection with the nature goddess Artemis, it also became associated with fertility and love, and found its way into marriage customs.

RIGHT: *Walnuts are extremely nutritious. They contain potassium, folic acid, protein and about fifty percent of their weight in oils.*

After a group of Pelasgian migrants settled in Latium, on the Italian peninsula, the goddess associated with the walnut became known to the Romans as Carmenta, derived from Latin *carmen* meaning "sacred song or oracle", and *mante*, "the revealer". This is a strong hint that her tree was used in oracles and divination in this region, too. In Roman legend, Carmenta had a son by Hermes, called Evander ("the benefactor of humankind"), and together they brought the alphabet, or more accurately, the art of writing, to the Romans. Pallatium, the name of the Pelasgian colony, has survived in the word "Palatine", the name of one of the seven hills of Rome. However, as male gods gained in status, Carya's nut became increasingly known by the Romans as *iuglans* (from *Jovis glans,* meaning the "acorn of Jupiter"), named after their principal deity.

In excavations of the Assyrian palace at Nimrud (now called Calah and in modern Iraq) wooden writing tablets made from walnut were found. Of all the precious woods used in the building of palaces – principally cedar and cypress, but also juniper, box (*Buxus sempervirens*), mulberry, pistachio and tamarisk – the Assyrians also chose the walnut to be associated with the art of writing. Later, the Romans introduced the walnut tree to areas north of the Alps (for example, the Netherlands), but it was too late for it to develop a distinct northern mythology, because Christianity was expanding its following and becoming the dominant religion. However, the walnut was widely planted for its nutritious nuts and medicinal leaves by monks during the Middle Ages. Its modern name derives from the German *welsche Nuss* or "foreign nut".

**Symbolism**: Confidence and mental wisdom

**Divine Associations**: Car (Pelasgian), Carya (Greek), Carmenta (Roman)

**Astrological Association**: Jupiter

**Superstition**: The seventh-century citizens of the town of Benevento in Italy lived in fear of their walnut tree because witches and the devil were believed to hold an annual dance underneath it. The tree was eventually cut down by St Barbatus (d. 682CE), but for a long time afterwards, the townspeople expected the devil to create an exact replica of the tree if any witches were to dance on the spot.

# Juniper *Juniperus*

*Juniperus*, the world's most widespread member of the Cypress family (*Cupressaceae*), comprises about 70 species of coniferous, evergreen, monoecious or dioecious trees or shrubs, which can be found in the northern hemisphere, from the subtropics as far north as the Arctic. The needle- or scale-like leaves are usually spreading on young branchlets and appressed on old ones. The male cones are yellow and catkin-like. The female cones are berry-like, glaucous, and have three to eight fleshy scales. They each contain one to twelve seeds.

An important tree in North America is the "red cedar", *J. virginiana*, which has adult scale-like leaves and purplish-blue-black, glaucous cones. It is known as the "red cedar" because of its fragrant red heartwood.

The common juniper (*J. communis*) is the main juniper found in the cooler parts of Europe. It can take the shape of a prostrate or creeping alpine, a dense, bushy shrub, or an erect small tree that reaches up to 30ft (9m) high. The ternate, linear, spreading, sharp-pointed leaves have a single white longitudinal band above and are weakly keeled below. The fruits are glaucous blue cones about ¼ to ½in (0.7–1.2cm) in diameter. They usually mature in their third year, and have three seeds.

In the Mediterranean, the Phoenician juniper (*J. phoenicea*) tolerates extremely dry conditions. It has scale-like leaves and yellow to red-brown fruits. The prickly juniper (*J. oxycedrus*) rarely exceeds 20ft (6m) in height and has linear leaves ½ to 1in (1.2–2.5cm) long.

RIGHT: *Junipers in the Lueneburger Heide, north Germany – scenery reminiscent of the post-Ice Age era 10,000 years ago.*

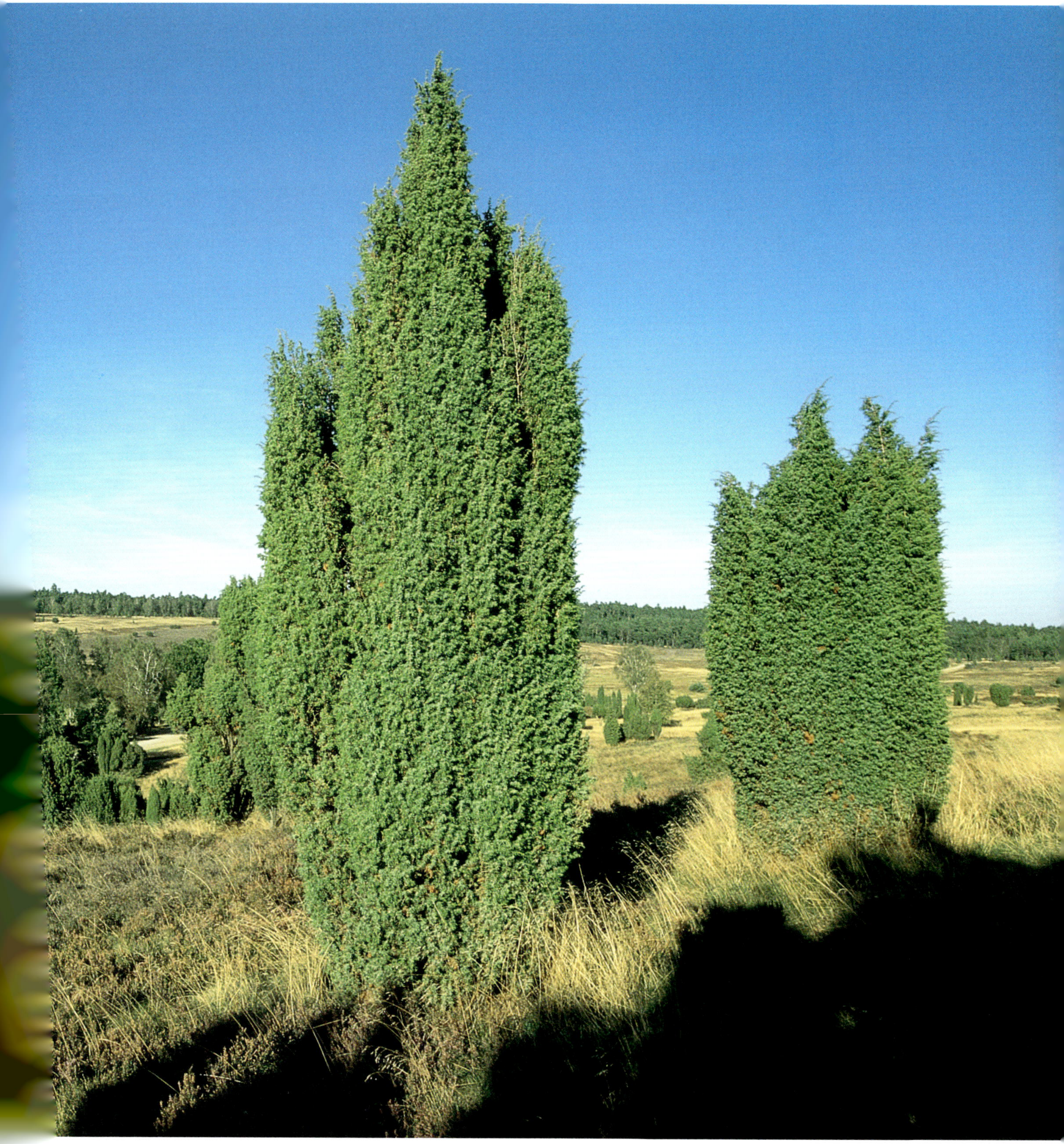

In the mountains of the Mediterranean region, no cedars and few firs are found higher than at 6,500ft (2,000m), but junipers have been recorded at up to 8,850ft (2,700m) in the Antilebanon mountains (Lebanon). And an 807-year-old tree (*J. turkistanicus*) was found in the 1970s in the mountains of Tajikistan at the uppermost tree line of 11,480ft (3,500m). Like the yew tree, the juniper is capable of extremely slow growth if survival requires it. A Phoenician juniper from the Verdon Gorge in France has a radius of nearly 3in (nearly 8cm) which took it no less than 1,140 years to grow. An annual radial growth of 0.06mm makes this one of the slowest-growing plants on earth.

## Practical Uses

The tall junipers of Greece and Asia Minor played an important role in the economy and building works of the ancient civilizations. The Syrian juniper (*J. drupacea*) grows as a narrow column up to 60ft (18m) high, but *J. excelsa* and *J. fœtidissima* surpass it with heights of up to 80ft (24m).

Greeks and Romans used the same word for cedars and tall junipers (Greek *kedros*; Latin *cedrus*) – an appellation perfectly deserved because while it is rare to find sound timber in a fir more than 300 years old, cedar and juniper can produce magnificent timber even after 600 years. And juniper wood shares with the cedar an aromatic scent, a resistance to insects and rot, a fine, straight grain and a reddish-brown hue. Except for a scent, the yew also shares these qualities, and all three genera were traded in the Old World as "cedar wood". This was the most expensive wood and only used for elaborate purposes, such as temple and palace roofs, clothes chests (because of the scent), coffins (sarcophagi) and burial chamber artefacts. However, the Phoenicians, who had no "cheap" wood in the mountains of Lebanon, used cedar and cypress for ship-building too.

Junipers also yield foliage that has medicinal uses, and (with the exception of *J. foetidissima*) edible, aromatic "berries", which are dried and used as food spice or medicine or as a characteristic ingredient in gin.

OPPOSITE: *A well-spread, creeping alpine form of the common juniper, pictured here in southern France, is one of several different forms that the juniper can take.*

RIGHT: *Junipers can easily be recognized by their spiky leaves and small round cones which appear like berries.*

## Natural Healing

Juniper berries strengthen the nervous system and stimulate appetite and digestion. Tea made from the berries makes an excellent urinary antiseptic; it is a key remedy for cystitis, while also having a warming and settling effect on the stomach. As the oils are fairly potent, juniper should not be used during pregnancy or by anyone suffering from kidney disease. Externally, the diluted essential oil is used as a warming treatment for arthritis and gout. The oil is also effective when rubbed onto the chest and inhaled to combat respiratory congestion. The tree essence helps us to renounce our past and to release old stresses.

## Culture, Myth and Symbol

Throughout Europe, the juniper was highly venerated. The Estonians traditionally worshipped the patron god of livestock under the juniper, and various widespread sayings in German-speaking regions remind us to take off our hats when passing either a juniper tree or an elder. Many legends and folk tales portray the juniper as a gate to other dimensions – for example, the dwelling places of fairies, giants or dwarfs. A German tale called "The Juniper Tree", which was collected by the Brothers Grimm, tells how the soul of a dead child rises from the juniper as a bird.

Leaving offerings to the local nature spirits under a juniper was a common practice that is still in evidence today. The tree's interesting German name, *Wacholder* (from Old High German *wachal*, "awake", and *tar*, "tree"), describes it as the "awake tree", because the tree has been perceived as a guardian on watch, acting as an intermediary between humankind and the invisible spirit world.

Another traditional way of communicating with the spirit world is the smoke offering. Smoke carries the prayers and blessings "up" to the higher, or "into" the subtler dimensions. Juniper smoke has been part of Celtic, Germanic, Slavic, Baltic, Finno-Ugric and Asian ritual, thus spanning the entire breadth of Eurasia. In the higher realms, it mingles with the "cedar", thuja and juniper offerings of Native North Americans. Tibetans too, offer juniper smoke in their temples for the blessing of all.

---

**Symbolism:** Cleansing, protection and humility

**Divine Association:** The spirit world

**Astrological Association:** Neptune

**Superstition:** In 19th-century Austria, if you wished to conjure up the devil, you were advised to bind juniper boughs to your hands and feet.

**Historical Spotlight:** The Middle Ages were a time of widespread deforestation in Europe. But one reason why the juniper is rare today is because at that time its acidic juice was discovered to be an effective contraceptive, so the Church encouraged the felling of junipers to protect the birth rate.

*OPPOSITE: A solitary, mature larch with unusual arched branches, near Peebles in southern Scotland.*

# Larch *Larix*

The genus *Larix* is a member of the Pine family (*Pinaceae*) and comprises about ten species of tall, deciduous conifers with spreading branches that grow in the colder parts of the northern hemisphere.

The common or European larch (*L. decidua, L. europaea*) has short, needle-shaped leaves arranged in beautiful rosettes, up to 1½in (3.7cm) long. The female cones are about the same length. American larch (*L. americana* or *L. laricina*) cones are only half this size, and have shiny, hairless scales. The Siberian larch (*L. sibirica*) has bright green, needle-like leaves and downy scales. Larch requires a cold climate, but nevertheless its young shoots are sensitive to spring frost.

## Practical Uses

Larch timber is fairly fire- and water-resistant. It became one of the main timber supplies for the fleets of the Roman Empire (along with pine, fir and cypress).

The larch is rich in resin which, unlike that of other conifers, remains liquid when heated, and is suitable for the production of pitch, as well as Venetian turpentine. Pitch was widely used to waterproof roofs, boats and ships.

## Natural Healing

A decoction of larch bark makes a soothing application for eczema and psoriasis. Both Europeans and Native North Americans, such as the Algonquin, Quebec and Iroquois peoples, have used needle or bark infusions to treat urinary tract infections, as well as bronchitis, colds and coughs.

The Bach Flower Remedy enhances self-confidence and helps to overcome obstacles. The tree essence balances heart and mind, will and desire.

## Culture, Myth and Symbol

In Alpine legend, the larch is the abode of the *Saeligen*, the "Blessed Ones", graceful otherworldly beings who are kind to people and protect animals. In different parts of the Alps, the *Saeligen* maidens have been described as spirit beings dressed in white or silver, dancing under old larch trees and singing the sweetest music.

In Siberian tradition, God made two trees at the creation: a female, the fir; and a male, the larch. The larch is one of the few trees that grows in the tundra, where a group of seven or more is considered to be a sacred grove. The Ostyak people used to make an offering every time they passed a larch grove. According to the Tungus tribe, the soul of the shaman is reared in the (otherworldly) Tuuru tree, and the rim of his drum is cut from a living larch tree, which is left standing to honour the Tuuru. During every shamanic trance-journey, a ritual "tree", made from a long pole of larch, is planted in the ceremonial tent and the shaman climbs up this World Tree to heaven.

**Symbolism:** Going beyond limits

**Divine Association:** The *Saeligen* (European Alpine)

**Astrological Association:** Neptune

**Historical Spotlight:** The larch was "discovered" by Julius Caesar (c.100BCE–44CE) when he laid siege to an Alpine fort built of larch, which he afterwards named *Larignum*. He was amazed that burning brushwood had no effect on the fort's timber walls. A generation later, larch was used during the construction in Rome of the palace of the emperor Augustus.

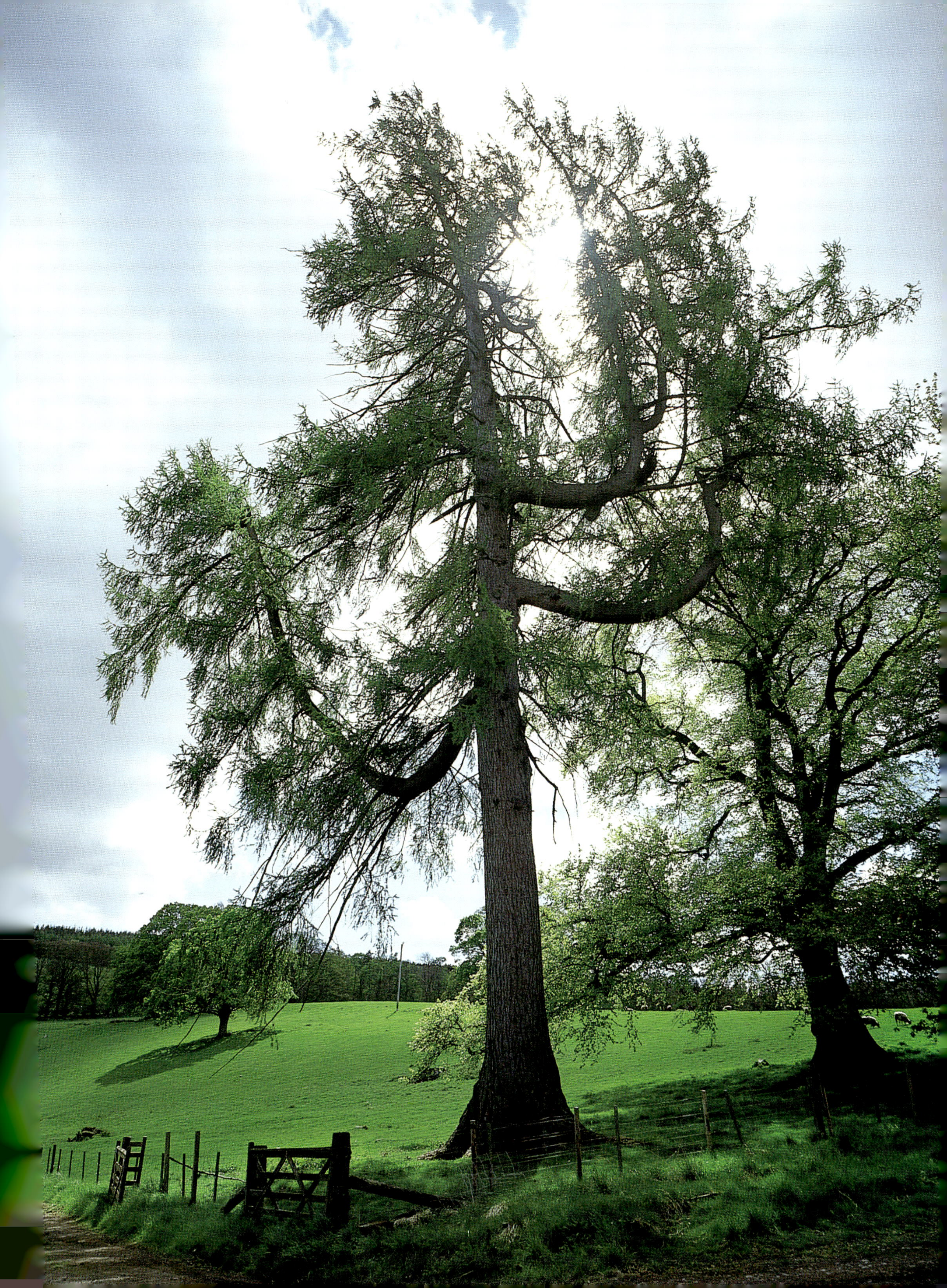

# Laurel *Laurus*

*Laurus* is a genus comprising two species of aromatic evergreens. The true laurel of antiquity is the laurel or (sweet) bay, *L. nobilis*, native to the Mediterranean region. It can grow up to 40ft (12m) in rich peaty soil with abundant moisture, but is of variable stature. Often it produces suckers at its base. The alternating, dark, glossy green leaves are lanceolate to elliptic in shape, and up to 4in (10cm) long. The small, yellowish, bisexual or unisexual flowers open in April. The male flower has 12 or more fertile stamens and its fruit is a black or dark purple berry.

## Practical Uses

The Greek writer Hesiod (seventh century BCE) describes farm tools made from oak, elm, and laurel wood. However, the laurel has been cultivated since ancient times for its aromatic leaves, which, known as "bay leaves", are widely used in cookery to flavour meat, poultry, soups and stews.

ABOVE: *The fruit and leaf of* Laurus nobilis.

RIGHT: *Laurel trees grow most vigorously in sunny locations, such as on this rocky hill, near the Riviera in southern France.*

ABOVE: *Laurel or bay leaves are one of the most versatile in cookery and are an ingredient in the French herb mixture* bouquet garni.

## Natural Healing

Tea made from bay leaves makes a warming and antispasmodic digestive tonic, both stimulating the appetite and helping digestion. (This is one of the reasons why the leaves have been so popular in cooking.) Externally the leaves can be chewed and applied to stings to help soothe the skin.

The essential oil extracted from bay leaves makes a warming rub to relieve arthritis and muscle tension, but it should be used with caution and in low dilution. Bay oil is a traditional remedy for sprains, bruises, and earache, and can also be used in inhalants to ease coughs and colds.

## Culture, Myth and Symbol

In Greek myth, a nymph called Daphne was pursued by Apollo, and for her safety was transformed into a laurel tree by Gaia, the earth goddess. Thereafter, Apollo wore a crown of laurel leaves in her memory. From this story developed the Greek and Roman custom of crowning master poets, and victorious athletes and warriors with a laurel wreath.

However, the ceremonial and ritual use of the laurel goes back much further into antiquity than this. When the Dorians swept through Greece from about 1100BCE onward, subduing the indigenous population and taking over their ancient religious sites, they found that the laurel was already established as the sacred plant at a site of worship on the slopes of Mount Parnassos. There, a laurel tree and a spring had appeared close to a deep fissure in the earth.

According to legend, Apollo later established his oracle on this site. Known as the Oracle of Delphi, it became the most famous and widely-consulted oracle in the Greek world. The high priestess and oracular medium was called the Pythia, named after the spiritual guardian of the area, a female dragon named Python. The priestesses who interpreted the earth oracle chewed laurel leaves and inhaled the fumes of their laurel smoke offerings (which is why their contemporaries believed that the laurel could induce prophetic trance states).

**Symbolism:** Earth's calling

**Divine Associations:** Gaia, Apollo, Daphne (all Greek)

**Astrological Association:** Neptune

**Historical Spotlight:** In 393CE, when Greece was a Roman province, the Christian emperor Theodosius destroyed the pagan Oracle of Delphi and its sacred laurels, as well as the sanctuary of Eleusis. He also abolished the Olympic Games.

# Apple *Malus*

*Malus*, a genus in the large rose family (*Rosaceae*), comprises about 25 species of small deciduous trees of the northern temperate zone. Apple leaves are softer and more downy than those of the pear (*Pyrus*). The flowers have five styles as against the solitary styles in the flowers of plum trees (*Prunus*).

The wild apple tree of northwestern Europe is the crab apple, *M. sylvestris*. Its leaves are ovate to broadly elliptic, toothed, and glabrous at maturity. The white or pink-white flowers are followed by greenish-yellow, sometimes red-flushed, fruits which are smaller than 2in (5cm) in diameter and crowned by the persistent dried-up calyx. The crab apple is one of the many parents of the orchard apple (*M. domestica*).

## Practical Uses

There are hundreds of varieties and cultivars of the orchard apple; the first-century Romans counted 30 different kinds, according to Pliny the Elder. Orchard apples have lost their thorns and have fruits considerably bigger and sweeter than those of the wild species. Interestingly, trees that escape the orchard and naturalize often grow thorns again.

In Asia varieties include the deep red apples of *M. yunnanensis* and the red and yellow ones of *M. kansuensis*, both native to western China, and the bright red fruits of *M. zumi* and the red and yellow apples of *M. floribunda* (Japanese crab), both native to Japan. Native North Americans, too, have used the fruits (and leaves) of apples, such as the Oregon crab apple (*M. fusca*), the Prairie crab apple (*M. ioensis*), and the sweet crab apple (*M. coronaria*) both as a food and for healing.

## Natural Healing

Apples are a good source of various minerals, such as potassium and iron, and vitamins, such as E and A, many of which are more abundant under or in the apple's skin than in the flesh itself.

These fruits help the body to detox, and are beneficial to the bowels, the liver and the brain. They are used to treat headaches, gout, rheumatism and high blood pressure, and are of special value to heart patients (apple with honey has been a remedy for heart problems since ancient times). The health benefits of eating apples indeed justify the English saying "An apple a day keeps the doctor away".

In Traditional Chinese Medicine, apples are categorized as cool, sweet and sour, and tone yin. They produce fluids, lubricate the lungs, enhance digestion and detoxification, and increase the blood sugar level.

In Ayurveda, apples are regarded as sweet and astringent. They increase *vata*, decrease *pitta*, and are suitable for *kapha* in small quantities. People with a *pitta* constitution should only eat sweet (not sour) apples, while those with a *vata* constitution should eat only the cooked fruit.

The Bach Flower Remedy of crab apple has an emotionally cleansing effect, as does the tree essence of the orchard apple.

## Culture, Myth and Symbol

With all its benefits, the apple tree has made a strong impression on the human imagination, and most stories and legends relate to its health-giving and sustaining properties.

The apple was already a symbol of fertility in ancient Greece, having been sacred to Demeter, the goddess of corn

**BELOW**: *Abundant fruit on an apple tree in an orchard in Dorset, one of many counties in southern England famous for their cider.*

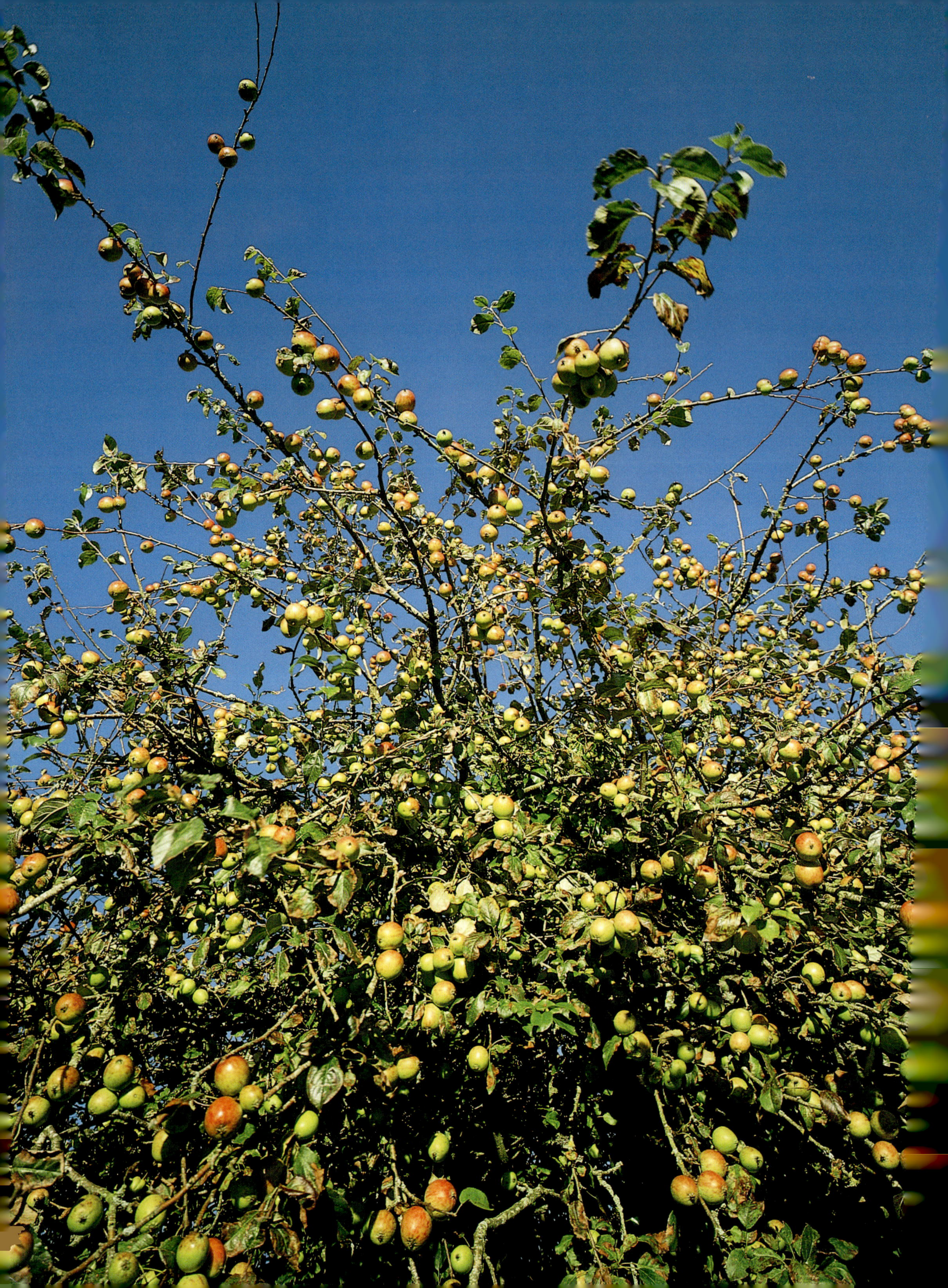

OPPOSITE: *The sensual fruits of the apple tree have been employed in human customs concerning love, courtship and fertility since time immemorial, hence its association with temptation in Christianity.*

and sustenance, and also (along with quince and the pomegranate) to Aphrodite, the goddess of love.

The apple's associations with fertility and marriage customs lasted down through the ages, becoming particularly pronounced in Europe during the Middle Ages and the centuries that followed. In many European fairytales, the eating of an apple ensures offspring. In France, during the Renaissance period, a young man would woo a girl by offering her an apple. In Transylvania (Rumania), there is a custom in which a red apple is waved at the bride at her wedding. A medieval love charm from Germany suggests writing certain letters on a "love" apple and then giving it to the object of your affection to eat. An Italian tale relates how such a love apple was eaten accidentally by a pig, with the result that subsequently the animal would not leave the wooer's side.

In Arthurian legend, Avalon is the Isle of the Blessed, the Celtic paradise into which King Arthur passes, mortally wounded, on a boat with three accompanying maidens or priestesses. "Avalon" stems from the word for apple (Welsh *afallen*, Scottish Gaelic *abhal*). In the real world, this place is believed to be related to Glastonbury (and its famous Tor or hill) in Somerset, England, which still has many an orchard (in Latin *avallonia*).

The apple was once such an important source of sustenance for ordinary people that many historical writers referred to every type of golden or red fruit as an "apple", resulting in the term becoming widely synonymous with "fruit". Hence the "apples" in some ancient Celtic legends now reveal themselves to be the red fruits of the yew tree, and the "golden apples" of the Hesperides are now believed to have been quinces (see Quince pp.78–81). Furthermore, the biblical "apple" (Latin *malum*) mentioned in the Book of Genesis, the one that Eve shared with Adam under the Tree of Knowledge, was invented by Cyprianus Gallus, a theologian in Gaul in 425CE. As a consequence of this, and also of the sexual connotations of its folklore, the apple became labelled as the "Tree of Temptation" by certain Christian sects. Some 19th- and 20th-century scholars have suggested that the apple referred to in Genesis is in fact a pomegranate because, unlike the apple, this fruit does grow in Palestine. However, the original Hebrew text simply mentions "a fruit" (*peri*).

According to a Saxon myth that was first recorded in the Middle Ages, the goddess of spring, Iduna, supplies the gods with fruits that give eternal life. This is an ancient theme connected with the Tree of Life, but we don't know whether or not we can trust the scribe's use of the word "apple" here. However, we *can* see this tale as a medieval way of paying homage to the apple by extolling its health-giving and life-enhancing properties.

**Symbolism**: Health and fertility

**Divine Associations**: Demeter, Hera (both Greek); Pomona (Roman); Frigga, Freya (both Germanic)

**Astrological Associations**: Sun and Venus

**Superstition**: In the 19th-century in Lower Saxony, Germany, the first bath water used by a newborn baby was poured over the roots of an apple tree to ensure that the child would have red cheeks, and, if it was a girl, large breasts too!

# Mulberry *Morus*

*Morus* is a genus of about seven species of deciduous, medium-sized trees and shrubs native to Asia, Africa and the Americas. Single trees bear one or both sexes, and the flowers are always unisexual.

The white mulberry (*M. alba*), native to western Asia, has heart-shaped to ovate-lanceolate leaves, often up to 6in (15cm) wide. Its sweet and edible fruits are whiteish changing to red-pink, or nearly black in some varieties. Native to the central and eastern United States, the red mulberry (*M. rubra*) is rather rare in cultivation. Its rounded, downy leaves turn bright yellow in the autumn; its fruit is red. The small but long-lived black mulberry (*M. nigra*) is native to western Asia. It develops a wide-spreading crown and a gnarled trunk with age. The heart-shaped leaves are rough above and downy below. Its delicious fruits are deep red.

## Practical Uses

For at least 5,000 years the white mulberry tree has been the home of the Chinese silkworm. The black mulberry was also widely grown in Italy for raising silkworms until the 15th century, after which it was replaced by the white mulberry.

## Natural Healing

Black mulberry fruits have been used to treat sore throats, coughs, and constipation. A juice of the astringent, unripe berries was also used as a mouthwash. Today, the mulberry tree is little used in Western herbal medicine.

Traditional Chinese Medicine uses the fruits, leaves, twigs and root bark of the white mulberry. The leaf dispels "wind heat" to clear the liver and brighten the eyes. The fruit is used to moisten and nourish the yin, while the twigs disperse "wind" and promote a smooth flow of Qi through the meridians. The bark cools and purges "lung heat".

## Culture, Myth and Symbol

In ancient Chinese cosmology, the centre of the universe is *kien-mou* ("erect wood"), the Tree of Renewal. At the beginning of time it united the Nine Sources (the realm of the dead) with the Nine Heavens. In some Chinese traditions, this World Tree is identified as *k'ong-sang*, the hollow mulberry. It is a hermaphrodite, because it dates back to before the separation of yin and yang, male and female, and it represents the Tao, or the all-encompassing cosmic order. Hence a sacred mulberry grove, *sang-lin*, was planted outside the eastern gate of the early royal capitals of China.

The mulberry is also a common sight in the Islamic sanctuaries along or near pilgrimage routes in Arabia.

**Symbolism**: Connection and interdependence

**Divine Association**: The Tao

**Astrological Association**: Mercury

**Historical Spotlight**: In 1608 an English attempt to establish a silk industry failed because the leaves of the black mulberry instead of the white species were fed to the silk-moth larvae (*Bombix mori*).

MULBERRY

**OPPOSITE**: *The luscious, edible berries of the black mulberry tree, which has been cultivated since ancient times for its fruit.*

**BELOW**: *Black mulberries can grow up to 30ft (9m) in height, but even these thriving specimens in a park in Lewes, Sussex, England, are dwarfed by a stately tulip tree growing behind them.*

# Myrtle *Myrtus*

The genus *Myrtus* comprises mostly white-flowered, aromatic evergreens, growing in mild climates. They prefer full sun and well-drained soils, including chalk. The opposite leaves are entire and pinnately veined.

The common myrtle, known sometimes as the Greek myrtle (*M. communis* or *M. italica*), has a dense canopy of aromatic leaves, and when it blossoms in the summer it has a profusion of white flowers. The ovate to lanceolate leaves of the myrtle are up to 2in (5cm) long, and produce a strong scent when crushed. The flowers are about ¾in (1.8cm) across. The ovary has two to three cells, each containing many ovules. The purple-black berries are crowned with persistent calyx lobes.

## Practical Uses

The myrtle has been cultivated since ancient times for its edible berries. The Sardinians prepare their national drink, *mirto*, from it.

## Natural Healing

Myrtle is little used in herbal medicine, despite the fact that the leaves can be used as an astringent and as an antiseptic wash. *King's American Dispensatory* (1898) describes the diluted tincture as a useful douche for leucorrhoea and uterine prolapse, or as a relief for hemorrhoids.

## Culture, Myth and Symbol

The earliest mention of a sacred myrtle can be found in the ancient Sumerian text, the *Epic of Gilgamesh*, where myrtle is mentioned as a special tree in the grove of the gods.

In Greece, the myrtle was sacred to Aphrodite and was believed similarly to possess the power that she had of being able to create and perpetuate love. Hence it was employed in early times in marriage ceremonies, when festive myrtle wreaths were worn. It also played an essential role in many other religious rites – for example, the initiates of the Eleusinian mysteries were crowned with the "nuts" of Zeus and the myrtle of Aphrodite. The myrtle was said to have been brought from Paradise.

In the foundation legend of the city of Sida (at the southernmost tip of the Peloponnese peninsula), Artemis, the goddess of the wild forces of nature, was glimpsed as a hare disappearing into a myrtle tree. This was the place chosen for the city, and the tree was still revered at the time of the Greek traveller, Pausanias (second century CE).

Virgil tells us that when Aeneas arrived at the spot where Polydore, a young prince of Troy, had been murdered,

LEFT: *In ancient Greece, the radiant beauty of the myrtle flower was a symbol for Aphrodite, the goddess of love.*

he found a grove of cornel and myrtle there. After proposing a sacrifice to Venus (Aphrodite), Aeneas heard the ghost of Polydore speaking from the trees. Aeneas and his companions performed a proper funeral ceremony for the prince and his soul was then able to depart.

In ancient Rome, two myrtle trees dedicated to Venus – the Patrician Tree and the Plebeian Tree – grew in front of the Temple of Quirinus. Their respective growth was said to reflect shifts in the power balance between the senate (the Patricians) and the people (the Plebeians).

**Symbolism**: Unity

**Divine Associations**: Aphrodite, Artemis (both Greek)

**Astrological Association**: Venus

BELOW: *A flowering myrtle tree in full splendour. According to the Greek geographer and historian, Strabo (64/63BCE–c.23CE), the myrtle was used in ritual by the ancient Persians.*

# Olive *Olea*

*Olea* is a genus comprising about 20 species of tender evergreen trees, native to the eastern Mediterranean. The opposite, leathery leaves are sometimes silvery beneath. The small, white or whitish flowers appear in panicles, and are unisexual or bisexual. The fruit is a drupe with usually one seed. Olive trees can reach a very old age, but they require a deep, fertile and well-drained soil.

The common olive (*O. europaea*), which is native to Asia Minor, reaches 25ft (8m) or more in height. The elliptic to lanceolate leaves are up to 3in (7.5cm) long, and silvery-scaly beneath. Its flowers are fragrant. The oblong fruit grows to about 1½in (3.8cm) in length and turns a glossy black when ripe.

## Practical Uses

Since ancient times (and from c.3,700BCE onward in the region north of the Dead Sea), the olive has been widely cultivated for its oil-rich fruit. The immature green fruits are also harvested and pickled. The olive tree blooms in the spring; the harvest for table olives takes place in the autumn; and the harvest for olives used for their oil, in the winter.

Olive oil is the finest culinary oil, and it is one of the few safe to heat to a high temperature. There are many grades of oil but the best quality one is "cold-pressed extra virgin". The oil has also been used in medicine and cosmetics, and for lighting. During the Romans' occupation of Libya (106BCE–c.439CE), they constructed an aqueduct from Jebal to Leptis Magna (a distance of about 100 miles/161km) in order to transport olive oil in an ingenious way: it was poured onto water at one end to be carried to the other where it was skimmed off to be exported.

The first olive trees to grow in North America were planted in 1769 by Franciscan monks at their mission in San Diego, California.

## Natural Healing

The list of health benefits associated with the olive is long and impressive. For example, olive oil, which is high in monounsaturated fats and low in cholesterol, is recommended for the treatment of heart conditions; it also reduces gastric acidity and stimulates the secretion of bile.

In Traditional Chinese Medicine the olive is neutral and sweet, and affects the spleen and liver meridians. It is used to treat sore throats, diarrhoea and alcoholism.

## Culture, Myth and Symbol

In the Old World, the olive was of outstanding importance. The city-state of Athens, in particular, owed most of its prosperity to the olive (in Greek, *elea*) and revered it accordingly. The ancient mother tree of all the olives cultivated in Attica stood at the heart of the Acropolis, next to the temple of Athena. Contrary to the sexual connotations of the fig and the apple, the symbolism of the olive is sexually neutral. In accordance with its deity, the virginal aspect of Athena, known as Pallas Athena, the olive yields "virgin" oil. This is the quality that makes it fit for temples and palaces. Athena was the goddess who inhabited the olive tree, and she was also the guardian and patroness of the city of Athens.

The olive was intrinsic to the foundation legend of the city. Both Athena and Poseidon wanted to bestow their name upon the newly founded city. As a gift, Poseidon offered a horse, Athena an olive branch. The council of gods decided

OLIVE

**BELOW**: *From ancient times to the present, the productive olive tree has been the basis for many economies in the Mediterranean.*

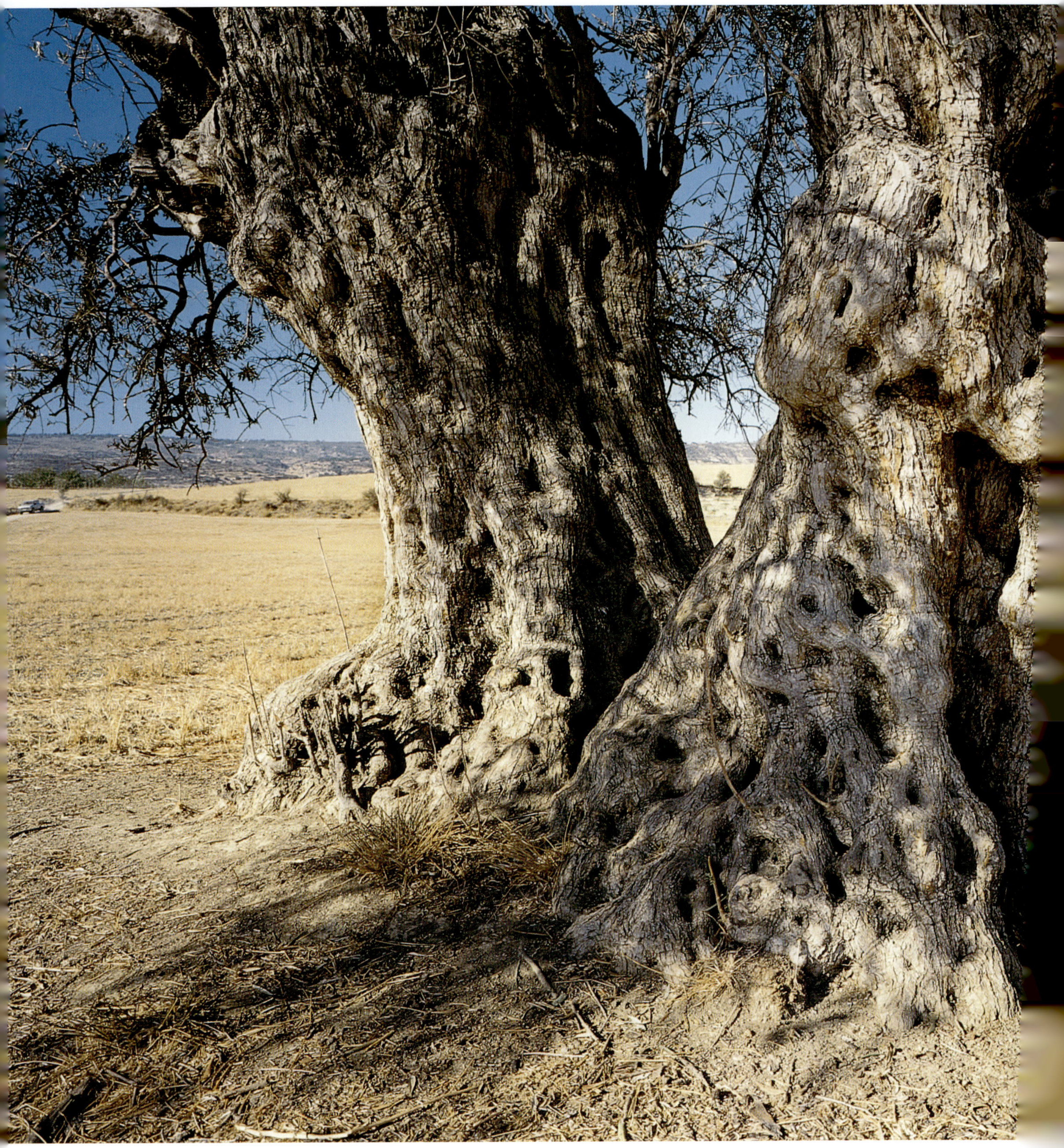

**LEFT**: *Olive trees can live up to 2,000 years. Old specimens, such as this one in Cyprus, tend to have impressively gnarled boles.*

to grant the privilege to Athena, for the horse is a symbol of war, while the olive is one of peace. The olives of the Acropolis' mother tree were harvested, and their oil was used to fuel a consecrated golden lamp next to it, which burned all year, day and night, on the sacred mound. This tree, together with Athens' other olives sacred to Athena (on the Aerophag and in the Academy), were called *moria*, "given as heritage (by the gods)".

In ancient Greece, the olive tree was protected; its wood was used only for cult statues. Merely harming an olive tree resulted in a court summons and heavy penalties. When the Epidaureans were told by the Oracle of Delphi to carve two cult statues from a certain olive tree from the Athenian district, they had to ask permission diplomatically.

The palaces and dwellings of Minoan Crete (from c.2,000BCE) were illuminated by an abundance of elaborate olive oil-fuelled lamps. The Homeric Greeks used olive oil (in Greek *elaion*) as a base for creams and perfumes to rub on their own bodies as well as on statues of the gods.

In Moroccan Islamic tradition, the olive tree is the World Tree itself, the centre and column of the world, the symbol of the universal human being, and of the Prophet. One of the names of God, or another sacred word, is said to be written on each of its leaves. The Koran describes Allah as "the light of the heavens and the earth", like a sacred lamp "lit from a blessed olive tree neither eastern nor western. Its very oil would almost shine forth, though no fire touched it." (Sura 24:35)

In the great Temple of Jerusalem, which was roofed and panelled with wood from the cedars of Lebanon, Solomon used olive wood for the frame of the outer door, the double door of the inner shrine and the two cherubim that towered behind the altar in the Holy of Holies. The olive doors and the cherubim were overlaid with gold (1 Kings 6:23–35). Using olive wood was a statement about eternal peace – the deep peace of the timeless space within the human soul. Because this is an inner quality, the olive wood on Solomon's Temple doors was not outwardly visible, its surfaces being clad entirely in the purest of metals – gold. In this way, gold (the metal of the sun, which represents the human Higher Self) had the olive at its core – thus serving as a symbol for the peace of the immortal soul, in Hebrew tradition *Adam Kadmon*, or the universal human being.

Furthermore, it is the olive (Hebrew *zayit*) that has always provided the base oil for the sacred anointing of kings and priests (see Myrrh pp.64–5), and for the "last ointment" of the dead. And the Messiah is the "Anointed One", who will lead the human soul from exile into the true peace of being at one with God.

**Symbolism**: Perfect peace

**Divine Associations**: Athena (Greek), the Messiah (Judaism), Jesus Christ

**Astrological Associations**: Sun and Moon

**Historical Spotlight**: During a Persian invasion (480BCE), the stronghold of Athens was burnt down and the fire reached the mother olive tree. But it is said that it put forth shoots the very next day, and the Athenians rejoiced and took this as a sign of hope. The tree was still thriving and the lamp still alight when Pausanias visited over 600 years later.

ABOVE: *The fragrant white flowers of the olive appear in panicles.*

*Christos* is Greek for "the Anointed One". The Roman Catholic Church today still consecrates the Oil of the Catechumens – the holy oil used in the sacrament of baptism. Olive oil is a key ingredient in this holy oil, which must be sanctified by the bishop of the diocese. The consecration ceremony is held on the Thursday before Easter, and it requires the assistance of twelve priests and seven deacons, who bow to the oil when it has been blessed.

Olive oil is also the traditional fuel used in the Jewish seven-branched candlestick, the *menorah*, which represents the Tree of Light. The Apocrypha mentions a gift of an olive branch from the Temple of Jerusalem (2 Maccabees 14:4), which seems to suggest that there was a living olive tree that grew in the Temple, rather like the one at the Acropolis. This would make sense – what better oil could you have for anointing the priests and providing fuel for the *menorah* than that derived from a sacred tree?

And in Jesus' darkest hours of doubt on the night before his torture and crucifixion, he turned to the olive tree for comfort. After the Last Supper, he "went as was his custom to the Mount of Olives" (Luke 22:39), and his followers knew the place well, for "Jesus often met there with his disciples" (John 18:2). It was in the peaceful olive garden of Gethsemane, on the sacred Mount of Olives, that an angel appeared to him and gave him strength.

The olive is also intimately linked with the dove that became a symbol of peace through the biblical story of Noah and the Ark. When the dove returned with an olive leaf in its beak (Genesis 8:11), Noah knew that land was appearing again above the waters and that God had made a new peace with humankind.

ABOVE: *In many places the hand-picking method of harvesting olives means little has changed for millennia. Nets are placed under the tree to prevent the fruits from hitting the ground and splitting open.*

OPPOSITE: *A stately date palm reaching skyward, which enables its sweet fruit to gain the maximum benefit from sunlight. The trunk is covered with the bases of old leaf stalks that have been pruned.*

# Date palm *Phoenix dactylifera*

*Phoenix* is a genus of about 17 species of dioecious palms found in tropical and subtropical Africa and Asia. The date palm (*P. dactylifera*) can grow to 100ft (30m) in height. Its slender trunk is covered with the bases of old leaf stalks, and produces suckers unless pruned. The upper part of the crown bears the erect-ascending foliage, the lower part comprises the down-curving leaves. The leaves are glaucous, the single pinnae are narrow and stiff, and up to 18in (45cm) long. The dates are about 2in (5cm) long with a slender, often pointed seed, coated in thick, sweet, edible flesh.

## Practical Uses

Having been propagated in northern Africa and western Asia about 6,000 years ago, the date palm is probably the oldest cultivated plant in the world. Dates are known as the "bread of the Sahara". Today, the date palm is commercially grown in Iraq, north Africa, California and Arizona. Various varieties and hybrids are planted as ornamentals.

The wood of the date palm is soft and fibrous, and the poorer people in ancient Egypt used split palms to roof their houses, or to build fences or rafts. The leaflets can be woven into mats, baskets and many other household items.

## Natural Healing

The fruit flesh is quickly converted to sugar in the human body, thus raising blood sugar levels and insulin secretion. People who live in the Sahara also roast and grind the fruits and seeds to make "date coffee", which is traditionally taken with milk. The milk lowers the absorption rate, so that the blood sugar level does not rise too quickly.

Dates are beneficial for treating intestinal problems, constipation, a weak heart, and also help the body to rid itself of toxins from alcohol.

In Traditional Chinese Medicine, dates are warm and sweet, and affect the liver, lung and spleen meridians. They tone yin energy, and the blood, and are useful for a weak stomach, palpitations, and nervousness. In Ayurveda, they decrease *pitta* and increase *kapha*. Those with *vata* constitutions can eat fresh dates but should avoid dried ones.

## Culture, Myth and Symbol

In ancient Egypt, the date palm was the abode of the goddess Nephtys, who offers a tray of dates and the water of life to the deceased. However, the tree usually depicted in ancient Egypt as the Tree of Life was the sycomore fig. From about 1000BCE the Tree of Life in Assyrian art increasingly assumes the shape of the date palm. A winged disc above the tree symbolizes the presence of the supreme deity. Palace reliefs show the high priest adoring the tree, while holding what looks like the cone of the male date palm. Today, this is believed to indicate a fertilization ceremony. The fertilization of the female palm is a process in which humankind has assisted since ancient times. A single male tree produces enough pollen for 25–50 females, and female trees can sometimes be seen to lean distinctly toward their male neighbour. However, it seems that from quite early in history, date-growing peoples in the Near East, such as the Mesopotamians, began brushing the female trees with male flower bundles to ensure fertilization.

The date palm took its Latin name from the mystical bird, the phoenix, which builds its nest, but also its pyre, out

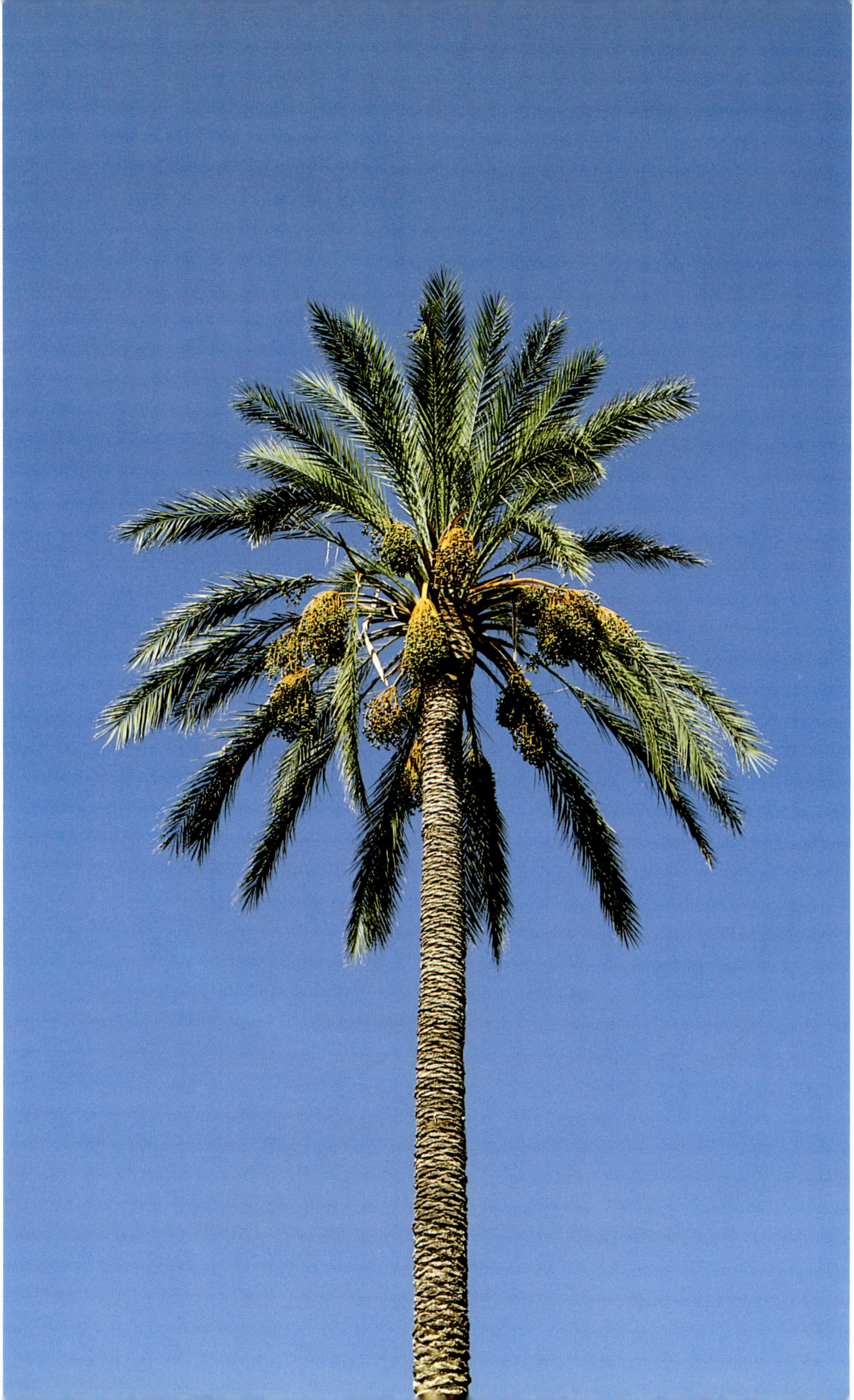

**BELOW**: *A mature palm with rich clusters of ripening dates.*

RIGHT: *Dates are not only delicious, but also nutritious – they are good sources of B-vitamins such as thiamin, riboflavin, biotin and folic acid, as well as iron, potassium, magnesium and other minerals.*

of myrrh and frankincense. After its death by fire the phoenix rises again from the ashes, for another life cycle of 1,461 years. (This period corresponds with the celestial rhythms of Sirius, the Dog Star, sacred to Isis. Its precise celestial position heralded the annual Nile flooding.)

On the island of Delos there was a sacred date palm said to have sheltered the births of Artemis (the moon goddess) and Apollo (the sun god). But palms did not grow in mainland Greece, and their fruits were imported from Phoenicia, the "land of the date palm". The significance of this tree for humans is expressed in the Greek word for it, *palma*, which also denotes the palm of the hand. Dates were called "fingers" in both Greek (*dactyli*) and Latin (*digiti*).

In Jewish history, Deborah was a wise and powerful prophetess and judge, and "it was her custom to sit under the palm tree of Deborah between Ramah and Bethel in the hill country of Ephraim" (Judges 4:5). The palm became a symbol of justice and righteousness. For the Feast of Tabernacles, palm fronds are among those boughs used to build ceremonial booths; they are also used for rejoicing (for example, at Jesus' arrival in Jerusalem). Palms were grown at many places: Jericho was called the "city of palm trees" (Deuteronomy 34:3). The Hebrew word for palm, *tamar*, has long been a popular first name for women.

According to Arabian legend, Allah had some spare clay left after creating Adam, and so he made the date palm, which, along with the camel, was traditionally regarded as the most precious gift to humankind. The Koran tells of how Mary gave birth to Jesus under this tree, which offered its fruits to her (Sura 19, 23). Palm trunks were used for the columns of the first mosque in Medina, and the early Islamic holy warriors were buried under palm trees. Calif Abu Bekr (*c*.573–634CE), the closest companion of the Prophet Mohammed, incorporated "Do not destroy palm trees" into his ten commandments. In the 19th century there were sacred palms in Oman, Nakhlah (Saudi Arabia) and Nejran (Yemen). The latter was an ancient tree oracle, which was decorated with fine garments and jewels at its annual feast.

In pre-Islamic lore, Baal was the life-giving spirit of the land, and life-giving trees in the desert (such as palms at oases) were called Baal trees. In the tradition of the Prophet, sacred trees are called *dhat anwat* in Arabic, meaning "trees to hang things on".

**Symbolism**: Sustenance and trust

**Divine Association**: Baal, the spirit of the land (Phoenician and ancient Arabian)

**Astrological Association**: Jupiter

**Historical Spotlight**: The Romans liked omens. In 48BCE a date palm shoot broke through the stone floor in the temple of Nike-Victoria (the goddess of victory) at Tralleis in Asia Minor. It quickly grew into a young tree next to the bust of Julius Caesar, who took it as a good sign regarding his impending battle against Pompey. Needless to say, he won.

# Spruce and fir *Picea* and *Abies*

The genera of spruce (*Picea*) and fir (*Abies*) are close relatives within the pine family (*Pinaceae*). Many traditions, both practical and spiritual, have not distinguished between them, hence they are considered here together.

The spruces (*Picea*) make up a genus comprising about 35 species of large coniferous, evergreen, monoecious trees distributed throughout the northern temperate regions, particularly in eastern Asia. The branches are borne in whorls. The male and female cones are pendulous and grow on the same tree – the mature female ones fall when still intact. The shoots and branchlets are rough to the touch, owing to the numerous peg-like leaf-scars. The Norway or common spruce (*P. abies*) is the one most commonly in cultivation today, and is popularly known as the "Christmas Tree". The botanical name of the genus, *Picea*, stems from the Latin *pix*, meaning "pitch".

The silver firs (*Abies*) differ from the spruces in having disc-like, comparatively smooth leaf-scars and erect cones which break up while still on the branch. Most firs have a conical shape and linear, needle-shaped leaves which are usually flattened. In many species, the erect female cones display amazing hues of violet or purple when young. Most firs are sensitive to air pollution, and are therefore severely endangered today. The European silver fir (*A. alba*) is native to the Alps, and has a smooth gray bark when young. The last wild silver fir in Bavaria, Germany, died early this millennium because of the general level of air pollution.

## Practical Uses

Many Native American peoples, such as the Paiute, use spruce and/or fir boughs as flooring in sweat houses and the Malecite and Micmac use them for camping bedding. The Algonquin shred and pound roots to make cords and ropes, while the Cree and Micmac use the wood for framing timbers, toys, paddles, tent frames, cabins and roofing. The resin produces pitch, which the Malecite and Ojibwa utilize in waterproofing roofs and canoes. Europeans in the mountainous Mediterranean and the Alpine regions used spruce and fir in much the same way, but the trees were only introduced to some areas, such as Britain, after the Middle Ages.

The lightweight timber of the Greek fir (*A. cephalonica*) and the Cilician fir (*A. cilicica*) was used for the construction of Greek and Roman houses, as well as for ships – the long, straight trunks of up to 90ft (27m) were a prime choice for ships' masts. Today, spruce is considered one of the best woods from which to make musical instruments, because of its qualities of resonance.

## Natural Healing

The high amounts of resin and essential oils in conifers (particularly in the buds) have made spruce and fir useful for treating gout and rheumatism, coughs, colds and other respiratory infections since ancient times. An invigorating spruce bath (6–7oz/150–200g of needles boiled in 1¾pts/1ltr of water, and added to the bath) stimulates circulation.

Native North American tribes, such as the Algonquin, Tsalagi, Kwakiutl, Bella Coola and Ojibwa have produced antiseptic, dermatological, gynecological, diaphoretic and laxative aids, as well as cough, tuberculosis, and rheumatism remedies from various spruce and fir species, particularly the balsam fir (*A. balsamea*), the giant fir (*A. grandis*), the white spruce (*P. glauca*), and the sitka spruce (*P. sitchensis*).

RIGHT: *In the natural history of the planet, the conifers pre-dated deciduous trees. While young spruces and firs have a triangular shape with the apex at the tip, older specimens, such as these Douglas firs, have more open, rugged crowns.*

The tree essence of silver fir boosts empowerment, creativity and healing. The essence of the Norway spruce brings clarity, trust and an understanding of change.

## Culture, Myth and Symbol

For the indigenous Siberians of the Altai mountains, the World Tree is a gigantic spruce that reaches from the navel of the Earth to the highest region of the heavens, thus connecting the three main layers of the universe: the spirit world, the earthly plane and the underworld. The Tatars believe that the World Tree has nine roots, and according to the Yakuts, shamans are born on this tree and reared in nests on its branches.

The spruce is also the centre of sacred teachings among the indigenous tribes of southern Canada, who call it the Peace Tree. Its lessons are: to co-operate and exchange with other life forms; to be connected with the earth and the heavens; and to exhibit a joyful and tranquil humility.

Many of the peoples in North America have ritual uses for spruces and firs. For example, the sitka spruce is employed in a variety of coming-of-age ceremonies and initiations for the adolescents of the Hanaksiala, Hesquiat, Nitinaht, and Kwakiutl tribes, while Tsimshian shamans, hunters, and fishermen use sitka boughs during preparatory and purification rituals. In general, native North American tribes believe that spruces and firs offer protection from malign influences.

According to Slavic tradition, the goddesses of the woodlands, Dziwitza and Boruta, often inhabit firs, while the King of the Forest (equivalent to the Green Man in Western tradition) dwells in the oldest fir of the region.

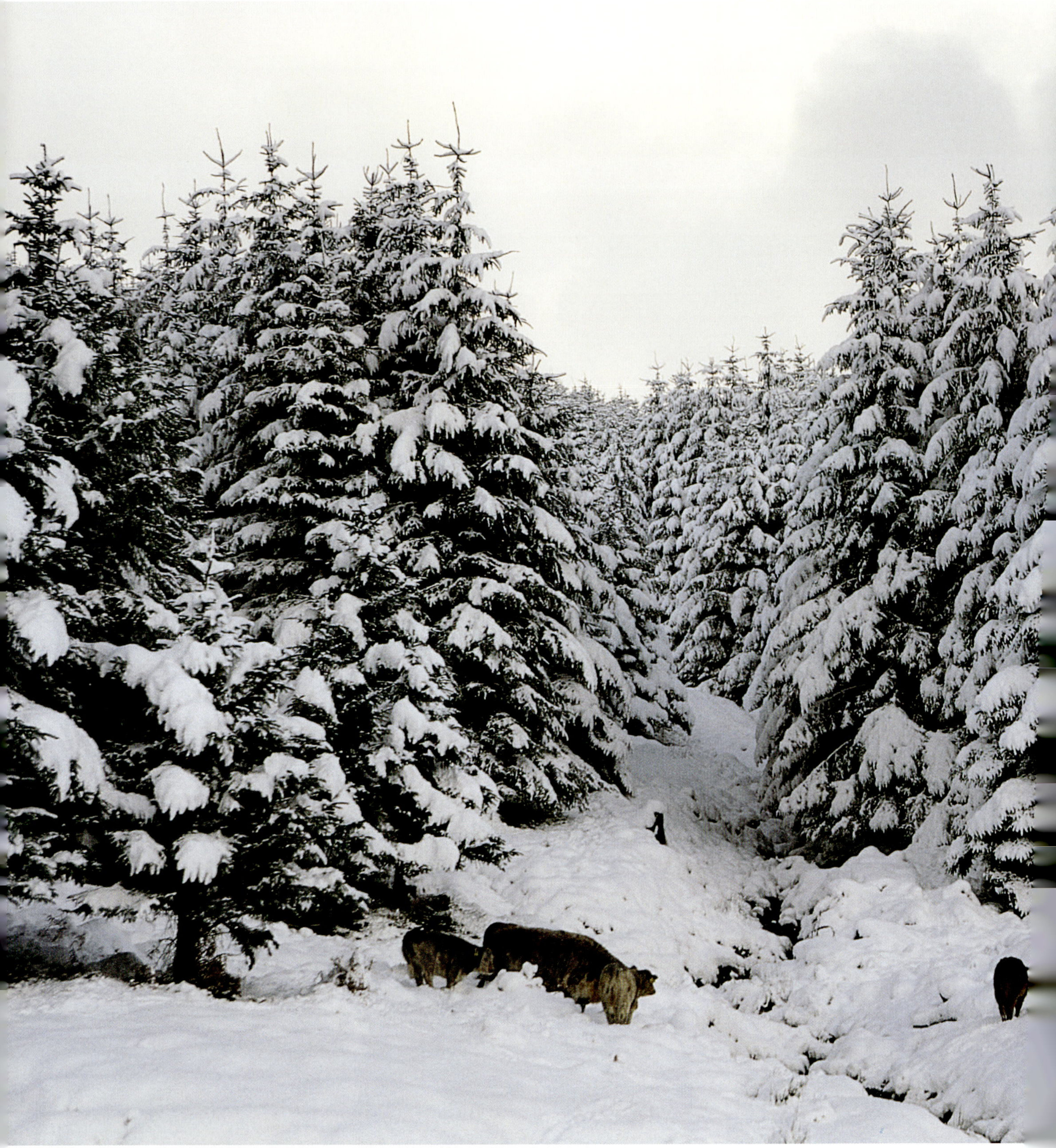

# SPRUCE AND FIR

*LEFT: Deep snow in Norway spruce woods near Glen Finglass, Scotland. The trees' sloping branches allow them to shed heavy snow.*

In ancient Phrygia and Greece, the fir (*elate*, "the lofty one") was sacred to Artemis, the moon goddess and patroness of childbirth. The participants in the procession of Dionysus waved fir boughs in her honour. The fir was also the birth-tree of Adonis, god of the Phoenician city of Byblos and, through his Mesopotamian origins the precursor of the pre-dynastic Osiris of Egypt. The annual death (autumn) and resurrection (spring) of the vegetation spirit were transferred by the peoples of the Near East to their fertility gods (such as Tammuz and Attis), the sons of the Great Goddess or Mother of the Universe (for example, Ishtar and Cybele). Evergreens have always been symbols of the continuity of life.

The accounts of the life of Jesus Christ not only come from the same geographical region (Asia Minor and the eastern Mediterranean region), but their major elements also fit this mythological pattern of death and resurrection perfectly (although the physical aspect of fertility has, of course, been replaced by a spiritual one).

It is no coincidence that we celebrate Christmas with a fir tree – the Tree of Light. Since ancient times, evergreens have been part of mid-winter ceremonies. This tradition dwindled in Christian Europe, then was revived in 18th-century Germany and spread across the Christian world.

**Symbolism**: Our connections with all life

**Divine Associations**: Osiris (ancient Egypt), Artemis (Greek), Dziwitza and Boruta (Slavic), the Great Spirit (Native North American)

**Astrological Association**: Saturn

OPPOSITE: *A veteran Scots pine bent by the strong wind on the shores of Loch Affric, Scotland.*

# Pine *Pinus*

The genus *Pinus* comprises more than 90 species of mostly tall, coniferous, evergreen trees which can be found throughout the temperate zone of the northern hemisphere. Young trees are usually conical in shape, but become bushy or flat-topped with age. The long, needle-like leaves are borne in bundles. Male and female cones grow on the same tree. The male cones are catkin-like and clustered; the female cones are cylindrical to nearly globose. There are two seeds to a scale.

In most species the seeds are released when ripening, but in a few species the cones remain intact until falling. The Monterey pine (*P. radiata*) often keeps its 6in- (15cm-) long cones intact on the tree for many years until a forest fire forces them to open (see Redwood pp.186–9). Pines like a good deal of light, and only a few species can tolerate smoke-polluted air.

The Scots pine (*P. sylvestris*) is the only pine native to northwestern Europe. It has a characteristic reddish bark, which fissures deeply with age. The twisted blue-green or gray-green leaves are borne in pairs and are 1–4in (2.5–10cm) long. The cones are about 3in (7.5cm) long and sit on short stalks. The Scots pine can thrive in almost any soil, but will not reach its maximum age or size (about 100ft/30m) in damp acid soil or shallow dry chalk.

## Practical Uses

Since time immemorial, pines have been important timber trees. Sometimes the Greeks used coastal pines (in Greek, *pytis*), such as the widespread Aleppo pine (or Jerusalem pine, *P. halepensis*), and the cluster pine (*P. pinaster* or *maritima*), but for house and boat building they preferred the tall and strong mountain trees (in Greek, *peuce*), such as the Austrian pine (*P. nigra*).

Many species yield edible nutritious seeds, for example the umbrella pine (*P. pinea*) in southern Europe. The nuts or pinyons can be eaten raw or roasted, in cakes, breads or on their own.

The lodgepole pine (*P. contorta*) received its name because the Blackfoot, Dakota, Montana, Paiute, Cheyenne and Thompson tribes make their tipi frames from its wood. And wherever fir or spruce do not yield enough resin for pitch production, pine saves the day.

## Natural Healing

Pine nuts are a good source of potassium, magnesium, vitamin E and carotenes. In Traditional Chinese Medicine they are regarded as warm and sweet, tonifying yin, and boosting the circulation.

Shoot or needle preparations (ointments, teas, baths and inhalations) are disinfectant, diuretic and relaxing. They can soothe coughs, clear the head of congestion, stimulate the lungs and improve circulation. The Bach Flower Remedy of Scots pine enhances self-acceptance and strength. The tree essence helps to develop penetrating insight in a balanced way.

## Culture, Myth and Symbol

The Blackfoot make "story sticks" from the wood of the lodgepole pine. These are given to children by tribal elders as a reward for doing small errands or chores. The number of notches on the stick indicates the number of stories that the child has "earned". The Hopi, on the other hand, apply

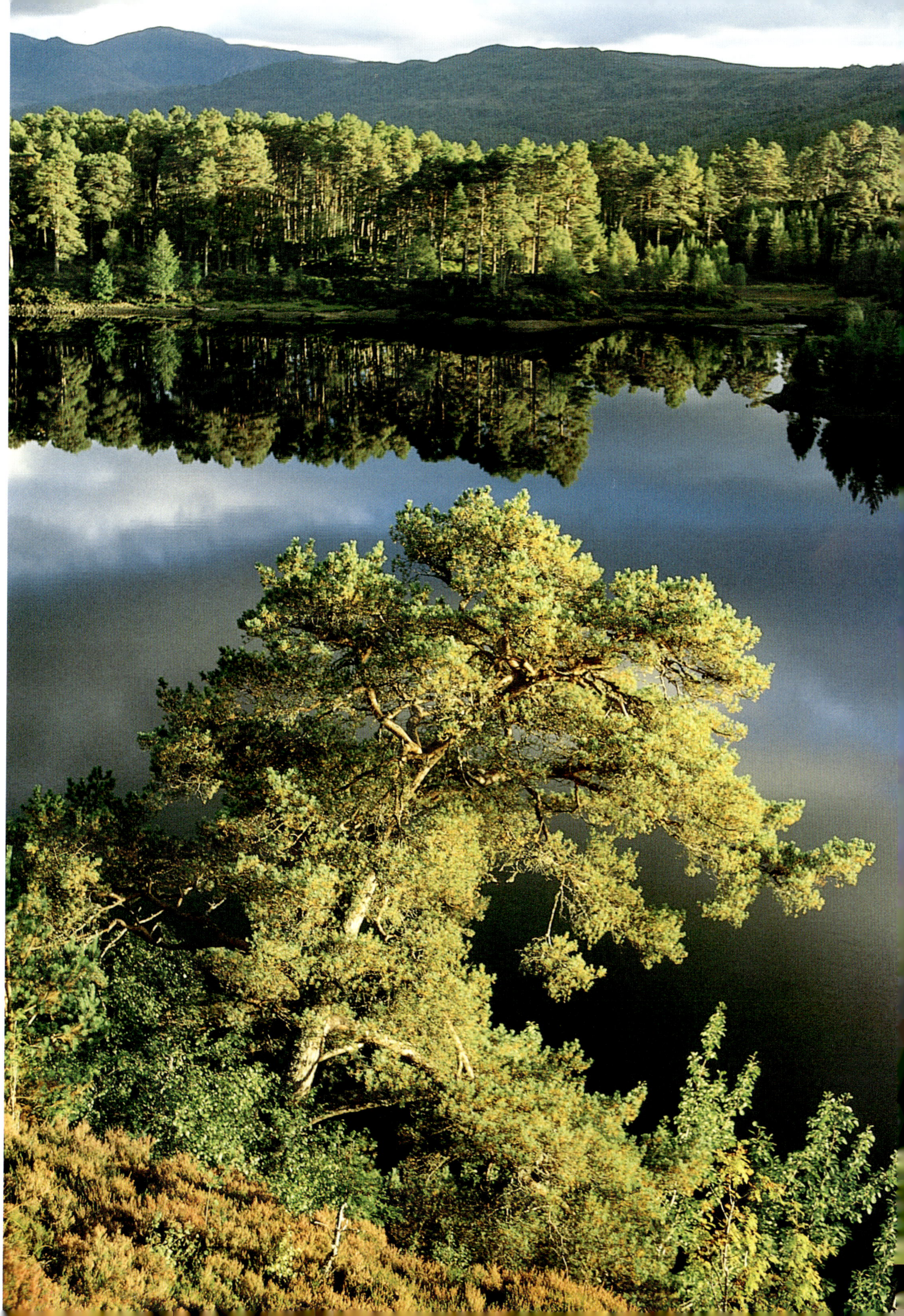

BELOW: *The "mother" Scots pine tree in Glen Affric, Scotland. Pines are exceptionally adaptable trees and have long been cherished as the homes of divine beings.*

two-needle pinyon "gum" to the forehead if necessary, as a protection from sorcery. In the War Dance, the Navajo used the needles of the same tree as a ceremonial medicine, and its pitch for body paint. The Kawaiisu hang a baby boy's outgrown cradle in a Ponderosa pine so that he will grow strong like the tree.

On the other side of the globe in China, Taoist hermits and monks living at high altitudes on sacred mountains cherish the pine for its nuts, which are among the few things eaten by the holy men. According to Taoist tradition these nuts can bestow eternal life.

Pine is the principal wood used for wall-panels in the royal burial chamber of the vast "Midas Mound" complex (c. eighth century BCE) at Gordium, Phrygia (modern western Turkey). And pine nuts (presumably from the Lebanon, as pines do not grow in Egypt), have been found in Egyptian coffins. The mighty Viking chiefs of the past were buried (on land) in their dragon ships made from pine, while in Scotland, clan chiefs and warriors liked to be buried under this tree. The pine is also the tree that features most frequently in the badges of the Scottish clans.

Similarly, in the ancient Mediterranean the pine was strongly associated with life force, vitality, death and resurrection, and particularly with the vigour of the spirit of vegetation: Pan in ancient Greece and Attis in Phrygia. In Greece, many an old pine tree was dedicated to Pan, the hairy and horned personification of the forces of nature, and would have a shrine or altar next to it, sometimes accompanied by a small sacred fire.

In Phrygian myth, the mother goddess Cybele has a son, Attis, whom she transforms into a pine tree at his death.

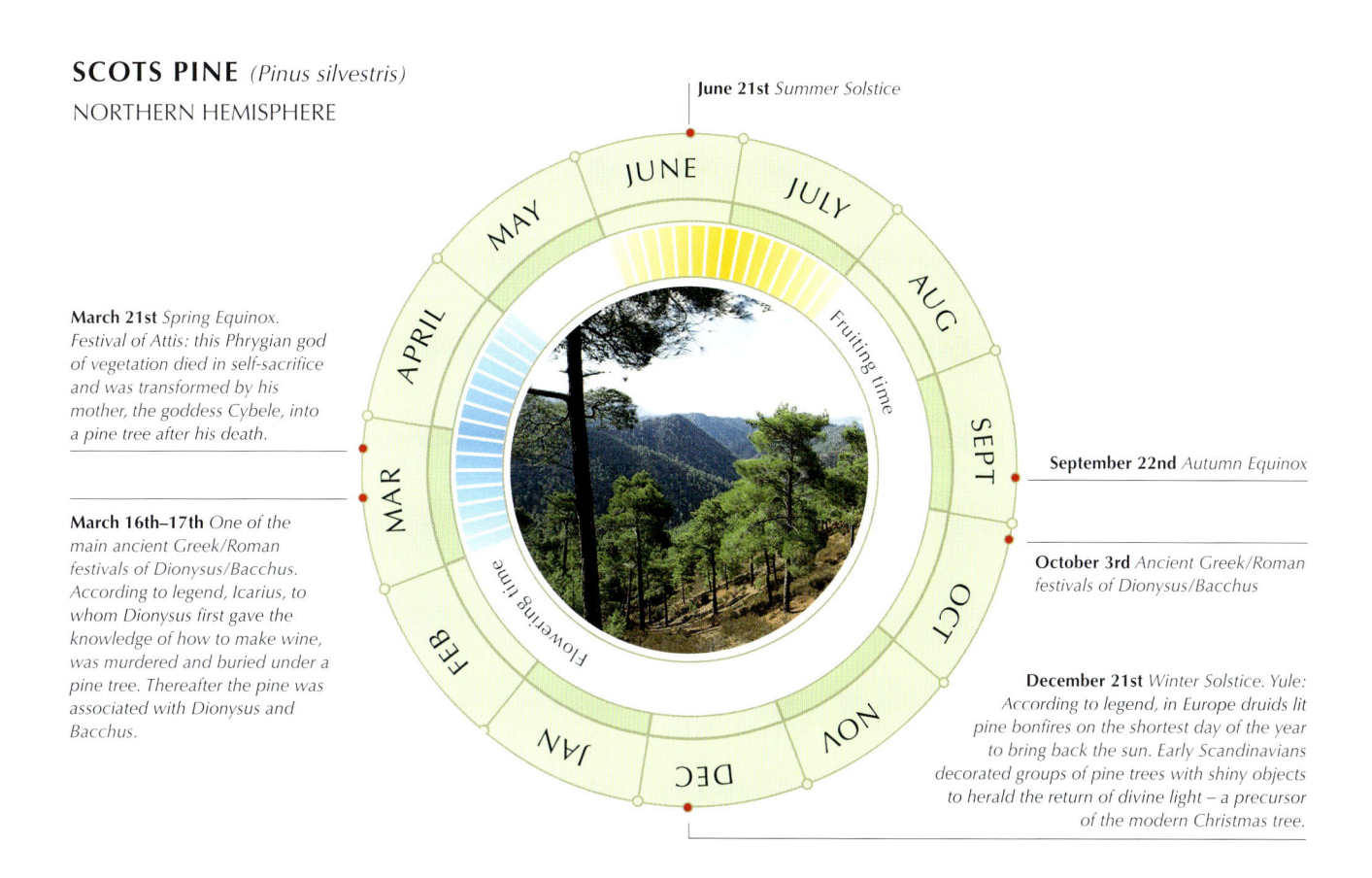

## SCOTS PINE *(Pinus silvestris)*
NORTHERN HEMISPHERE

**March 21st** *Spring Equinox. Festival of Attis: this Phrygian god of vegetation died in self-sacrifice and was transformed by his mother, the goddess Cybele, into a pine tree after his death.*

**March 16th–17th** *One of the main ancient Greek/Roman festivals of Dionysus/Bacchus. According to legend, Icarius, to whom Dionysus first gave the knowledge of how to make wine, was murdered and buried under a pine tree. Thereafter the pine was associated with Dionysus and Bacchus.*

**June 21st** *Summer Solstice*

**September 22nd** *Autumn Equinox*

**October 3rd** *Ancient Greek/Roman festivals of Dionysus/Bacchus*

**December 21st** *Winter Solstice. Yule: According to legend, in Europe druids lit pine bonfires on the shortest day of the year to bring back the sun. Early Scandinavians decorated groups of pine trees with shiny objects to herald the return of divine light – a precursor of the modern Christmas tree.*

(He died in self-sacrifice, which involved castration.) At his annual spring festival, a decorated pine was festively carried into the village. As part of this ancient fertility cult, the high priest of Attis would cut his own arm and offer his blood to the god. Other men would follow his example, to the music of cymbals, tambourines, flutes and horns. But whether the self-sacrificing dances culminated in self-castration we do not know – such stories could be exaggerations made by outsiders and later commentators.

According to Breton legend, the legendary wise man Merlin climbed the Pine of Barenton (from *bel nemeton*, "sacred grove of Bel"), just as shamans climb the World Tree. Here, he had a profound revelation and he never returned to the mortal world. In later versions, Merlin's *glas tann* was mistranslated as a "glasshouse". It is actually a living tree (from the Cornish *glas*, "(ever)green", and *tann*, "sacred tree"), and from these words the name of Glastonbury, in Somerset, England is derived. Hence, according to legend, it is a sacred tree in which the soul of Merlin awaits his return.

**Symbolism**: Vitality and continuity

**Divine Associations**: Pan (Greek), Attis (Phrygian) and Merlin (Celtic)

**Astrological Association**: Mars

**Historical Spotlight**: During the Romans' occupation of Israel, they generally made use of local Jerusalem pine (*P. halepensis*) and this is probably also the wood they used to make the crosses for most crucifixions, including that of Jesus Christ.

BELOW: *The leaves and small, inedible fruits of the terebinth.*

# Terebinth *Pistacia terebinthus*

*P*istacia is a genus of about ten species of deciduous or evergreen shrubs and small trees. The terebinth (*Pistacia terebinthus*) is native to the Mediterranean and Asia Minor. It is a small tree with aromatic, dark green, glossy, pinnate leaves and greenish unisexual flowers. The small inedible fruits turn from red-brown to dark purple. Another species, native to Israel, is the Palestine terebinth (*P. palaestina*).

The pistachio nuts we eat today grow on the pistachio or pistacia nut tree (*P. vera*), native to Iran and central Asia.

## Practical Uses

The terebinth yields tannins (used in the leather industry) and is the original source of turpentine.

## Natural Healing

Turpentine has traditionally been used as a treatment for lice. The resin has expectorant and anti-bacterial effects and hence has been made into an ointment and used as a chest rub for lung conditions.

## Culture, Myth and Symbol

Among the ancient peoples of the Near East, the terebinth was revered and deified. Many terebinth sanctuaries served as sites for worship, incense-burning and as burial places. Today, terebinth trees can still be found in sanctuaries along Islamic pilgrimage routes in Arabia.

In all Bible translations to date, the Hebrew word for the terebinth, *elah* (*alah*), which has a feminine ending, has been confused with *allon* (*elon*), meaning "oak", which has a masculine ending. (The most frequently used Hebrew words for "terebinth" and "oak" are given first, with their variations in brackets.) This has resulted in the mistranslation of many tree names mentioned in the Bible. For example, the "oaks" of Moreh (Deuteronomy 11:29), Shechem (Genesis 35:4), and the sacred grove at Mamre where Abraham received his calling from God (Genesis 18:1), were not, in fact, oaks, but terebinths.

Some of the mistranslations could have arisen also because there is another, hitherto-overlooked interpretation of the words *elah* and *elon* (and their variations): that of "sacred tree", as they stem from *el* (*al*), meaning "God". This is extremely significant because it indicates that *any* species of tree could be encoded by *elah* (*alah*) as a female "tree of God", or by *elon* (*allon*) as a male sacred tree.

OPPOSITE: *The terebinth tree at the catacomb of Agia Solomi, Greece, adorned with votive offerings in the form of cloth rags.*

---

**Symbolism**: Revelation

**Divine Associations**: Jehovah, Allah

**Astrological Association**: Mercury

**Historical Spotlight**: For centuries, the Terebinth of Mamre, said to have sprung from the staff of Abraham himself, was the centre of a huge fair (including stalls and social events). According to the Scottish scholar W.R. Smith, the Jews, Christians and Muslims all revered the tree as a "haunt of angels" and made offerings of wine, cake, coins and incense there. However, shortly after 324CE Constantine the Great replaced the tree with a Christian basilica.

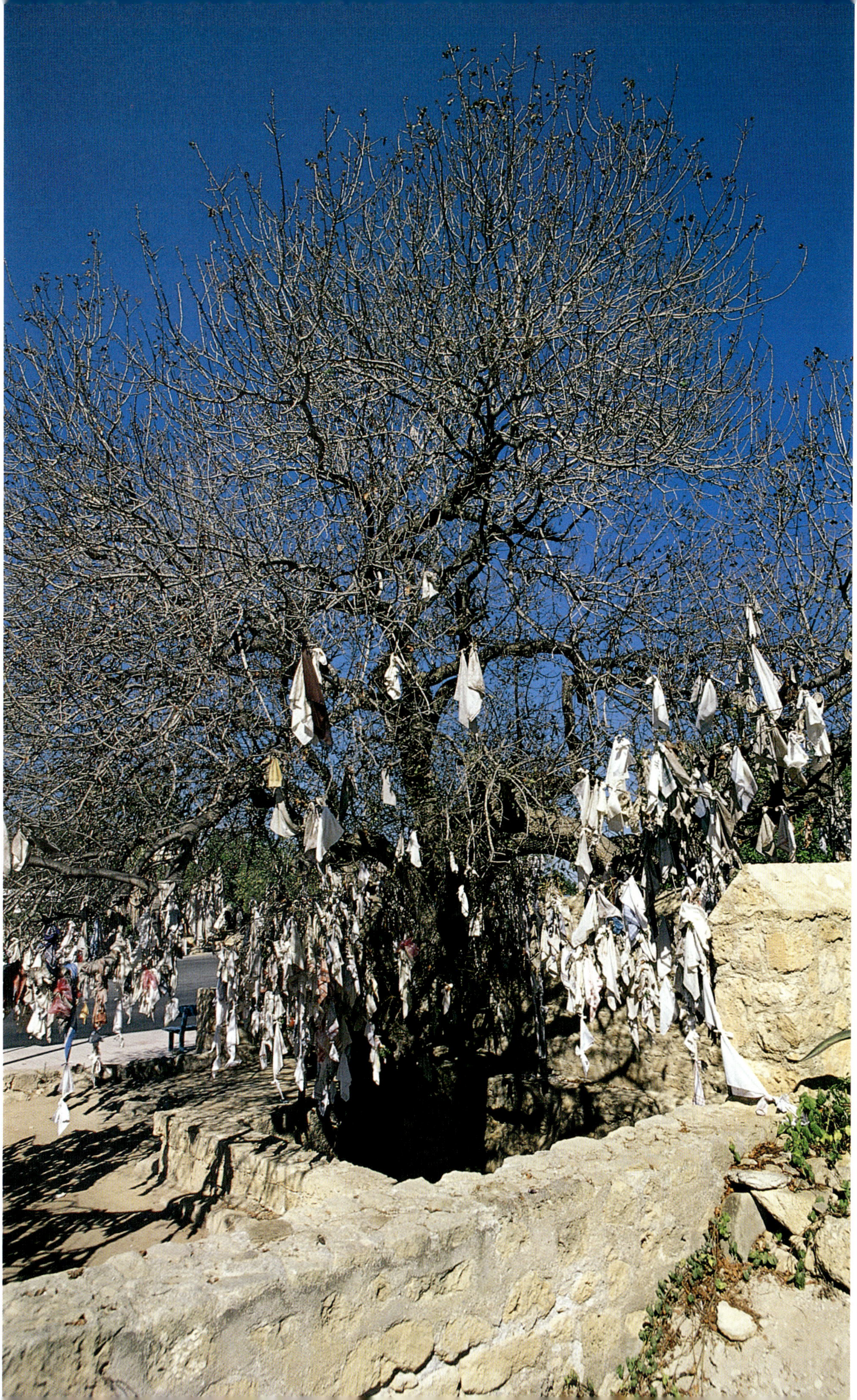

# Plane *Platanus*

The Oriental plane (*P. orientalis*), a native of southeastern Europe and western Asia, belongs to a small genus of about six species. It is a large, long-lived tree with dappled, flaking bark. Its leaves are deeply five-lobed, and between two and six bristly fruits sit in a cluster on one stalk.

Plane trees can tolerate polluted air as well as heavy pruning, hence the popular London plane (*P. acerifolia*), a hybrid between the Oriental and the American plane, is widely planted in cities.

## Practical Uses

The huge plane tree has been a popular shade tree in the Mediterranean since antiquity.

## Natural Healing

A poultice of freshly crushed plane leaves soothes sore and inflamed eyes, while a tea made from the leaves treats diarrhea. A decoction of the bark boiled in vinegar is a pain-relieving gargle for toothache. The tree essence prevents melancholy and over-analysis, and broadens points of view.

## Culture, Myth and Symbol

In ancient Armenia, the fire priests interpreted oracles from the movements of the branches of the sacred plane at Armavira, while in Persia, the plane tree was the guardian tree of the kings. Still today, many revered plane trees can be found shading village springs in the Near East.

In ancient Caria (southwestern Turkey), Zeus' symbol was the *labrys*, the double axe, and a plane grove was dedicated to him at Labraunda. Zeus' usurpation of the double axe, which was an ancient symbol of female power suggests that the grove was sacred to the Great Goddess prior to the Dorian invasion of c.1200BCE. The patriarchal victory over the older female deity is reflected in local legends in which male gods, particularly Zeus, harass, seduce or rape female deities. One such goddess is the Cretan Europa, who surrendered to Zeus inside an evergreen plane (a very rare variety – only 29 specimens were known to exist in 1980).

According to the myth of Heracles, a sacred plane grove stretched from Mount Pontinus to the sea near Argos. Shrines marked where Hades, Persephone and Dionysus had descended to the underworld. The Hydra, a water-monster, had her lair under one of the planes, and her seven heads symbolized the seven-fold source of the Amymone river. The associations with the underworld and water point again to the more ancient connection of the plane with the Great Goddess. The lore of the plane also links it with the sun and the moon, with the underworld and the heavens – a balance of opposites reminiscent of the Tree of Life.

---

**Symbolism**: Balance

**Divine Associations**: Zeus, Apollo Platanistios (both Greek); the Great Goddess

**Astrological Associations**: Sun, Pluto

**Historical Spotlight**: In 480BCE, while marching his army against Greece, the Persian king Xerxes was so entranced by a plane tree east of Sardes in Lydia (modern Turkey), that he stopped his troops to celebrate it. He adorned the plane with golden jewelry and other offerings and, according to Herodotus, appointed a gardener to care for it for its lifetime.

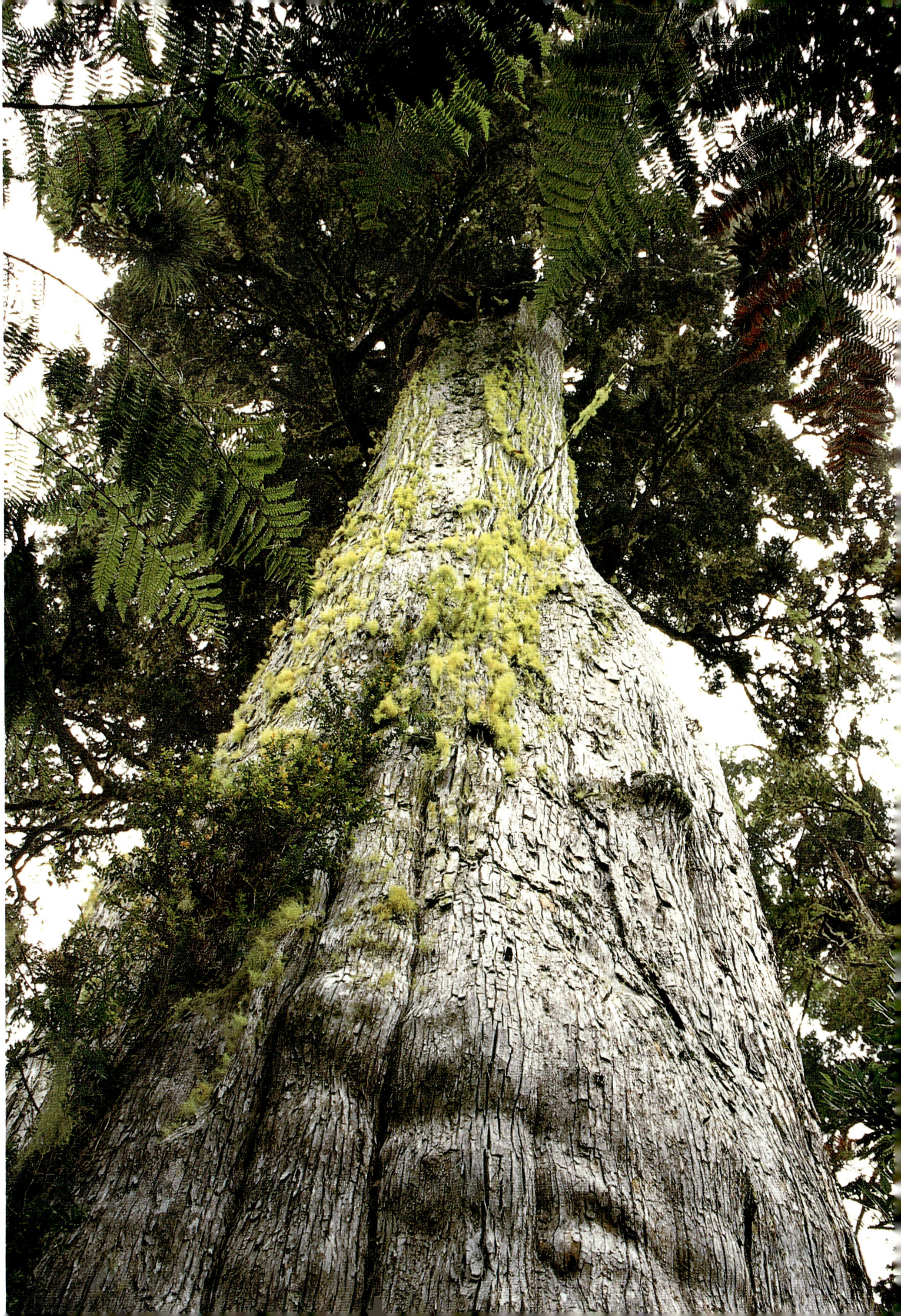

OPPOSITE: *A black poplar rising from an ivy-covered riverbank in Hertfordshire, England, its bark characteristically riven with clefts.*

# Poplar *Populus*

Part of the willow family (*Salicaceae*), *Populus* is a genus of about 35 species of dioecious trees found in the northern temperate zone. These include some of the fastest-growing of all trees, and they produce soft, white wood. The flowers appear in drooping catkins before the leaves. The fruits are small capsules, and the seeds are surrounded by copious hairs. Poplars are associated with damp stands, such as river valleys and floodplains.

The white poplar (*P. alba*), native from southeastern Europe to central Asia, has ovate and irregularly lobed leaves or toothed, larger leaves that are distinctly three to five-lobed. The black poplar (*P. nigra*), the only species native to northwestern Europe, is a large, heavy-branched tree with a deeply fissured trunk and hairless twigs. The bright green leaves are triangular to ovate, and slender-pointed. Both trees grow to a height of about 90ft (27m). The Lombardy poplar (var. "Italica" or "Pyramidalis"), a cultivar of the black poplar, takes the shape of a large, narrow column. Individual Lombardy poplars are usually male only.

## Practical Uses

Fast-growing poplars make ideal windbreaks, and are also usefully coppiced or lopped. Livestock like to eat poplar leaves, but only from trees that are cut early in the year and lopped frequently because this results in the leaves becomings softer and easier to chew.

In the Middle Ages, black poplar wood was favoured for building because of its fire-resistant properties. It is also used to make packing boxes, cotton-reels, clogs and matches.

## Natural Healing

Like willow and aspen, poplar bark contains salicylic acid, which makes it a useful anti-inflammatory and analgesic. The buds (high in resin and essential oils) have been used traditionally as an infusion to treat chest complaints, kidney and prostate problems, and rheumatism and gout. Externally poplar bark soothes burns, rashes, wounds and limb pains. The tree essence creates a sense of security.

## Culture, Myth and Symbol

In Greek myth Phaeton was the son of Helios, the sun. One day, he drove his father's chariot, but could not control the horses. An angry Zeus struck him dead with a thunderbolt. Phaeton's grieving sisters were changed into poplar trees.

The white poplar was associated with the dead. It was said to have originated on the banks of the Acheron river in the Greek underworld. A grove of black poplars in Aegaira (Achaia, in the northern Peloponnese) was sacred to Persephone, other groves were connected with Hecate; both were underworld goddesses. Homer mentions the black poplar being at the entrance to Hades, the realm of the dead – hence their link with graveyards. The Greek name, *aegaira*, became Latin *egeria*, and gave its name to the sacred grove of Nemi, near Rome. Here, a nymph by the name of Egeria inspired the first king of Rome to make his laws.

---

**Symbolism**: Descent, protection

**Divine Associations**: Hecate, Persephone, Hades (all Greek); Pluto (Roman)

**Astrological Association**: Saturn

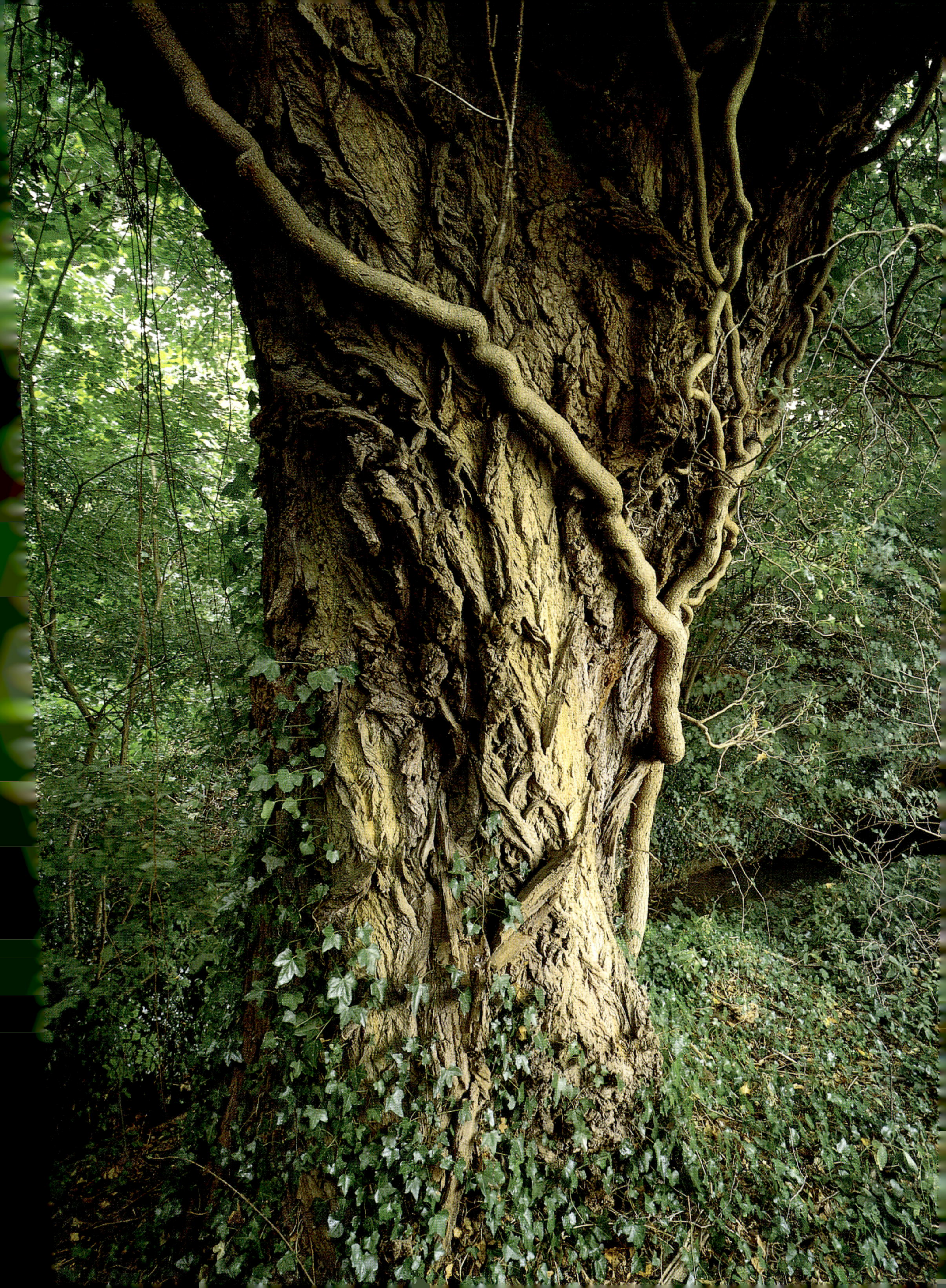

*OPPOSITE, ABOVE: A group of aspen closely interwoven, which often occurs due to the species' vivid suckering.*

*OPPOSITE, BELOW: Their long stalks mean the leaves "tremble" at only slight movements of air, speeding up the tree's metabolism of water.*

# Aspen *Populus tremula*

The aspen (*P. tremula*) is a medium-sized species of poplar, widely distributed in Europe and Asia, and extending to northern Africa. The leaves are prominently toothed and hang on long, slender stalks which cause the leaf to quiver in the slightest breeze.

The quaking aspen (*P. tremuloides*), its American equivalent, is mainly distinguished by its smaller, finely and evenly toothed leaves, its more slender catkins, and the pale yellowish bark visible on younger trees. This tree is one of the most widely distributed in North America, reaching from northern Mexico to Alaska.

## Practical Uses

Because the timber of poplars is light, tough, shock-absorbent and splinter-resistant, the Celts used it for battle shields. Today, aspen is one of the most common woods used in the match industry. In North America the Shuswap and the Blackfoot tribes make whistles from its branches.

## Natural Healing

The aspen contains salicylic acid – the forerunner of aspirin – which makes the leaves useful as an anti-inflammatory treatment and for pain relief in arthritis. The bark has been used in European tradition to make a stimulating tonic to treat weakness and as an astringent for diarrhea. In North America the Blackfoot tribe uses aspen preparations to ease heartburn, while the Bella Coola use them to treat gonorrhea and the Iroquois to cure worms. Blackfoot women take an infusion of bark scrapings when they are about to give birth.

The Bach Flower Remedy soothes unexplained worry and anxiety. The tree essence calms fear and brings laughter.

## Culture, Myth and Symbol

Because of their long stalks, poplar leaves seem to be in perpetual motion, making the whispering wind audible. Hermes, who rode the wind, is the messenger of the Greek gods, hence poplars featured as oracular trees in antiquity.

On Heracles' return from Hades (the underworld), he wove himself a wreath of aspen leaves. And in Olympia he lit a sacrificial fire of aspen wood to thank Zeus for his safe return. Ever since, it is said that the upper side of the leaves is dark because of the heat of Hades and that the underside is bleached silver, as a result of the sweat of the hero. Golden wreaths in the shape of aspen leaves have been found in 5,000-year-old graves in Mesopotamia.

Guarding the mythical rebirth of the sun, an aspen stood at the burial place of Velkhanos, the Cretan solar deity and precursor of the Roman god Vulcan. In North America, too, the aspen has strong solar associations. For the Navajo tribe, the tree is prominent in the Sun's House Chant, and the Cheyenne build the Sun Dance Lodge from its wood. The Thompson ritually wash their hunters (so that animals can't smell them), in a decoction of quaking aspen branches. This is also a protection against evil. The Hopi smoke aspen leaves ceremonially.

**Symbolism**: Ascent, protection

**Divine Associations**: Heracles, Hermes (both Greek), Vulcan (Roman)

**Astrological Association**: Mercury

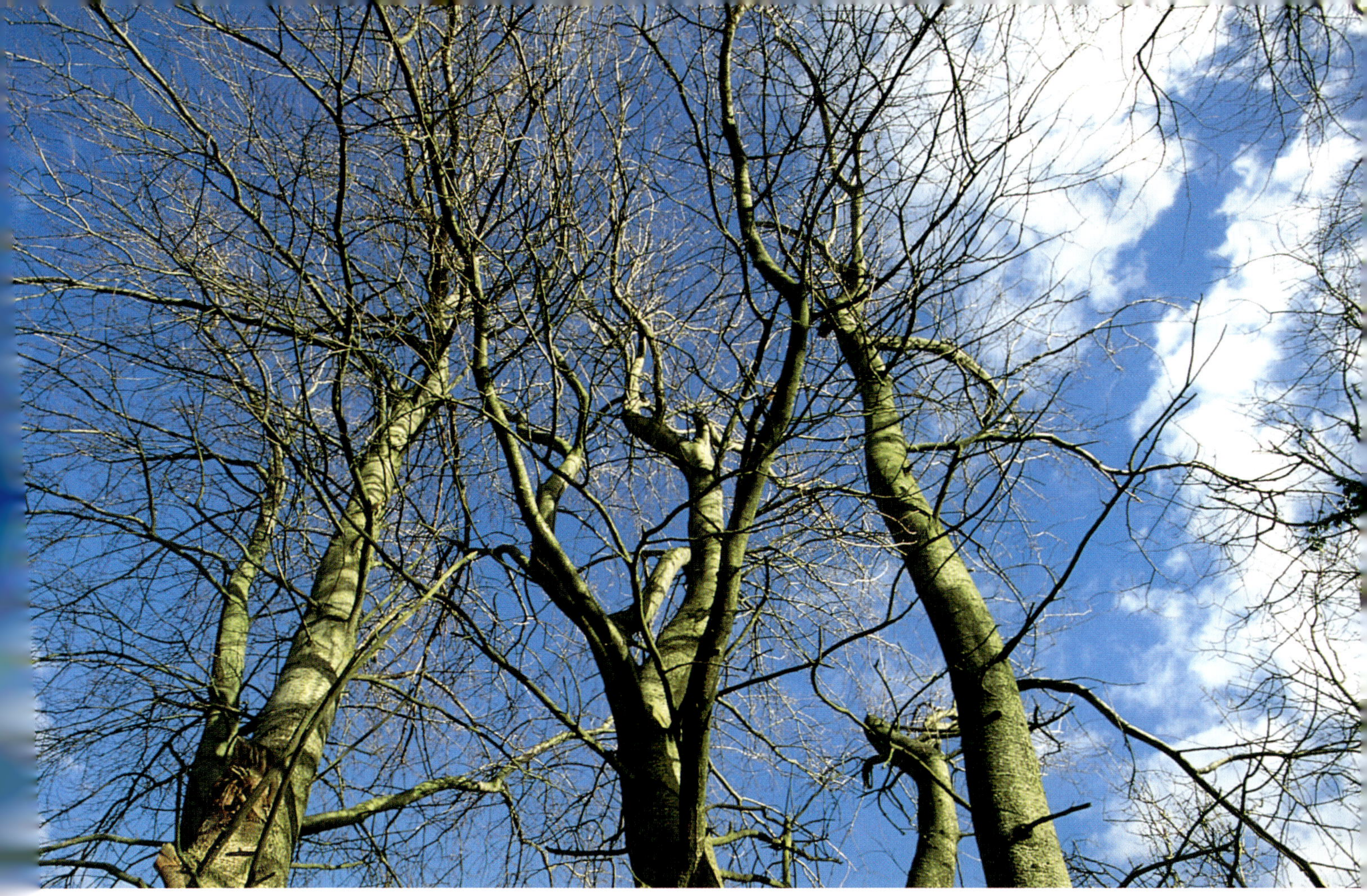

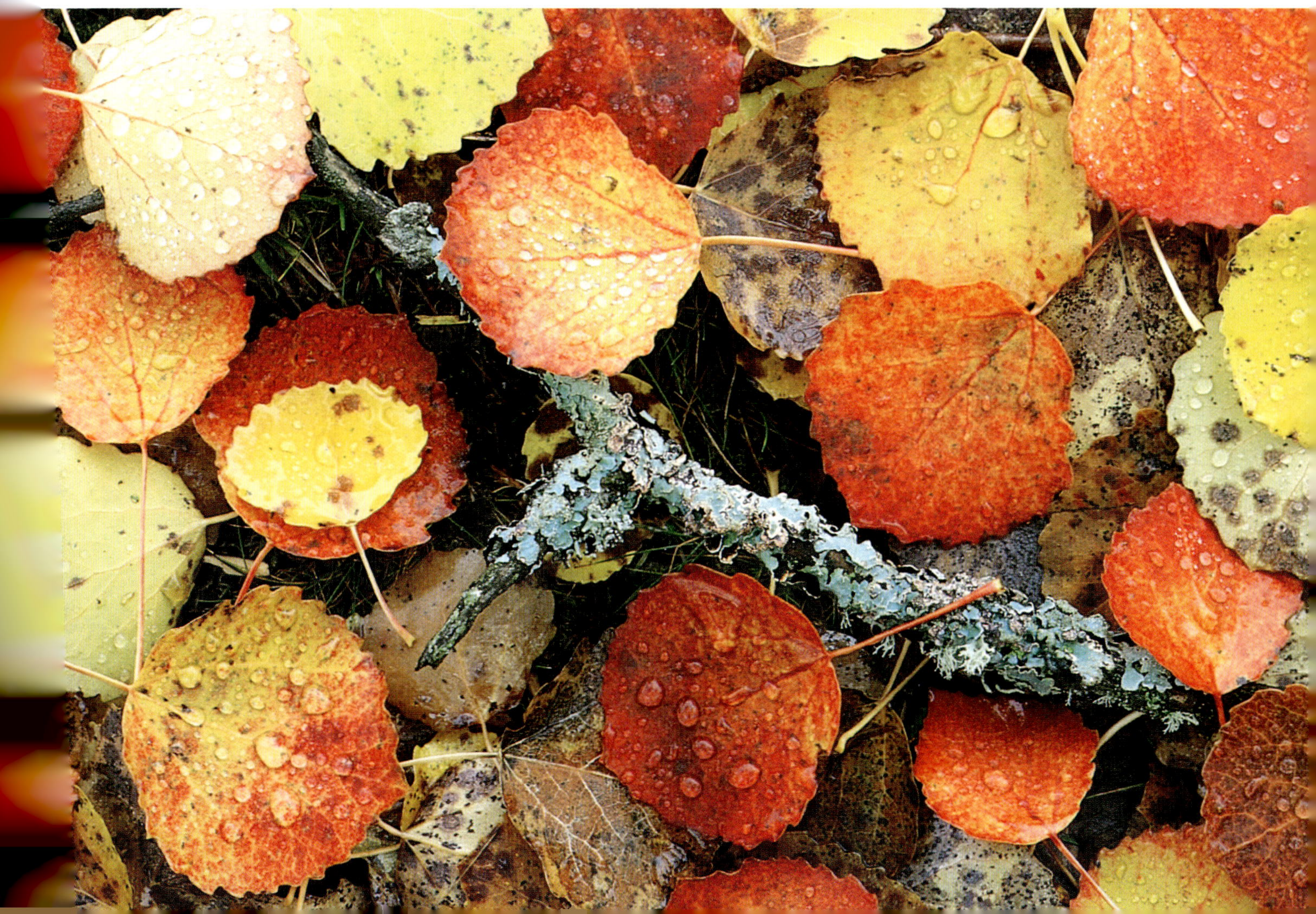

# Cottonwood
## *Populus deltoides*

The cottonwoods are various American members of the *Populus* genus (see also Poplar pp.156–7), most of which can reach a height of 90ft (27m). In spring, the female trees discharge masses of fluffy "cotton" from their fruit capsules. The Eastern cottonwood (*P. deltoides*) has a broad crown, its ovate leaves are glossy on their upper side and up to 7in (17.5cm) long.

### Practical Uses
The leaves of the Eastern cottonwood are used by the children of the Dakota, Omaha, Pawnee and Ponka tribes to make toy tipis and moccasins. The adult Omahas used this wood for the poles of the Buffalo Tent (in which a ceremony was held to ensure that the souls of hunted buffaloes lived on). The Navajo make cradles and ceremonial carvings out of the wood of the Rio Grande cottonwood (*P. deltoides ssp. wislizenii*), while the Lakota use the roots of the lanceleaf cottonwood (*P. acuminata*) to create ceremonial snake figurines and fire drills (to start fires). The Havasupai make their drums from hollow logs of Fremont's cottonwood (*P. fremontii*).

### Natural Healing
Like the leaves of the other poplars, cottonwood leaves are anti-inflammatory and analgesic. They are made into a decoction to treat bruises, wounds and insect stings. The Choctaw tribe use the steam from a decoction of stems, bark and leaves of the Eastern cottonwood as a snakebite remedy.

RIGHT: *A mature cottonwood in the Chihuahua Desert, Mexico. Not long-lived trees, cottonwoods survive, on average, for about 70 years.*

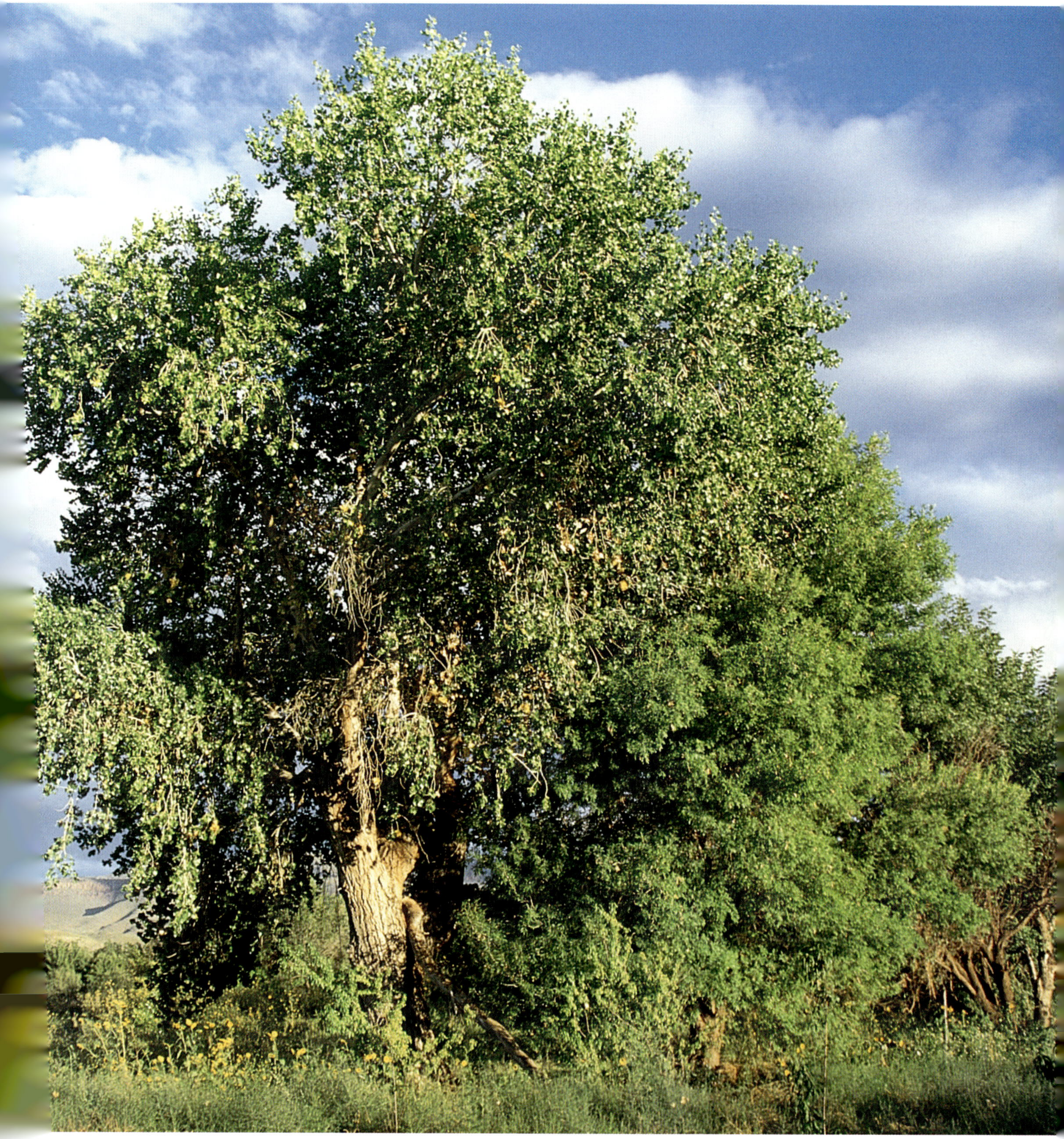

BELOW: *Like all poplars, cottonwoods have long leaf stalks which enable them to increase evaporation and maximize the amount of water and nutrients they assimilate.*

## Culture, Myth and Symbol

According to the great Sioux holy man and seer, Black Elk (1863–1950), the cottonwood was sacred to his tribe for a number of reasons. Long ago, the children played with its leaves and made playhouses with them, thus inventing the tipi. Grown people can learn from small ones because, as Black Elk put it, "The hearts of little children are pure, and, therefore the Great Spirit [the supreme being in Native North American tradition] may show them many things which are not revealed to older people. And in the lightest breeze the voice of *wagachun*, the 'rustling tree', can be heard. This we understand is its prayer to the Great Spirit, for not only humans, but all things and all beings pray." (Interestingly, when an upper limb of the cottonwood is cut crosswise, it reveals a five-pointed star, which represents the divine presence in many cultures, such as the Celtic Druids' pentangle, or the star symbol of the Sumerian goddess, Ishtar.)

One of the greatest rites of the Sioux Indians, the *wiwanyag wachipi* (Sun Dance) is held around a young cottonwood tree. Kablaya, the legendary hero who first taught his people the Sun Dance, said to the tree: "Of all the many standing peoples [trees], you O rustling cottonwood have been chosen in a sacred manner … for you will bring that which is good to all beings and all things."

The cottonwood tree for the Sun Dance is ceremonially chosen a year ahead of the ritual. During that time people visit the tree to say prayers of appreciation, and to make offerings of tobacco, prayer ties (small, cloth bundles filled with herbs, and tied to the tree while prayers are said), and the medicine people preparing for the ceremony even offer tiny pieces of their flesh. The dancers ready themselves by praying, fasting and participating in purification ceremonies.

A few days before the Sun Dance begins, the dancers cut down the tree, carry it to the ceremonial grounds and erect it in the middle of the arbor or ceremonial hoop – the round wooden construction in which the ritual takes place. The circular roof gives shade to the viewers while the dancers in the centre are exposed to the sun. Symbols of the elements (earth, air, fire and water) are ritually placed in the hole beneath the tree and attached to its branches and trunk, and thus the cottonwood becomes the Tree of Life.

*ABOVE: A venerable old cottonwood like this one would not be selected for the Sun Dance. Only very young trees are used.*

When the preparations are completed and the sun rises on the first day of the actual Sun Dance, the dancers enter the arbor through the eastern gate. They dance from sunrise to sunset for four days without food or water. Before the ceremony begins some dancers might tie a rope to one of the tree's high branches. During the ceremony these same dancers can choose to have their chest skin pierced with an eagle's claw, and tie the end of the rope to their piercings. Everyone within the sacred circle can offer their body and soul for the well-being of all people and all creatures.

Sadly, the ceremonies and traditions of many of the Native North American tribes have been lost. The Sioux have generously opened the Sun Dance to their brothers and sisters from other tribes as a means to help them reconnect with their own ancestral traditions and ceremonies. Today, there are about 1,000 Sun Dancers on Turtle Island (as the indigenous people call their continent), and only native-blood participants are permitted. Non-natives rarely witness a truly traditional ceremony, although outsiders are sometimes invited to attend as honorary guests.

**Symbolism:** Honesty, humility, and self-sacrifice

**Divine Association:** Wakan Tanka, the Great Spirit or Supreme Being (Native North American)

**Astrological Association:** Sun

**Historical Spotlight:** The suppression of Native North American culture resulted in a total ban of the Sun Dance in 1883. It went underground until Frank Fools Crow, ceremonial chief of the Teton (Sioux), and other elders challenged the US government by refusing to send their young men to fight in the Vietnam War without a proper ceremony. Risking high penalties, they performed a public Sun Dance in 1974, and afterwards won back religious freedom for the Indian nations.

OPPOSITE: *The largest wild cherry tree at Studley Royal, Yorkshire, England. In England, cherry blossom was traditionally used to decorate churches at Easter.*

# Cherry *Prunus avium*

The large genus *Prunus* comprises more than 400 species of deciduous trees and shrubs (including the plum, the almond, the apricot and the peach) growing in the northern temperate regions. The alternating leaves are mostly serrate; the white or pink flowers are bisexual. The fruits are drupes with a fleshy outer layer that surrounds a hard stone or pit containing the seed.

The wild cherry (*P. avium*) is a medium-sized woodland tree native to Eurasia, and naturalized in North America. It has smooth gray bark that turns mahogany-red with age and peels in horizontal stripes. The white, cup-shaped flowers are borne in clusters and open with the leaves in late April to early May. The glossy reddish-purple fruits are small and bitter or sweet to the taste. The wild cherry is the ancestor of most of the sweet cherry cultivars.

## Practical Uses

Cherry trees have long been grown not only for their edible fruits and as ornamentals, but because the fine-grained wood is highly sought after for furniture, musical instruments (particularly woodwind), carving and turning.

## Natural Healing

Wild-cherry bark makes a pleasantly flavoured cough remedy, often prepared as a syrup and particularly helpful for dry coughs. In Traditional Chinese Medicine, cherries are considered warm and sweet, affecting the heart, spleen and stomach meridians. They improve circulation and counteract "cold" disorders, such as arthritis and rheumatism.

## Culture, Myth and Symbol

Cherry blossom, *sakura*, is the unofficial national flower of Japan. Most of all, its delicacy symbolizes purity and beauty, and its annual blossoming in April heralds the return of spring and generally indicates a bright future. Hence the Japanese school year, as well as the fiscal year, start at this time. Cherry blossom features strongly in ceremonial events, such as weddings. For example, *sakura-yu,* a tea-like drink made with salt-preserved cherry blossom and hot water, is served at weddings and other celebrations.

In April, weather forecasts monitor the 40-day period of *sakura zensen*, the "cherry blossom front". And when the flowers open, millions of Japanese people flock to the parks and riversides to admire them. For example, in Tokyo's Ueno Park there are 1,100 cherry trees and in the city of Kyoto, about 1,000 cherry trees line the Tetsugaku-no-michi, the Path of Philosophy. The custom of *isakura-gari*, "cherry blossom viewing", is believed to have begun early in the Heian Period (794–1185). Ever since, Japanese gardeners have carefully cultivated and cross-fertilized varieties of

ABOVE: *Cherry blossom is popular at weddings, especially in Japan.*

*P. serrulata* and *P. speciosa*. And today, there are some 300 kinds of *sato sakura*, "blossoming cherry trees". The word *sakura* is a combination of *sa*, which refers to the deity of the rice plant, and *kura*, "divine seat". It is also closely related to *sakuya*, the general word for blooming.

The cherry is sacred to the mythical princess Konohana Sakuya Hime, the younger daughter of the mountain god Oyama Tsumi. She married Ninigi, the grandson of the sun goddess, and her three children became the progenitors of humankind. Between the 14th and 16th centuries she became the principal goddess of Mount Fuji, where she is still worshipped in Shinto shrines at the base of the volcano.

Throughout the ages, cherry blossom has been a great source of inspiration for Japanese artists, writers and poets particularly on the themes of beauty, purity and decay. The cherry blossom embodies traditional Japanese values such as simplicity and virtue, and when the petals fall unwithered, they demonstrate perfection, even in death.

**Symbolism**: Beauty and purity

**Divine Association**: Konohana Sakuya Hime (Japanese)

**Astrological Association**: Venus

# Blackthorn  *Prunus spinosa*

The blackthorn or sloe (*P. spinosa*) belongs to the large genus of *Prunus*, and is a native to Eurasia and north Africa. In western Europe, especially the British Isles, it is a familiar sight in hedges. It is a deciduous, dense and rigid shrub which produces suckers and forms dense, impenetrable thickets. The small white flowers appear in April, before the leaves. The blue to blueish-black fruits are globose, about ½in (1.3cm) in diameter, and astringent to the taste.

BELOW: *Impenetrable blackthorn thickets are safe havens for birds.*

## Practical Uses

Blackthorn thickets and hedges make excellent wind-breaks and provide a safe shelter for birds. The fruits (sloes) have traditionally been used in western Europe for flavouring liquor, such as sloe gin or port. The old custom of leaving the sloes on the bush until the first frost softens the skins a little has become obsolete in a time of changing weather patterns and global warming. Instead, the sloes are picked when they ripen in late September or October.

## Natural Healing

In pre-industrial Europe, the fruits, rich in vitamin C and tannin, were a traditional remedy for inflammations of the mouth and throat, while the leaves and flowers, which have diuretic properties, were used to clear excess fluids and toxins from the body. The tree essence stabilizes emotions and stimulates hope and joy.

## Culture, Myth and Symbol

The blackthorn's scented white blossoms, and their contrast with its dark, spiny branches, symbolize the general theme of light and darkness with which this plant has been associated since ancient times. The dangerous, long spikes and the red "blood" that flows in the veins of the blackthorn tree enhance the dramatic effect even further. The blossoms, the fruits and the crimson sap display the three colours of the Great Goddess: white, black and red. And as its name suggests, this tree has been associated with the dark aspects of life, such as night, death and the underworld.

Ancient shamanic societies cultivated world views that assigned value to both sides of the dualistic opposites, such

*ABOVE: The white flowers contain nectar and have a subtle, musky scent to attract the insects on which the tree depends for pollination.*

as life and death, light and darkness, mind and body and so on, and the blackthorn was a guardian of the balance between them. But with the advance of dualistic religions such as Zoroastrianism and Manichaeism, which separate the world into "good" and "evil", came the demonization of the blackthorn tree. Where once it had provided magical protection *against* negative influences, it now became the emblem of evil forces.

The blackthorn became associated with witches who were said to use it in all kinds of black magic, and with Satan himself who reportedly used blackthorn spines to prick his followers with his "mark of the devil". The pyres used by the Spanish Inquisition to burn heretics at the stake often contained blackthorn wood. However, some rural customs that employ the blackthorn as a protection against evil still survive today, particularly in eastern Europe.

In medieval Europe, the blackthorn was believed to be the tree from which Christ's crown of thorns was made, despite the distinct probability that it did not grow in Jerusalem. Scholars today agree that Christ's crown of thorns was most probably made from either the spiny shrub, aptly named Christ thorn (*Ziziphus spina-christi*), or the thorny burnet (*Sarcopoterium spinosum*), a dwarf-shrub that is common around Jerusalem.

**Symbolism**: The balance between light and darkness

**Divine Association**: The Great Goddess

**Astrological Association**: Saturn

**Historical Spotlight**: As late as 1683, a blackthorn tree near Pritzwalk (in Brandenburg, Germany) continuously attracted crowds of people who believed it had healing powers. On November 17th that year, Duke Friedrich Wilhelm ordered its felling, "for we are not fond at all of such superstitious dealings".

# Pomegranate *Punica granatum*

Two species native to southeastern Europe and southern Asia form the small genus *Punica*. The one species in general cultivation is the pomegranate (*P. granatum*), a large shrub or bushy tree that can reach a height of about 20ft (6m). The branches are sometimes spiny. The oblong to lanceolate leaves are up to 3in (7.5cm) long, entire, hairless and glossy. The spectacular funnel-shaped flowers are up to 1½in (3.75cm) across, and appear solitary or clustered at the ends of the branchlets in the late summer or early autumn. The fruit is up to 5in (12.5cm) in diameter and of a brownish-yellow to reddish colour. The thick skin protects a multitude of seeds, each one enclosed in a juicy, edible pulp.

## Practical Uses

The pomegranate has been cultivated since ancient times for its edible fruit, and as an ornamental. Its bark and rind also yield ingredients for ink, and for tanning.

## Natural Healing

The fruit juice has been used to soothe indigestion, while the rind has been used in India for diarrhea and dysentery. Pomegranate bark has a long tradition of being used to combat worms (in combination with a laxative). However, there are parts of the plant other than the fruit that contain highly toxic alkaloids, and hence should not be used in healing without professional supervision.

## Culture, Myth and Symbol

When Dionysus, the son of Zeus and Semele, was born, jealous Hera plotted for the Titans to abduct the baby, cut him into pieces and boil him in a cauldron. From the blood of the baby Dionysus grew the first pomegranate tree. Later, Dionysus' grandmother, Rhea, re-assembled his body and revived it (just as the Egyptian goddess Isis did with Osiris). Thus Dionysus is called "twice born", and the parallels to shamanism (the cutting and boiling is how Siberian shamans often describe the "inner" journey of their initiation) suggest an ancient initiation rite has been encoded in this myth. Indeed, the cult of Dionysus' is much older than the cultivation of the vine, which is the plant that he was primarily associated with in ancient Greece.

Being a symbol of fertility, the pomegranate was also sacred to the love goddess Aphrodite, and in the Near East to the goddess Astarte. Other female deities who also guarded the fruit of life, such as Athena, and Hera in her temple at Argos, were portrayed holding a pomegranate in the hand.

A Greek myth tells that Rhoeo, the nymph of the pomegranate and the daughter of Chrysothemis, came to Greece as a seed in a chest. Apollo made her son a prophetic priest and king of Delos, which suggests that there may have been a pomegranate sanctuary on this island (as such localized myths often indicate a regional cult practice).

The pomegranate is also connected to Persephone, who personifies the revival of nature in spring, but is also the goddess of the underworld. She could have left the underworld

---

**Symbolism**: The fruit of life

**Divine Associations**: Dionysus, Aphrodite, Hera, Persephone (all Greek); Astarte (Syrian, Phoenician)

**Astrological Associations**: Venus, Mars and Pluto

**ABOVE**: *Pomegranates thrive in temperate to subtropical climates with cool winters and hot summers. High temperatures during the five to seven months when the fruit ripens give it the best flavour.*

**RIGHT**: *The fruit of the pomegranate contains little sacs, each filled with juicy, sweetly acidic pulp surrounding an angular seed.*

for good, but Hades tricked her by asking her to eat seven pomegranate seeds before departing, which condemned her to stay. Zeus effected a compromise that meant she returned to Hades for four months – the winter season – every year.

For the tribes of Israel, the flowering of the pomegranate symbolized the arrival of spring. Hence pomegranates, along with grapes, were chosen by the scouts Moses sent to explore Canaan to show the bounty of the "Promised Land".

In the Temple of Solomon (c.1100BCE), the fruit of the pomegranate (in Hebrew, *rimmon*) gave its shape to the ornamental golden bells and the carved capitals of its columns. The pomegranate was also embroidered onto priestly garments (Exodus 28:33–4).

OPPOSITE: *In April, the showy white flowers of the pear tree appear, blossoming earlier than those of its fellow fruit tree, the apple.*

# Pear *Pyrus*

About 20 species of small to medium-sized, deep-rooted, deciduous or semi-evergreen trees of Eurasia and northern Africa constitute the genus *Pyrus*. The white to pink-white, bisexual flowers appear in April, before or with the leaves. As members of the rose family (*Rosaceae*), the flowers have five petals. The fruit is a pome, the flesh of which contains stone or grit cells. The common pear (*P. communis*) is a long-lived tree. Its elliptic to oblong-ovate, leathery, short-pointed leaves are 1–2½in (2.5–6.3cm) long.

## Practical Uses

Many cultivars are grown in orchards for fruit, or as ornamentals. In the first century CE the Romans knew 39 pear varieties. Today there are over 3,000, but the most familiar are probably those preferred by the fruit trade, such as William, Conference, Bartlett and Packham's Triumph.

Pear wood is used for cutlery and in wood-turning, and to make musical instruments such as flutes and harpsichords.

## Natural Healing

In Western medicine, a decoction from pear bark has long been used as a mild analgesic for bruises and sprains, while the easily digestible, nutritious fruit is helpful in convalescence. Pears are rich in fibre, vitamins (particularly A, B, and C), minerals and trace elements (such as potassium, iron, magnesium, calcium). Their cooling quality counteracts internal inflammations.

In Traditional Chinese Medicine, pears are cool, sour and sweet, and they stimulate the liver and stomach meridians. Beneficial in treating chesty coughs, digestive and urinary problems, pears tone yin and regulate the heart. In Ayurveda, they are cooling, sweet and astringent, increase *vata* and reduce *pitta* and *kapha*.

## Culture, Myth and Symbol

In ancient Greece, the pear was sacred to Hera, Zeus' wife, queen of the Olympian gods, and the goddess of marriage and childbirth. Timber from the pear tree was the first choice for making wooden idols of her, and one of her names was Hera Apia, from *apios*, "pear tree".

The ancient custom of planting a tree after the birth of a child is known in many parts of the world. In the Swiss canton of Aargau, people used to plant an apple tree for a boy, and a pear tree for a girl. In post-medieval Swabia (Germany), the afterbirth was buried underneath the tree as well, as a blessing for the child.

In the early 20th century, the pear tree was still believed to be the protector of cattle in Circassia (northwestern Caucasus). Once a year a young tree was chosen, cut, stripped of its branches and festively brought to the homestead where it was adorned and celebrated like a god.

Like the apple, the pear has always had a strong connection with children, fertility and prosperity. But while the apple often appears in male-female customs concerning courtship and marriage, the pear tends to be associated solely with the female gender.

**Symbolism:** Good health and fortune

**Divine Association:** Hera (Greek)

**Astrological Association:** Venus

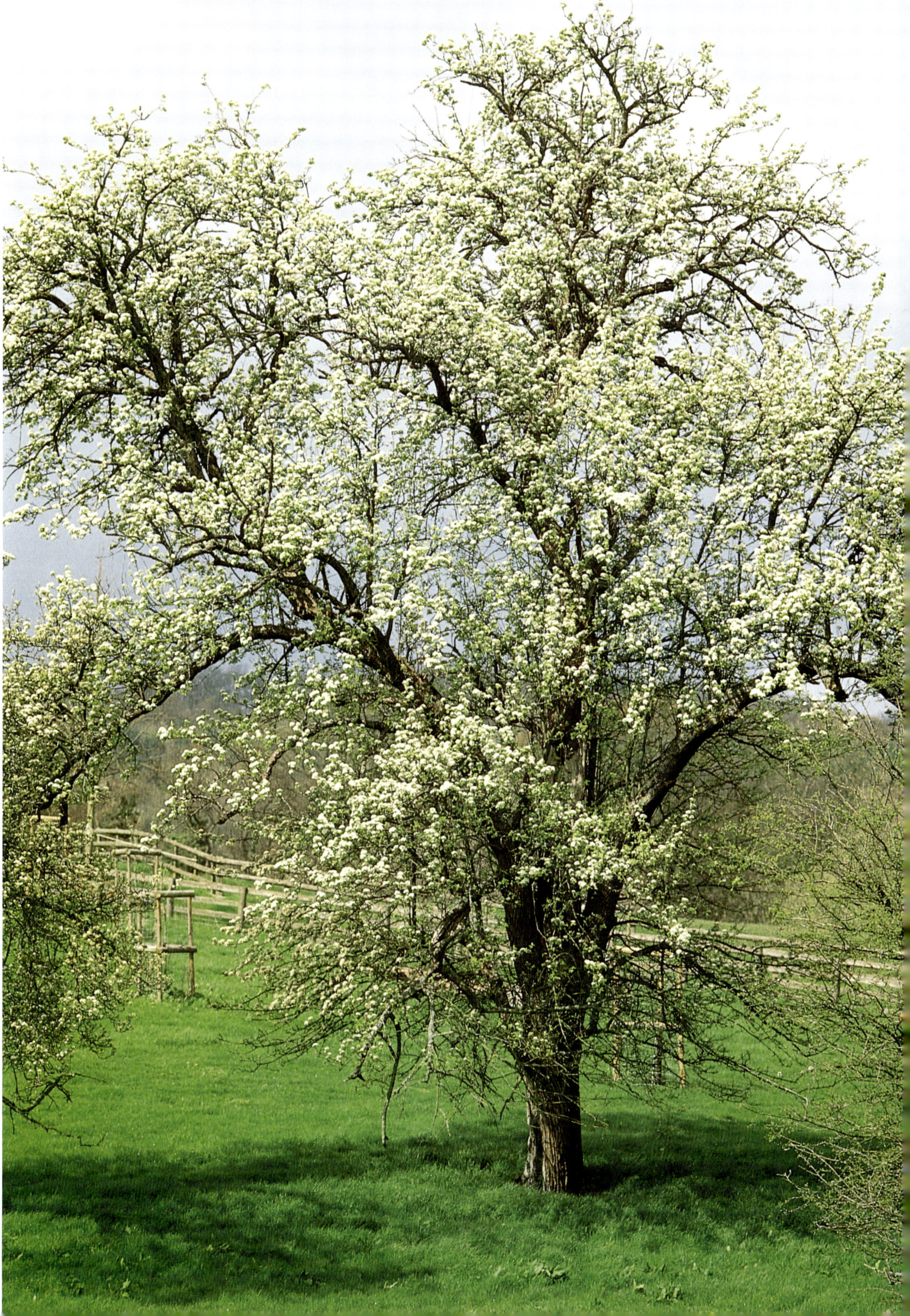

OPPOSITE: *Torn and shaped by weather and time, the ancient hulk of the Stinton Oak in Dorset, England, speaks of centuries gone by.*

# Oak *Quercus*

The oak (*Quercus*) is a large genus of more than 450 species of monoecious, deciduous or evergreen trees, native mainly to the northern temperate zone.

The common oak (*Q. robur*) is a large, long-lived, deciduous tree native to Europe and the Caucasus, Asia Minor and northern Africa. As a lone tree, it develops a broad head of rugged branches. The leaves are mostly sessile, shallow-lobed, and auricled at the base. The unspectacular flowers, male catkins and female spikes, are only about 1in (2.5cm) long and pale green. The fruit, the acorn, is a nut surrounded at the base by a cup-like involucre. One to several acorns are borne on a slender stalk. The common oak is a pioneer tree, and its seedlings invade open grassland rather than shady forests.

The sessile oak (*Q. petraea*) is very similar to the common oak, but can be distinguished by its rather large, long-stalked leaves, and its sessile fruits (hence the name). It is deciduous, and native to western, central and southeastern Europe, and Asia Minor.

The holm oak (*Q. ilex*) is a large and majestic evergreen tree that can grow up to 60ft (18m) in height. It has corrugated bark and ovate to lanceolate leaves which are leathery, entire or toothed, and shining dark green above and greyish-green beneath. The fruit cup encloses about half of the rather short acorn. Native to the Mediterranean, it has also been cultivated in the warmer parts of the British Isles, such as Cornwall, in the south-west.

## Practical Uses

The Old English word for a field, "acer", has Anglo-Saxon origins. The Saxons and others engaged significantly in

ABOVE: *An "oak apple" or gall is formed by the tree to protect itself when a gall wasp lays its eggs in the bark.*

"masting" – pasturing livestock, such as pigs, cattle and sheep, in the woods to feed on acorns and beech nuts. Masting has been important in rural economies throughout the oak's area of distribution since early history. And in the Middle Ages, estimates of the value of woodland were based on the number of pigs the mast could feed.

Wood-pasturing is still practised in the Iberian peninsula, where the savannah-like *dehesa* (Spain) and *montado* (Portugal) form the largest open forest in western Europe (about 12,355,000 acres/5 million ha). The trees (the cork oak and particularly the live oak, *Q. rotundifolia*), widely-spaced at 100–150 trees per acre (40–60 trees per ha), produce about 1,100lbs/500kg of acorns per hectare per year. Feeding on grass, mushrooms and acorns on an area of about 2½ acres (1 hectare), an Iberian black pig doubles its weight from about 154 to 308lbs (70 to 140kgs).

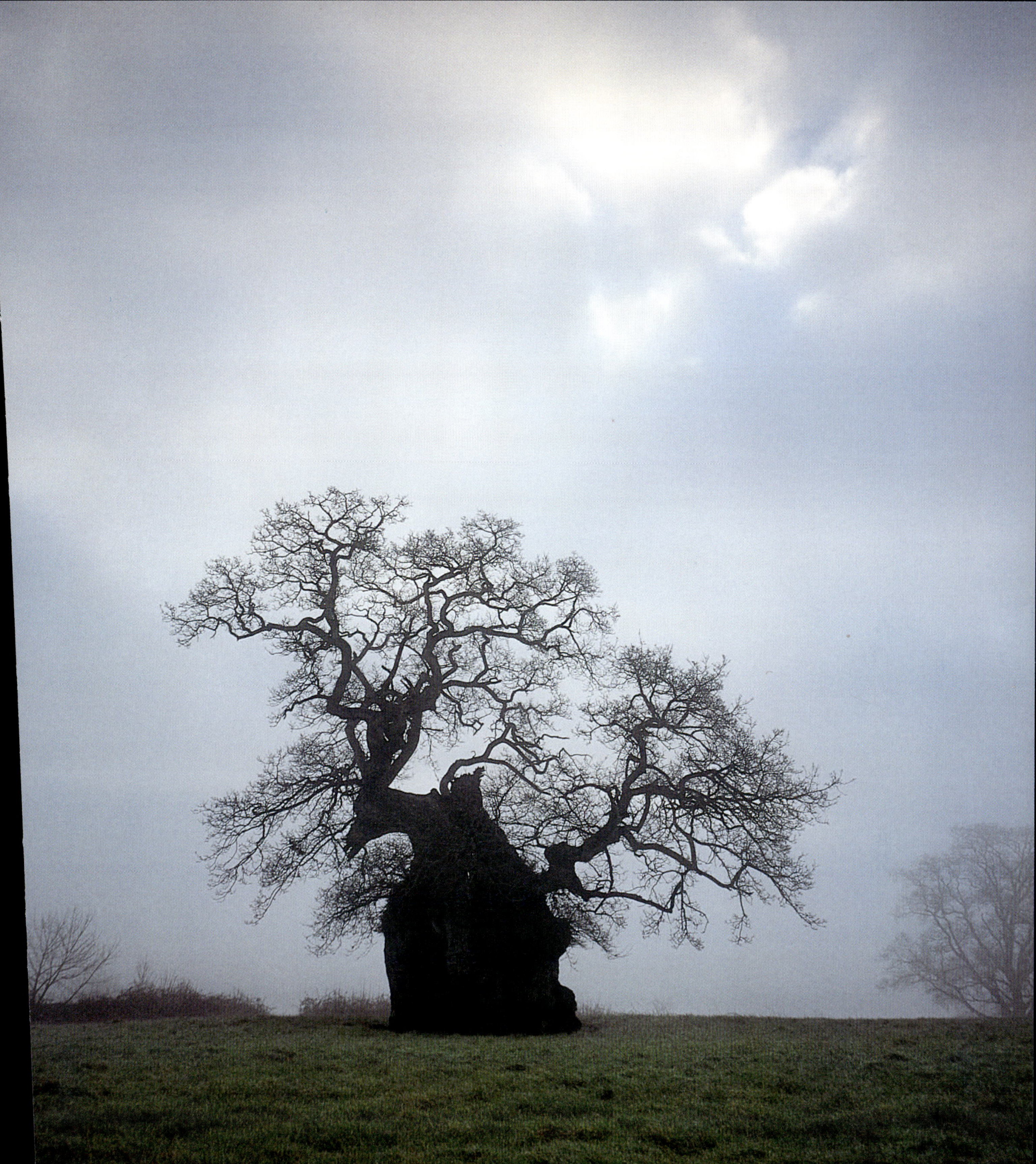

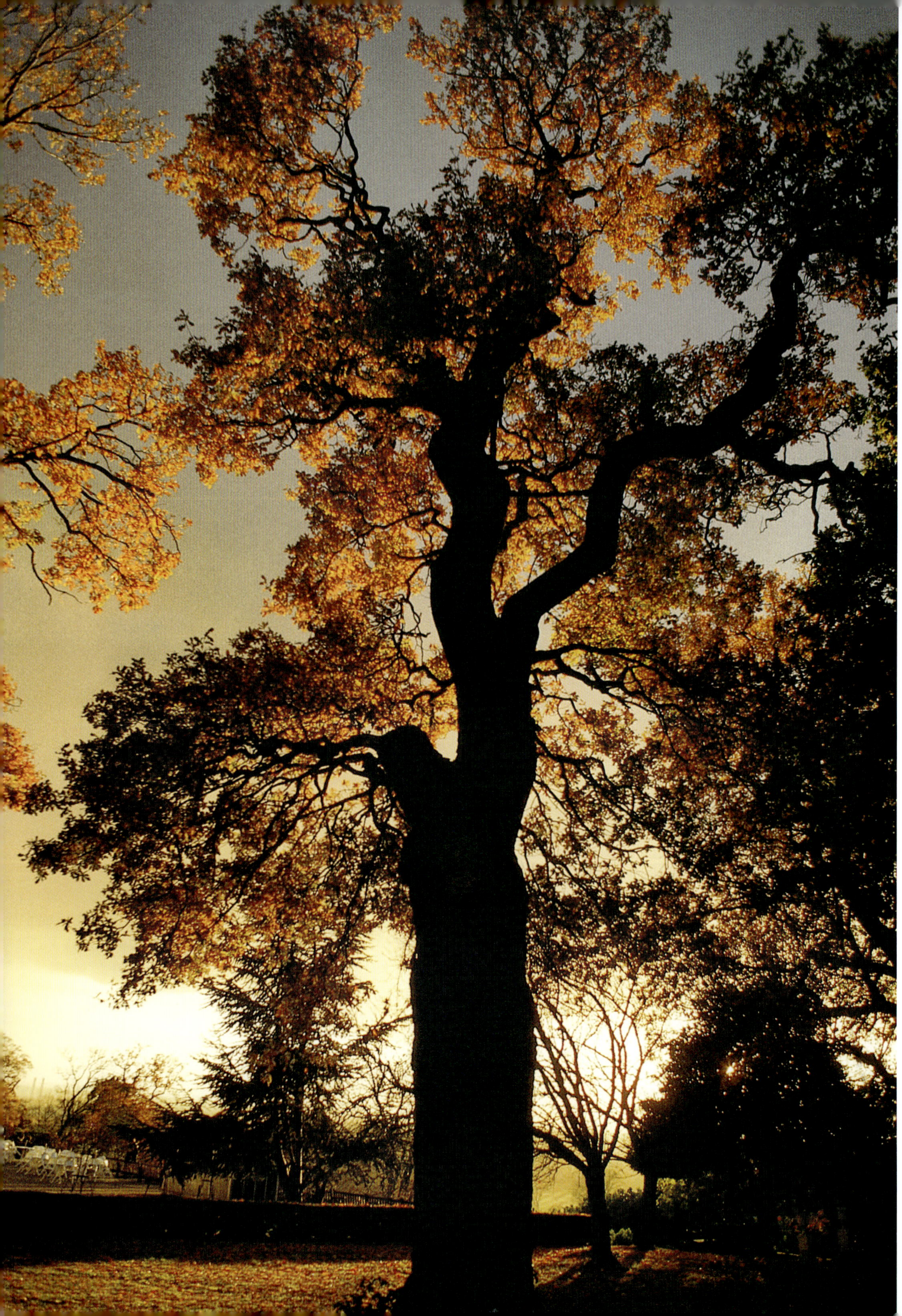

OPPOSITE: *An oak gloomily lit by a brewing storm – a fitting image for a tree once strongly linked to the weather gods.*

Cork is a fire-resistant outer bark that can be peeled off a living cork oak (*Q. suber*) tree every nine years (once the tree is 25 years old). It is used for wine bottle stoppers, and the lesser grades provide insulation and floor tiles. The lifespan of a cork oak is 150–200 years, and an average tree produces enough cork for about 4,000 bottle stoppers per harvest.

In pre-Classical Greece, acorns formed part of the staple diet of the human population. Many Native American tribes still roast and grind acorns for use in bread or to make a beverage. Acorns were also made into ersatz coffee in many European countries during the two world wars.

In the northern temperate zone, oaks are mainly planted today as ornamentals and for timber. The hard, tough and durable wood has always been widely appreciated. The bark of some species also yields dye and tannins, which are used in the leather industry.

## Natural Healing

Common oak (*Q. robur*) bark, which is strongly astringent because of its tannin content, has been traditionally taken in a tea to combat diarrhea and dysentery, and used externally to treat hemorrhoids, inflamed gums, wounds and eczema. A decoction of acorns and oak bark used to be considered an excellent antidote to poisoning. The tree essence boosts energy levels and the ability to manifest our goals.

## Culture, Myth and Symbol

Across the whole of Bronze-Age Europe, Indo-European cultures associated the oak tree with their weather gods, particularly those of thunder and lightning: because of its

ABOVE: *Leaf and acorn of the common oak (left) and the holm oak.*

strong electrical currents, its deep tap root and its tendency to grow above subterranean watercourses, the oak is indeed struck by lightning more often than other trees. The oak was sacred to sky gods such as the Slavic and Baltic Perun(as), the Norse Thor, the Saxon Donar, and the Celtic Taranis. The main significance of weather gods lies in their effects on the harvest, which was essential to human survival. Zeus (the Roman Jupiter) was a lightning god who became the principal deity in ancient Greece. His career started in the famous oracular grove of Dodona, and his tree was the oak.

Apart from its agricultural importance, the oak also had associations with war among all cultures from ancient times until fairly recently – for example, the oak's thunder god was invoked to use his power of lightning to strike an enemy, or its tough wood was used in the construction of fortifications or battleships. In the 17th and 18th centuries the oak rose to military fame once more, when the nations of western Europe felled their oak forests to build large fleets.

However, the oak itself is not a "warrior". It provides a habitat for over 500 species of insects and other invertebrates, not to mention many birds and mammals. Together

*ABOVE: This Bronze Age site on the coast of Norfolk, England, is the remains of an ancient offering made to the Earth Mother consisting of oak tree trunks sunk vertically into deep shafts in the ground.*

with the long list of economic benefits it bestows, the oak seems to have a rather caring, paternal quality. It is not surprising then, that the ancient Gauls and the Romans associated the oak with Mars Silvanus, the god of agriculture and healing. The oak was an important presence in the farmyard, where it had a nurturing role. It was with reluctance that the oak god resorted to arms, but Mars was nevertheless eventually transformed into a war deity and the cultural history of the oak reflects this transition from the plough to the sword.

In later centuries and further north, for example in Great Britain and Germany, Silvanus frequently manifested as the Green Man or Herne the Hunter. Two important legendary figures associated with the oak are King Arthur, who gathered his knights around the Round Table (which, it is said, was made of oak), and Robin Hood who lived among the oak trees of Sherwood Forest. Both King Arthur and Robin Hood embody a balance of the two sides of oak lore: the caring, paternal qualities and the ability to fight ruthlessly when justice demands it.

However, over the last few centuries the significance of the oak in ancient cult practices has been vastly overemphasized. In the Middle Ages, European translators of foreign manuscripts tended to call every significant tree an "oak" (just as every red fruit was to them an "apple"). Thus, the "oaks" mentioned in the Bible have to be read not as oaks, but as "sacred trees" (see Terebinth, pp.150–51).

# OAK

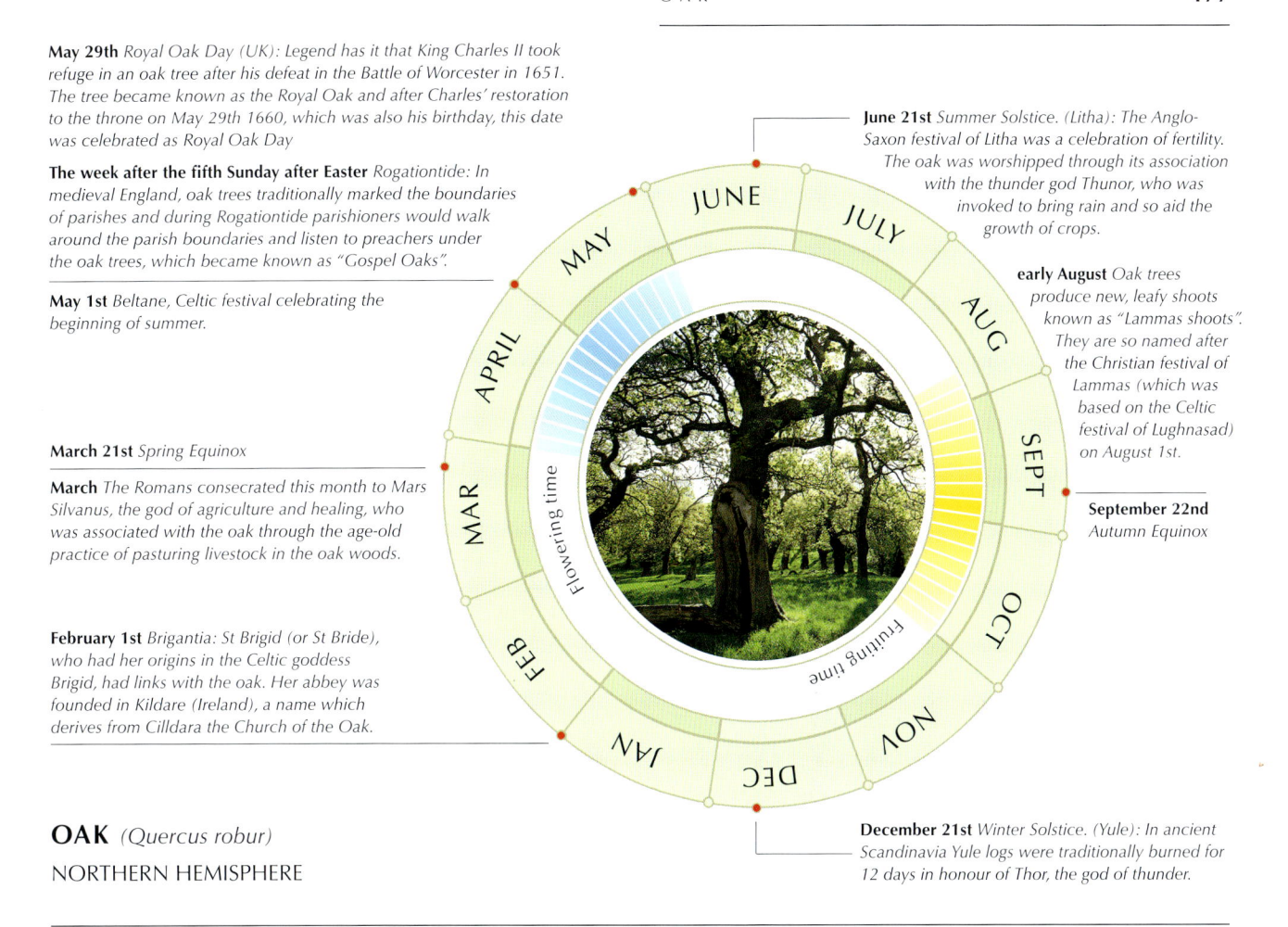

**May 29th** *Royal Oak Day (UK):* Legend has it that King Charles II took refuge in an oak tree after his defeat in the Battle of Worcester in 1651. The tree became known as the Royal Oak and after Charles' restoration to the throne on May 29th 1660, which was also his birthday, this date was celebrated as Royal Oak Day

**The week after the fifth Sunday after Easter** *Rogationtide:* In medieval England, oak trees traditionally marked the boundaries of parishes and during Rogationtide parishioners would walk around the parish boundaries and listen to preachers under the oak trees, which became known as "Gospel Oaks".

**May 1st** *Beltane,* Celtic festival celebrating the beginning of summer.

**March 21st** *Spring Equinox*

**March** The Romans consecrated this month to Mars Silvanus, the god of agriculture and healing, who was associated with the oak through the age-old practice of pasturing livestock in the oak woods.

**February 1st** *Brigantia:* St Brigid (or St Bride), who had her origins in the Celtic goddess Brigid, had links with the oak. Her abbey was founded in Kildare (Ireland), a name which derives from Cilldara the Church of the Oak.

**June 21st** *Summer Solstice. (Litha):* The Anglo-Saxon festival of Litha was a celebration of fertility. The oak was worshipped through its association with the thunder god Thunor, who was invoked to bring rain and so aid the growth of crops.

**early August** Oak trees produce new, leafy shoots known as "Lammas shoots". They are so named after the Christian festival of Lammas (which was based on the Celtic festival of Lughnasad) on August 1st.

**September 22nd** *Autumn Equinox*

**December 21st** *Winter Solstice. (Yule):* In ancient Scandinavia Yule logs were traditionally burned for 12 days in honour of Thor, the god of thunder.

**OAK** *(Quercus robur)*
NORTHERN HEMISPHERE

---

Although the sweet acorns of the live oak, (*Q. rotundifolia*), were a vital part of the diet in ancient Greece, the oak itself was sometimes elusive, which is because the "acorns of Zeus" also referred to other edible nuts, such as walnuts and sweet chestnuts. Roman writers often confused *drys*, the Greek word for oak, with *drus*, meaning "sacred tree" – the etymological closeness of these words hints at possible prehistoric associations between the oak and divinities.

The modern, unjustified cliché that expresses a strong connection between Celtic druids and the oak actually owes its existence to Pliny the Elder (23–79CE), a Roman military commander and administrator, who wrote books on natural history. It was he who conjured up the image of the druids of Gaul cutting mistletoe from oaks with golden sickles. Pliny was not even present in Gaul and had only heard a report of this practice. He even stated that it happened throughout Gaul, completely ignoring the fact that tribes such as the Averni ("Alder People") or Eburoni ("Yew People") held different trees sacred. Pliny also suggested that the very word "druid" may have derived from the Greek *drys* – which it did not (see Introduction, pp.8–13).

**Symbolism:** Sovereignty; rulership; power

**Divine Associations:** Thunder gods: Perun(as) (Slavic, Baltic), Taara (Estonian, Finnish), Thor (Norse), Donar (Saxon), Taranis (Celtic), Zeus (Greek), Jupiter (Roman). Agrarian deities: Mars Silvanus (Roman and Celtic), the Green Man (Anglo-Celtic)

**Astrological Association:** Mars

OPPOSITE: *A green willow bough swaying gently in the breeze completes an idyllic lake- or riverside setting.*

# Willow *Salix*

*S*alix is a huge and diverse genus of 300 or more species of fast-growing shrubs and trees, varying from tiny creeping alpines in high altitudes to large and noble lowland trees throughout the temperate zones but mainly in the northern hemisphere. Almost all willows are at home in water meadows, chalky or otherwise, and similar damp conditions. The leaves are mostly lanceolate in shape. Most willow species are dioecious. The small flowers are borne in dense catkins, which, depending on the species, open before or after the leaves. The fruits are small capsules bearing downy seeds. Most willows respond well to cutting and pruning, by regenerating vigorously.

The white willow (*S. alba*) is a familiar and elegant tree in water meadows and at riversides. It reaches up to 75ft (23m) in height. Its lanceolate leaves are up to 4in (10cm) long, finely toothed, and silky white underneath. The catkins appear with the leaves. The goat willow or great sallow (*S. caprea*) is noticeable in early spring when its large, yellow, male catkins appear. The female trees with their silver catkins are known as "pussy willow" (which are not to be confused with the American tree of the same name, *S. discolor* – a tree that doesn't grow as high as the goat willow, having leaves that are not lanceolate but broadly ovate to oblong, and about 4in/10cm long).

## Practical Uses

Willows are grown as ornamentals, for screens and shelter, and for stabilizing riverbanks. Traditionally, willows have also been pollarded to make leaf fodder – either fresh or stored for the winter. However, the long and extremely flexible branches of the willow mean that its practical uses are manyfold: wickerwork is used to make baskets, furniture, wattle-and-daub walls and fences. In modern "green" technology, willows are planted as "reed beds", which help to purify and recycle water naturally, while also providing habitat for wildlife.

## Natural Healing

Salicylic acid – the anti-inflammatory and pain-relieving ingredient in aspirin tablets – was first discovered in the salicin in willow bark. Although this bark does not share all the properties of aspirin (for example, it has no blood-thinning effect), tincture of willow bark is still used today for treating arthritis, musculo-skeletal pain and fevers. The tree essence of the white willow enhances the awareness of our deeper selves and has a spiritually cleansing effect.

## Culture, Myth and Symbol

Since ancient times, willows have been associated with the moon and the feminine. The sphere of the willow encompasses activities that are receptive and reflective. Prophecy and divination (particularly with the help of water, as in scrying, or looking into a well, brook or bowl of water when in a

*Prophecy and divination, healing, white magic, poetry and music were the domains of the moon priestesses in the willow groves.*

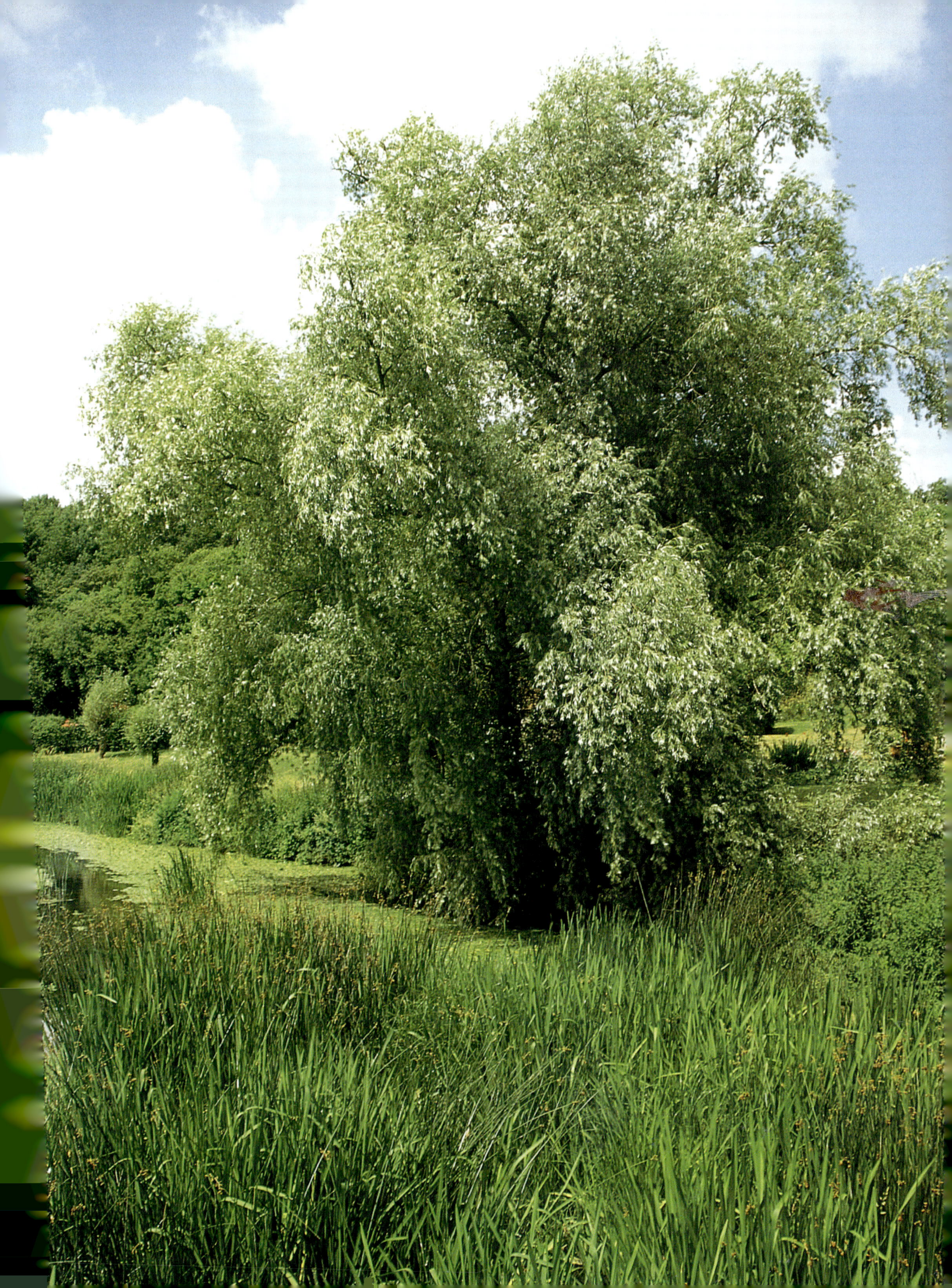

trance-like state), as well as healing, white magic, poetry-writing and music-making activities, were the domains of the moon priestesses in the willow groves.

Belili, the Sumerian goddess of love, the moon and the underworld, resided in willow trees, springs and wells. In ancient Greece, Persephone had a grove of aged willows, and the priestess Circe guarded a willow grove dedicated to Hecate, the goddess of death and transition. An image of the moon goddess Artemis was found in a willow thicket at Sparta, and Hera, the Queen of Heaven, was said to have been born under a willow tree at Samos, where appropriate rituals were held annually.

The willow was sacred to poets. The Nine Muses, priestesses of the moon goddess, resided on Mount Helicon, which was named after Helike (from the Greek for "willow tree"), the willow spirit. We can reasonably assume that similar associations existed in Celtic, Germanic and Slavic cultures, but because these traditions were transmitted orally we have no record of them if they died out before they were written down.

However, in Irish legend the willow appears in a significant role – as the provider of wood for harps. In the old bardic tradition of Celtic Europe, the harpist was an entertainer/historian and his instrument was a sacred object. Like the druids, the bards underwent rigorous training in many disciplines (although that of the druids was more complex and lasted longer), including natural law, philosophy, language, poetry, verse and grammar, composition and music. Their task was to relate the ancient myths and legends to the

LEFT: *The graceful catkins of the white willow.*

# WILLOW

**WILLOW** (Salix alba)
NORTHERN HEMISPHERE

- **June 21st** Summer Solstice
- **May 1st** The festival of Beltane was named after Belin the Celtic sun god who was derived from Bel, the Sumerian god of willows. Bel had supplanted Belili the ancient Sumerian goddess of the moon, and the underworld.
- **April 23rd** Festival of Green George. Celebrated by the Roma people of Rumania, in this festival a man representing "Green George" wears a willow wicker frame covered in vegetation. He appeases the water spirits (with which the willow is associated), so that he can fertilize the land and ensure the continuation of growth.
- **mid-March–mid-April** Palm Sunday and Easter. In Russia willow branches are consecrated on Palm Sunday in Orthodox churches instead of palm leaves.
  In Celtic Europe, according to Druid lore, the earth and the sun hatched from two scarlet snake eggs, which were concealed in a willow tree. The eggs were represented by red-painted chickens' eggs in the spring rituals and were eaten at Beltane. This practice gave rise to the modern tradition of Easter eggs.
- **September 22nd** Autumn Equinox
- **September–October** The Feast of Tabernacles: Ancient priests in Jerusalem called the willow tree "Jehovah's tree" because of its connection with water and rain. During the Feast of Tabernacles there was a "Day of the Willows" when participants carried willow branches.
- **December 21st** Winter Solstice

---

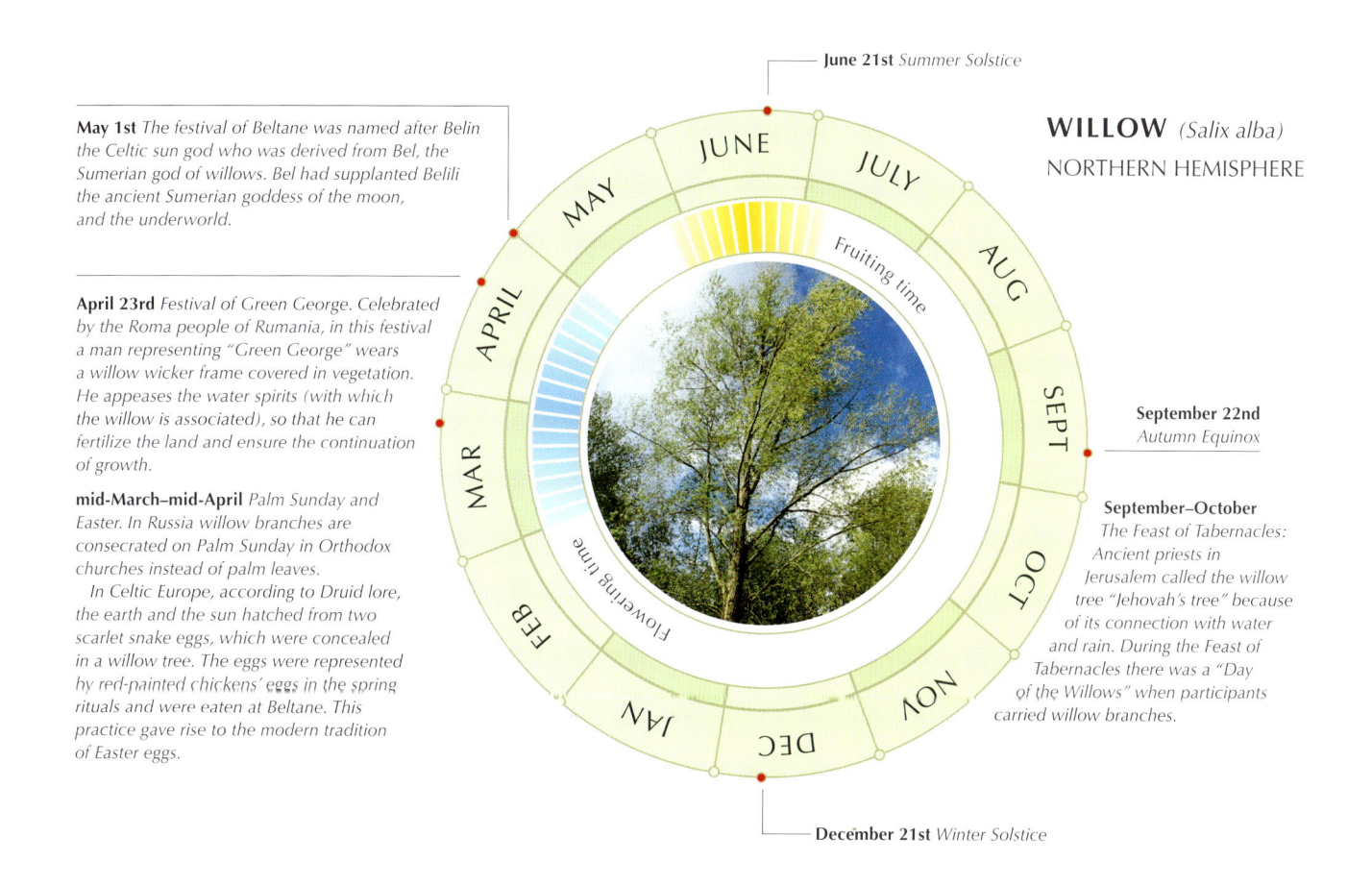

people, and, in so doing, keep alive an awareness of their ancestors and the invisible realms of the spirits, fairies and other supernatural beings. The harp was the instrument through which they engendered in the people a sense of beauty, belonging, gratitude and respect for all life.

Archeological finds confirm that willow wood was used to make harps. The most famous historical Celtic harp, the so-called "Brian Boru", is now exhibited at Trinity College, Dublin. Named after the high king of Ireland (died 1014), it probably dates from the 15th century and has a pillar and head-piece of oak, a sound-body of willow and is strung with brass. Once again, the willow is the resonating feminine vessel that receives the vibration of the string and gives birth to music. For the Chinese, too, the willow represents the feminine, yin, grace and the moon.

**Symbolism:** Resonance and harmony

**Divine Associations:** Belili (Sumerian); Persephone (Greek)

**Astrological Association:** Moon

**Superstition:** Psalm 137, "By the waters of Babylon we sat down and wept ... On the willow trees there we hung up our lyres", caused generations of European poets to interpret the willow as a symbol of mourning and despair.

**Historical Spotlight:** In Jewish tradition, the willow (S. alba and S. acmophylla), is one of four species of tree used in the Feast of Tabernacles to give thanks for the harvest. "... Take the fruit of citrus trees, palm-fronds, and leafy branches [myrtle], and willows from the riverside, and rejoice before the Lord your God for seven days." (Leviticus 23:40).

OPPOSITE: *An elder in blossom demonstrates how the plant became identified with the ancient White Goddess, guardian of the home.*

# Elder *Sambucus*

*Sambucus* is a genus comprising about 20 species of small trees and shrubs (and also some perennial herbs), widely distributed in the temperate and subtropical zones.

The common elder (*S. nigra*), native to Eurasia and northern Africa, is a large shrub or small tree with a rugged, fissured bark. The opposite leaves have five- to seven-toothed, elliptic leaflets, each up to 5in (12.7cm) long. The flattened heads of fragrant, white or cream-hued flowers are up to 8in (20cm) across, appear in June, and during the summer they develop into heavy bunches of small, glossy black fruits (berry-like drupes) borne on bright red stalks. Elder thrives on nitrogen-rich soils, such as waste dumps of organic matter, and thus has been an accompaniment to human settlements from early history.

## Practical Uses

In western Europe, elder is a common plant in hedgerows and gardens. For millennia, all parts of the elder have been used as medicine, and it has been dubbed "the medicine chest" by country people. The young twigs have a centre of spongy pith and, hollowed out, have been used to make pipes, pea-shooters and the like. However, although the heartwood of mature elder growth is surprisingly hard, it is not used commercially.

## Natural Healing

All parts of the elder can be used in medicine. Traditionally, the inner bark has been used as a purgative and an emetic, while the leaves have been applied to bruises, sprains and headaches. Today it is primarily the blossoms and berries which are used in medicine. The blossoms make a delicious tea that has an anti-inflammatory effect on the sinuses, and also helps hayfever. Combined with yarrow, the blossoms are an excellent treatment for colds because they tone the mucous membranes, promote perspiration and thus lower temperatures. The berries have potent anti-viral effects and stimulate the immune system, and are best taken as a hot decoction (optionally with honey and ginger).

The tree essence brings stability and forgiveness. It is good for times of change, and also for fretful children.

## Culture, Myth and Symbol

The elder is rather small in stature (in fact, none of the trees that have made the strongest impressions on the human soul – the birch, the rowan and the yew – are particularly tall), but the size of its body of traditions and folklore is probably second to none of all the European trees.

The traditional personifications of the elder spirit, the Scandinavian Hyldemoer ("Elder Mother") and the old German Frau Holle ("Mistress Elder"), are late expressions of the archaic White Goddess, a benevolent deity of light, life and wisdom. In some regions (for example, in Bavaria), the goddess of the elder was revered as Perchta or Bertha, a name deriving from the Indo-European *bher(e)g*, "shining white" (see also the Irish goddess, Brigid, p.42).

To the tree of her choice the goddess gave an abundance of healing power, which people have benefited from since ancient times. Imbued with her benevolent spirit, the elder has also been the traditional guardian tree of the household and farmyard. In countries as diverse as Russia, the Baltic States, Germany, Scandinavia and the British Isles, and throughout the ages, it was said that the good "house

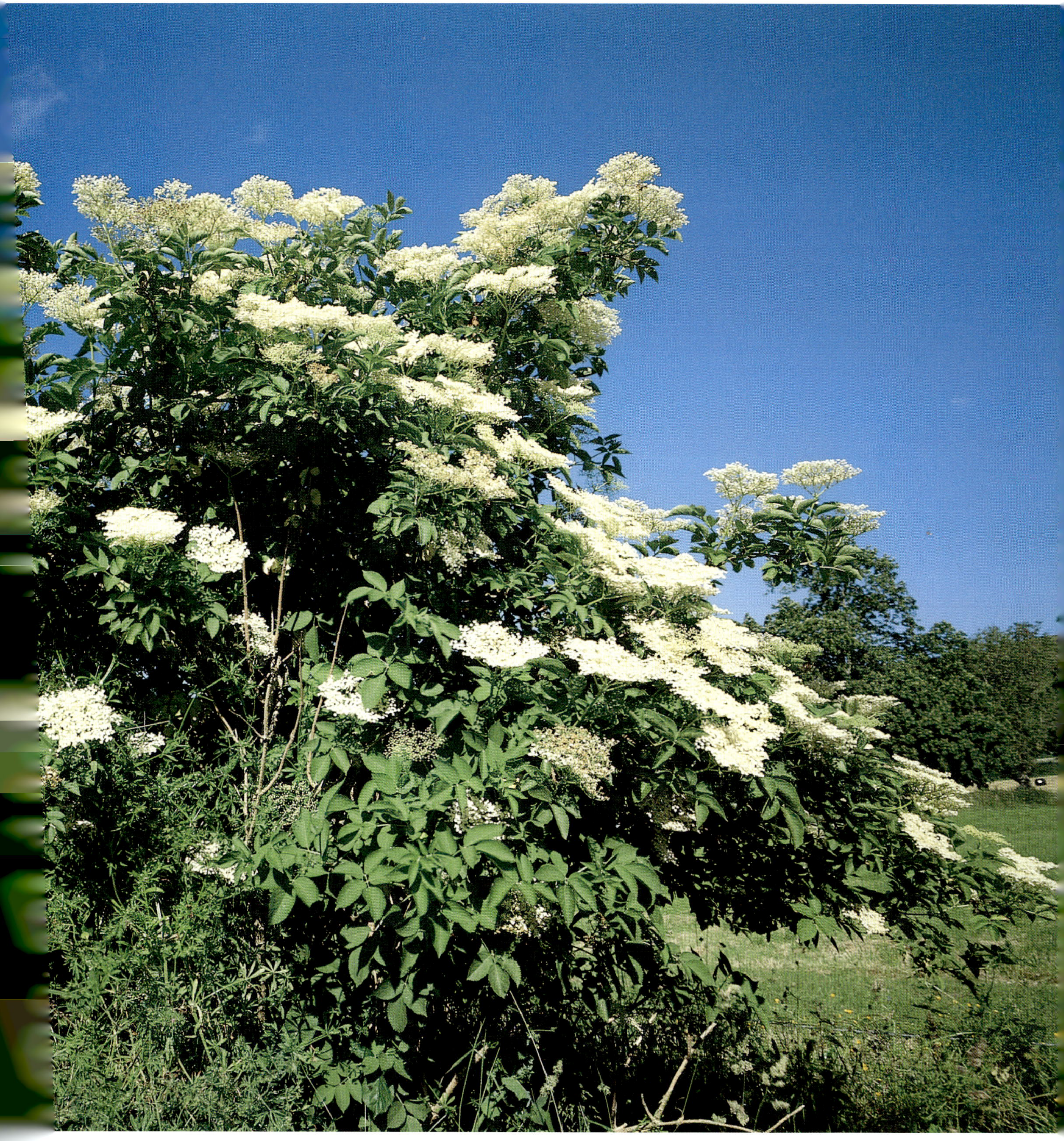

**BELOW**: *The blessings of the elder berries lie in their healing power: they have potent anti-viral effects and also stimulate our immune system.*

spirit" of the home resided in the elder bush, and as recently as the 19th century it was a widespread custom to bring her an offering of water, milk or beer, together with cake or bread, at least once a week and even daily.

Only those in dire need would ever take a piece of wood from an elder tree. "Lady Elder, give me some of thy wood; then I will give thee, also, some of mine when it grows in the forest," was a saying from northern Germany that referred to death and the decomposition of the human body in the earth. And even at the turn of the 20th century, "Hats off to the elder!" was still commonly said as a sign of respect in Switzerland and southern Germany.

A Russian tradition has preserved the powerful and archaic association of the elder with healing. Whenever a village was threatened by a dangerous epidemic, the local women would use a plough to draw a furrow around the settlement, to act as a barrier against malevolent forces. This course of action was accompanied by an ancient ceremonial song which invoked the mythical image of the cauldron of rebirth that contained "every life under the sky". The cauldron was surrounded by the old elders, the mythical ancestors of all elders on earth:

> "The old elders sing –
> They sing of life, they sing of death,
> They sing of the whole human race.
> The old elders bestow
> Long life on the whole world;
> But to the other – bad death,
> The old elders command
> A long and far journey.
> The old elders promise
> Eternal life
> To the whole of mankind."

The advance of Christianity led to changes in many such folk traditions. In some cases, trees that had been most venerated in pre-Christian times were recast in a negative light once the religion became established. Thus, in the popular imagination, the physical setting of the elder as its actual character gradually became associated with evil, witches and devils. For example, in some regions, Lady Elder was said to steal children or cut up people, and in Bavaria, the image of the goddess Perchtha (see p.182) mutated into one with long, iron fangs.

However, while superstitions flourished, countless remnants of the old and innocent veneration of the elder survived, leading to the seemingly contradictory mixture of affirmative and condemnatory customs that has fascinated anthropologists ever since.

**Symbolism**: Healing and abundance

**Divine Association**: The White Goddess

**Astrological Association**: Moon

**Superstitions**: In medieval Europe, there was a superstitious belief that the elder had acquired the unpleasant scent that characterizes its leaves because it had been the tree on which Judas Iscariot had hanged himself. However, in Baden, southern Germany, it was said that the odour was the legacy of Mary having dried the infant Jesus' soiled garments in its branches.

*OPPOSITE: The rust-coloured bark of these colossal giant redwood trunks in Sequoia National Park, California, is highly fire-resistant.*

# Redwood *Sequoia* and *Sequoiadendron*

A monotypic genus, *Sequoia* is named after Sequoyah (1770–1843), the son of a Tsalagi (Cherokee) chief's daughter and a white fur trader, who lived in Georgia in the eastern United States and invented the Cherokee alphabet. Redwoods are all that remains of a worldwide forest of the Cretaceous period (c.144–c.66 million years ago).

The Californian redwood or coastal redwood (*Sequoia sempervirens*) is a gigantic, coniferous, monoecious, evergreen that can exceed 330ft (100m) in height. Several coastal redwoods have reached an age of 2,000 years, and the oldest known specimen, felled in 1934, was dated at 2,200 years.

The immense trunks of coastal redwoods are protected by a thick, fibrous and fire-resistant outer bark, which is reddish-brown, soft and spongy. The branches are slightly drooping, yew-like, and bear two kinds of leaves: the terminal and fertile shoots have scale-like leaves up to ½in (1.3cm) long, the other branches bear linear, needle-like leaves up to 1in (2.5cm) long, and mostly spreading in two ranks. The female cones are ovoid or globose, and have 15 to 20 woody scales which bear three to seven ovules each. The tiny seeds mature in one year. The coastal redwood is native to the coastal region of the United States from southern Oregon to central California.

The giant redwood or giant sequoia (*Sequoiadendron giganteum*) was formerly considered to be of the same genus, but is now considered a monotypic genus of its own. Although they resemble each other closely, the giant redwood has only ovate to lancoelate leaves, appressed or slightly spreading, and ¼ to ½in (0.6–1.2cm) long. Its ellipsoid female cones are larger (2–3in / 5–7.5cm long), have 30 to 40 hard and woody scales, and the seeds take two years to mature. The giant redwood is native to the western slopes of the Sierra Nevadas in California.

As a young tree the giant redwood develops a conical shape, while older trees have more widely spaced branches and are down-swept. Despite its name, it never grows quite as tall as the coastal redwood, but has a greater girth. The famous "General Sherman" tree, with a height of 311ft (95m), has a diameter at the base of 25ft (17.6m). With a total estimated weight of more than 1,200 tonnes, it is a strong contender for the title of as the world's largest living thing, and at about 2,700 years old, one of its oldest too. However, the greatest reported age of a giant sequoia, is c.4,000 years.

*LEFT: Dusk mist issues from the giant redwoods at Kings Canyon National Park, California, the largest remaining grove of these trees.*

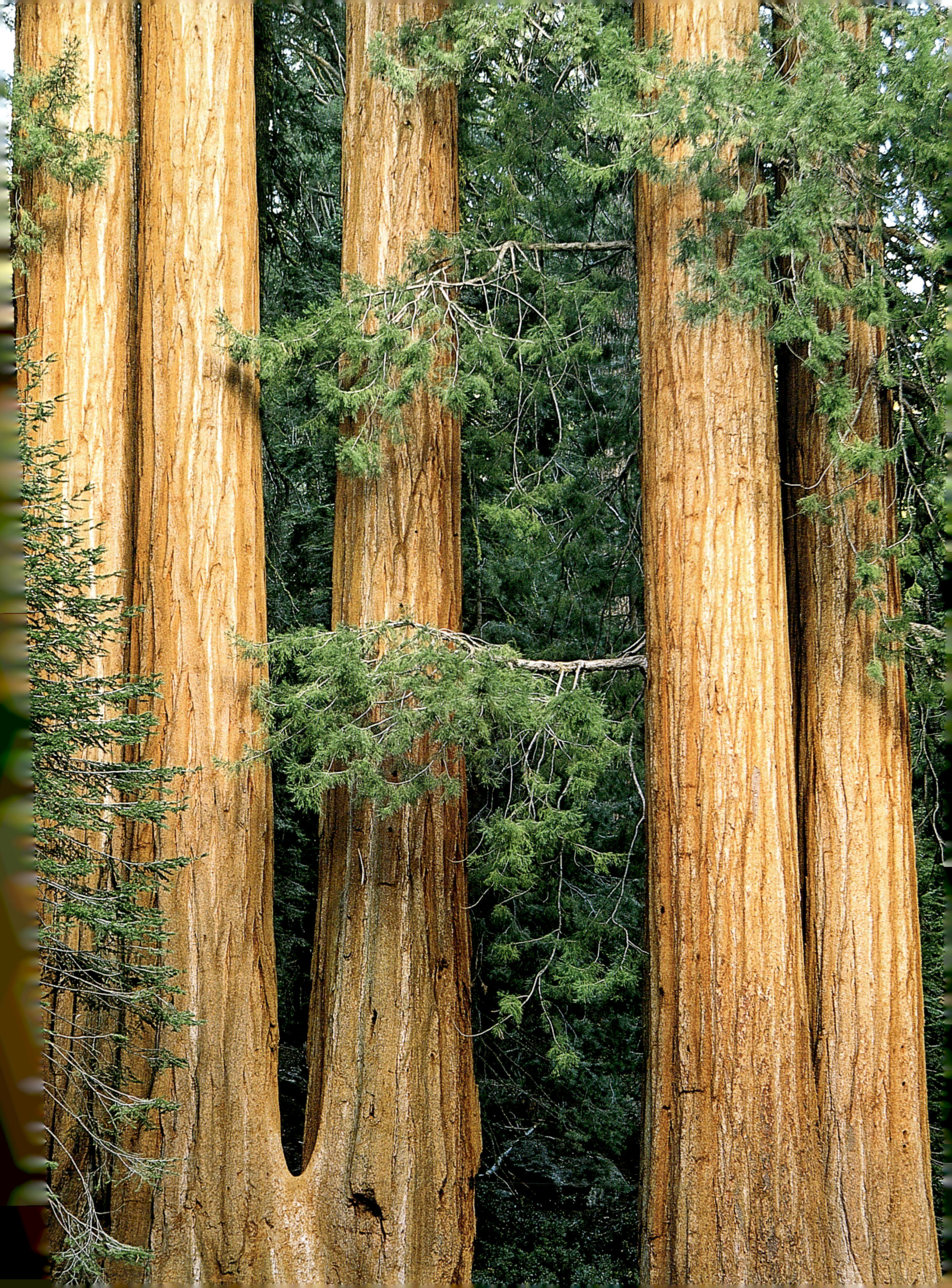

ABOVE: *An ancient coastal redwood tree in the Redwood National Park that lies on the border of Oregon and northern California on the Pacific coastline of the western United States.*

*… no botanist has discovered what triggers redwood seeds to burst open and scatter. But ask a native woman and she might tell you that when she sings to the trees, dozens of cones respond without fail.*

## Practical Uses

The indigenous peoples used only naturally fallen timber, never harming living trees. The Mendocino, Yurok and Tolowa tribes made redwood canoes by hollowing out trunks with fire and working with simple tools of horn and stone. When Europeans came with saws, axes and dynamite, it took three of them at least a week to bring down a giant redwood. In this way, the boomtowns of the mid-19th century Gold Rush were built. Today, as chainsaws and heavy machinery are used in clearfelling, environmentalists fight to preserve the remaining four percent of redwood forest.

## Natural Healing

Native North Americans have a long tradition of using the redwood for healing. For example, the Pomo and the Kashaya

*ABOVE: The giant redwood known as "General Sherman" stands in the Sequioa National Park, California. With an estimated weight of 2.7 million lb (1,200 tonnes) it is one of the largest living things on earth.*

tribes use poultices of warmed, new redwood foliage for earaches and take the gummy sap with water as a stimulant and a tonic. The Houma drink inner bark infusions to treat jaundice and to purify the blood.

## Culture, Myth and Symbol

Sadly, the original lore of the redwoods has disappeared with the culture of the indigenous peoples of California. Turning to the trees themselves, perhaps even more striking than the size and age of the giant redwoods is their unusual process of reproduction. After two years of maturing, the seeds cling to the branches for up to 20 years, and no botanist has discovered what triggers them to burst open and scatter. But ask a native woman and she might tell you that when she sings to the trees, dozens of cones respond without fail.

These giants have a special relationship with lightning, which they need to be struck by in order to stop growing. When struck, a substantial part of the upper crown falls to the ground and burns to cinders, leaving the tree unharmed.

Laurinda Reynolds, a Tsalagi storyteller in the convention of her ancestors, lets the giant sequoias speak for themselves in a traditional teaching story, *Peaceful Giants*:

"It's all a part of growing in balance. We grow in balance above and below, and we balance the outside with the inside. We grow in balance with time, too. Today, we use what we prepared yesterday, last season, even during the past year. Today we prepare for tomorrow, for the next season, and even the years to come. We balance the past and the future by what we are doing in the present moment."

**Symbolism**: Balance

**Divine Associations:** Heaven and Earth

**Astrological Association:** Jupiter

**Historical Spotlight:** The discovery that the coastal redwood was a new botanical species was made in 1794 by the Scottish botanist Archibald Menzies (1754–1842). Redwoods were first introduced to Europe in St Petersburg, Russia, in 1840, and three years later they were brought to England.

# Rowan *Sorbus*

*Sorbus* is a genus of about 85 species of deciduous trees and shrubs widely distributed in the northern hemisphere. Being members of the rose family (*Rosaceae*), the species of *Sorbus* produce flowers with five petals.

The rowan, European mountain ash or quickbeam (*S. aucuparia*) is native to Europe and Asia Minor and grows up to 50ft (15m) high. Its gray-brown twigs are downy when young, but later turn hairless. The pinnate leaves, up to 10in (25cm) long, have 11 to 19 (but usually 13 to 15) sharply toothed, oblong leaflets. The tree produces flattened heads of small white flowers in May, and dense bunches of bright scarlet fruits during the autumn – a feast for the many birds which are the major dispersal agents for the seeds. The rowan is a tolerant and versatile tree that grows in a multitude of soils and conditions at up to 3,200ft (about 975m) above sea level. Only the juniper and some small willows can grow at a higher level.

The service tree (*S. domestica*) is native to southern and eastern Europe. It has a rough, scaly bark, and sticky winter buds. Its pinnate leaves, composed of 13 to 21 leaflets, turn yellow to orange-red in autumn. The fruits are about 1in (2.5cm) long, pear- or apple-shaped, and green but tinged red on the side that faces the sun.

The American mountain ash (*S. americana*), native to eastern North America, is smaller than the European species, has 11 to 17 narrow-lanceolate leaflets which are sharply serrate, gray-green beneath, and hairy when young.

**RIGHT**: The "Rannoch rowan" grows on a rock in the highlands of Scotland where, historically, it was taboo to use any part of the tree for other than ritual purposes (except the berries, to make a drink).

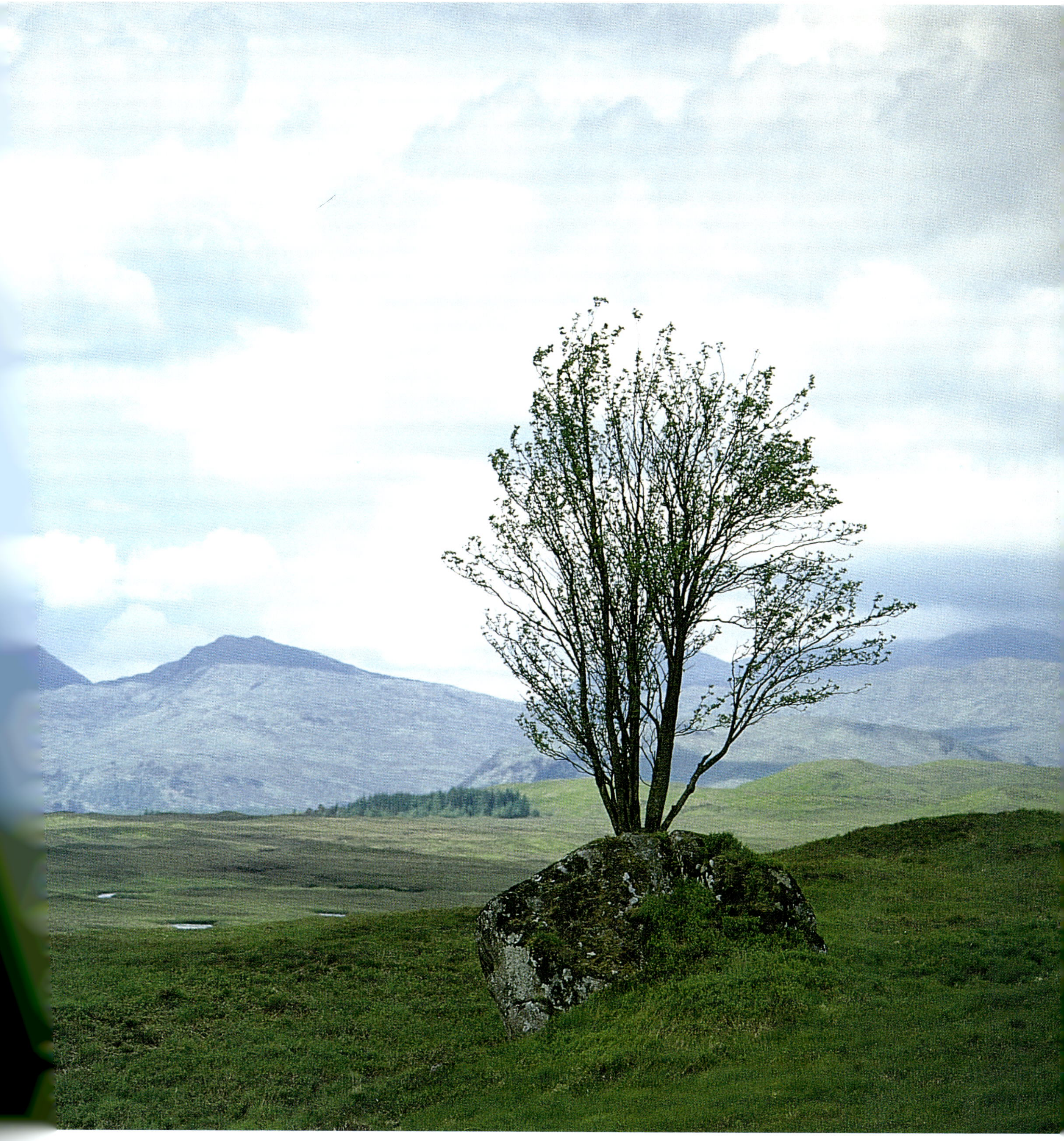

*For the Germanic and Norse tribes, the rowan was sacred because it saved the life of Thor, the mighty thunder god himself.*

**Practical Uses**

The hard wood has been used to make spinning wheels, tool handles, stakes and pegs, dowsing and divining rods.

**Natural Healing**

In European herbal tradition, the astringent properties of rowan have been applied in a variety of ways. A decoction of the bark was used internally to treat inflamed or irritated mucous membranes of the digestive tract (for example, in gastritis and diarrhea), and externally for cuts, sores, ulcers and skin problems, and for bleeding gums and sore throats.

Contrary to common belief, rowan berries are not poisonous, although more than eight or ten berries eaten raw would upset the stomach lining, owing to the parasorbic acid they contain. But this acid is destroyed by boiling, which makes rowan jam and jelly delicious ways in which to consume the nutritious berries. They are blood-cleansing and strengthen the immune system.

A flower remedy made from rowan can be used in healing to help promote a protective and nourishing aura of energy around the patient. The tree essence helps to attune us to the energies of nature.

**Culture, Myth and Symbol**

In all regions where rowan is native, it used to be one of the most revered trees, and far into the Christian age it retained its significant role in popular magic, as a provider of protection, usually in the form of a living tree planted near the house, or by means of a few small boughs cut and fixed over doors, gates or fireplaces. Sometimes, a talisman carved from dead wood was used, but usually a piece of bark sufficed.

Small crosses made from rowan twigs, each tied with a red ribbon, were once widespread in the British Isles. These were usually hung above the door at Eastertide or on May Day. In Bohemia, small bundles of rowan twigs were hung outside windows and on the roofs of houses to protect from lightning. In northern Germany, butter-paddles were made from rowan wood to counteract spells that would spoil the butter, while in Ireland, a rowan sprig was placed inside the house to protect it from fire spells, as well as to prevent ghosts from entering and the dead from rising. But above all the rowan was the sovereign protector of milk, and hence it was always found close to cow sheds.

Scottish tradition did not allow the rowan, or *caorann*, to be cut, except for ceremonial purposes, such as providing wood for a funeral pyre, or to make the threshing tool. In Germanic and Norse lore, the rowan was sacred for two reasons: first, because it saved Thor, the mighty thunder god, from being washed away in the river of the underworld. (Hence, the tree was seen as an effective protector against lightning.) And second, the rowan was considered sacred because the first woman was made from its wood.

The English name, rowan, stems from the Norse *runa*, meaning "a secret", or "to whisper", which is also the origin of the word "rune". This hints at a deeper layer of meaning:

**May 2nd** *In many parts of Western Europe, it was traditional to deck milksheds with rowan to protect the milk and cows from evil influences, and for shepherds to make their flocks pass through rowan hoops.*

**mid-March–May 1st** *In the British Isles it was customary to hang small bunches of rowan twigs tied with a red ribbon outside the windows and on the roofs of houses at Easter or on May Day, according to the region.*

**March 21st** *Spring Equinox*

**February 1st** *Brigantia/Imbolc The rowan is associated with the Celtic goddess Brigid (who later became the Christian St Brigid or St Bride) through her role as patron of spinning and weaving – spinning wheels were traditionally made from rowan.*

**ROWAN** (Sorbus aucuparia)
NORTHERN HEMISPHERE

**June 21st** *Summer Solstice On Midsummer's Night in Britain it was customary for travellers to wear a sprig of rowan or to place it on their horse's bridle as protection against being kidnapped by fairies.*

**September 22nd** *Autumn Equinox*

**December 21st** *Winter Solstice According to Icelandic myth, the frost-covered rowan tree is symbolic of divine light shining through at the darkest time of year.*

---

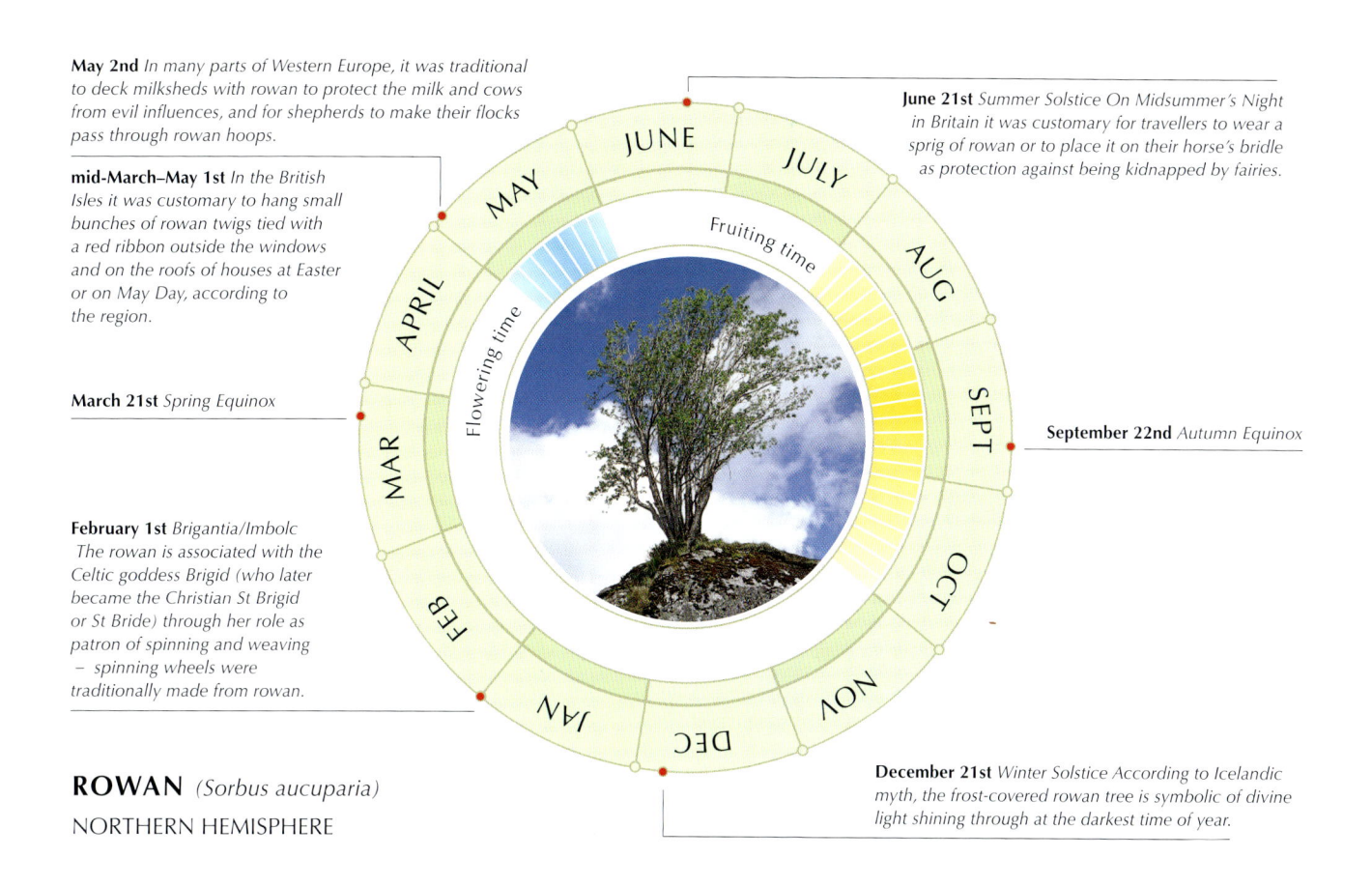

the tree whispers secret inspiration into our hearts. It was also the sacred tree of the ancient Irish goddess Brigid, the patroness of crafts, particularly spinning and weaving (hence spinning wheels were made from rowan wood). Brigid is also the muse of poets and bards. In the bardic tradition, the rowan is known as the "Tree of Inspiration". Its strong connection with druids is also reflected in the alternative Irish name, *fid na ndruad*, the "wizard's tree". In Wales, the rowan is believed to guard the soul's passage through the gate of death, and so is traditionally planted in graveyards, alongside the yew, which performs the same role.

The rowan's Anglo-Saxon name, *cvicbeam*, meaning "life tree", is related to "quickening". This was a tradition known throughout Europe, in which livestock were gently beaten with a soft rod of rowan (or sometimes of hazel or willow) every spring, to stimulate their life force and to bless them. But there is more to the "life tree". In the Irish legend of Diarmuid and Grainne, the fleeing lovers find shelter (*protection* once more) in a wonderful quicken-tree, which was also referred to as the "beautiful Druid tree" that had grown from a "berry of the Land of the Ever-Living Ones" (the elves). The rowan's legendary ability to restore youth to old people clearly identifies it as yet another example of the archetypal Tree of Life.

**Symbolism:** Protection and inspiration

**Divine Associations:** Brigid (Irish); Thor (Norse and Germanic)

**Astrological Associations:** Sun, Mercury

# Tamarisk *Tamarix*

*Tamarix* is a genus of about 54 species of deep-rooted shrubs or small trees, native to Europe, Asia and northern Africa. Tamarisk trees have graceful, slender, greenish branches and minute, scale-like leaves with salt-secreting glands, a feature which enables these trees to withstand the salt spray in coastal locations. The tiny, white to rose-coloured flowers are borne in simple or compound racemes. The fruit is a capsule that contains many seeds, with a tuft of hairs at the apex.

The leafless tamarisk (*T. aphylla*), native to northern Africa and the eastern Mediterranean, is a richly-branched, evergreen tree that grows to a height of about 30ft (10m), and has pale pink to white flowers. Its leafless, intensely green branches are the photosynthesizing and transpiratory organs. More common is the Nile tamarisk (*T. nilotica*) which grows in almost every deep *wadi* (watercourse) of the desert, and also in marshes.

## Practical Uses

A species of tamarisk, *T. gallica* (which is native to southern Europe but also naturalized along stretches of the English coast), became the popular choice from which to make crab-pot bases in the British Channel Islands. This was because its wood had the ability to withstand the long-term effects of salt water.

**Symbolism:** Protection

**Divine Association:** Osiris (ancient Egyptian)

**Astrological Association:** Saturn

## Natural Healing

In ancient Egypt the orchard of Pharaoh Tuthmosis I (who reigned 1528–1510BCE) included tamarisk trees, but unfortunately their medicinal use has not been passed down to us. In China, the branchlets and leaves of *T. chinensis* are officially classed as medicines because their salicin content is effective in treating fevers, headaches and arthritic pains. Its diuretic properties are useful in combatting bladder problems, and clearing toxins from the body.

In England, the famous herbalist Nicholas Culpeper (1616–54) advocated using a decoction of tamarisk (*T. gallica*) to treat a range of ailments from varicose veins and heavy menstrual bleeding to jaundice, colic, snake bites and even leprosy. He also recommended using the ashes to soothe blisters caused by burns.

## Culture, Myth and Symbol

In a version of the ancient Egyptian myth of the death and resurrection of Osiris, the sarcophagus containing the dead body of this ancient vegetation deity floats down the Nile river and finally comes ashore on the coast of Phoenicia. Immediately, a tamarisk tree grows up around the coffin and encloses it in its trunk. The local king and queen come to hear about the majestic and sweet-scented tree and decide to have it fashioned into a pillar for their palace. Meanwhile, Isis, Osiris' divine sister-wife, has been searching the earth far and wide for her beloved and finally finds the palace and the enchanted tamarisk column. She removes the coffin from the pillar and takes Osiris home.

The tamarisk shares the task of protecting the body of Osiris with the acacia, which, after this initial episode in his story, takes over the task of providing him with magical shelter. Hence, mortals too valued the tree for its perceived protective powers.

The tamarisk was often used in purification ceremonies, and the smoke was believed to keep away snakes. The great healing power of the tamarisk was also known in ancient Israel, where, for example, it was used to cleanse lepers and their houses (Leviticus 14:4; note that the scriptures sometimes call it "cedar" instead, but this tree did not grow in the region).

As a foreigner in the land of the Philistines, Abraham "planted a tamarisk tree at Beersheba, and there he invoked the Lord" (Genesis 21:33). When King Saul of Israel and his sons had fallen in the battle against the Philistines, the people of Jabesh took their mortal remains home, buried them under a tamarisk and fasted for seven days (I Samuel 31:13). However, in the other version of this event (Chronicles 10:12), the tamarisk (in Hebrew, *eshel*) was replaced with "terebinth" or "female sacred tree" (in Hebrew, *elah*).

ABOVE: *The small surface area of its leaves reduces transpiration and enables the tamarisk tree to live in dry and hot conditions.*

BELOW: *The greenish tamarisk branches blend almost seamlessly into the minute scale-like leaves. The flowers are tiny too.*

# Montezuma cypress
## *Taxodium mucronatum*

*Taxodium* is a small genus of two species of monoecious conifers, found in river and lake margins and swamps in the southeastern United States and Mexico. The short, linear leaves are flattened or awl-shaped and appear radially on the branches of persistent varieties but in two opposite ranks on deciduous ones. Male and female flowers grow on the same tree – the male ones hang in long, drooping catkins from the ends of the branches. The short-stalked cones have woody, shield-like scales. The seeds ripen during the first year.

The small to medium-sized Montezuma cypress (*T. mucronatum* Ten.) was named after the last Aztec emperor, Montezuma II (1466–1520). It has short leaves which are persistent in warm climates, or deciduous in trees planted in colder climates. The most famous specimen is in Santa María del Tule, near Oaxaca, Mexico. With a bole measuring 119ft (36.3m) in girth, "El Tule" is one of the world's largest trees, estimated to be between 2,000 and 4,000 years old. The other species in this genus, the bald cypress (*T. distichum var. distichum*) is a tall tree that sheds its leaves in autumn.

### Practical Uses
Both species are important for their strong and durable timber but are also planted as ornamentals. The Seminole Indians have traditionally used the wood of the pond cypress (*T. distichum var. imbricarium*, also known as *T. ascendens*) to make houses, canoes, paddles, coffins, medicine bowls, arrowheads, drums, ox yokes, mortars, ball poles and dolls.

### Culture, Myth and Symbol
Ancient Mesoamerican religions were based on belief in a life force inherent to all beings, and the cycles of time marked by the movements of celestial bodies. This led the ancients to formulate complex calendar systems, which determined sowing and harvest times and also elaborate rituals, including human sacrifice, in an attempt to maintain the balance of human destiny and the forces of nature.

An integral part of the cosmology was the sacred *ceiba* or "Tree of Life". The ancient Mexican people, the Zapotecs, believed that their ancestors had been born from old trees. Indeed, the myth of humans having descended from trees can be found across the Americas.

The present town of Santa María del Tule has a hispanicized name derived from the Aztec *tollin* or *tullin*, a generic term for aquatic plants. The modern Mexican name for the Montezuma cypress, *ahuehuete*, is also an old word, meaning "ancients of the water". Many ancient specimens are found in dry locations, demonstrating that much of Mexico has become desert over the last 2,000 years. The survival of El Tule has been assisted since 1952 by an underground irrigation system to water its roots. There is little doubt that the church of Santa María del Tule was built on the site of an Aztec place of worship. In 1586, the Spanish chronicler José Acosta attested that "people gathered to perform their

---

**Symbolism**: Balance and fertility

**Divine Associations**: Chalchiuhtlicue, Coyolxauhqui, Coatlicue/Cihuacóatl (all Aztec)

**Astrological Association**: Moon

ceremonial dances and superstitions" there. In 1834, the last ceremony incorporating ancient ritual elements was performed underneath El Tule, involving the sacrifice of a dove and a special dance in honour of the tree.

But exactly which forces or deities were worshipped in ancient times underneath the swamp cypresses? This question leads us away from the well-known sun worship of Mesoamerica, to the forces of the earth, the underworld and the waters that complement the solar fire.

Aztec tradition has many deities associated with such forces. One is Chalchiuhtlicue ("jade skirt" or "lady precious green"), the goddess who rules the waters of the earth: the rivers and streams, lakes and other freshwater. Her husband is Tlaloc, the rain god. She unleashed the flood that destroyed the Fourth World of the Aztec calendar (we are presently in the Fifth). Another nature deity is Xochiquetzal ("precious feather flower"), the goddess of the earth, of flowers and plants, and of love. She is also the patron of pregnant women, childbirth, prostitutes and artisans. Her twin brother,

ABOVE: *El Tule, a gigantic tree with a heavily fluted trunk, dominates the churchyard of Santa María del Tule in Mexico.*

Xochipilli, presides over love and games, beauty, song and dance. There is also Coyolxauhqui ("golden bells"), the goddess of the moon. She presides over all the star deities and has great magical powers.

All these are divine children of Coatlicue ("serpent skirt"), the goddess of life and death, mother of the stars, the gods and mortals, also called Teteoinnan ("Mother of the gods") and Toci ("our grandmother"). She is a manifestation of the earth goddess Cihuacóatl ("snake woman"), also called Tonantzin ("our mother"). The serpent in Aztec religion is a symbol of fertility, of the underground waters and the world ocean from which the tree rises. Ancient swamp trees are a perfect symbol of the *ceiba*, the Tree of Life, as they root deep in the life-giving waters and reach up to the life-giving sun, thus connecting the nine layers of the underworld and the 13 heavens of Aztec cosmology.

# Yew *Taxus*

A small genus of eight species of evergreen trees, *Taxus* is distributed throughout the northern temperate region and as far south as Central America and Sumatra. The eight species are very similar and there is a greater range within *T. baccata*, the common yew, than there are differences between the species. Hence, some botanists regard the other species as subspecies of *T. baccata*. Furthermore, with its red fruits and lack of resin, the yew is not a true conifer.

Yews are densely-branched trees. As solitairs their width is often greater than their height, which rarely exceeds 50ft (15m). However, straight columns topping 100ft (30m) have been reported in the mountain forests of Caucasia.

The needle-like leaves are ½in to 1¼in (1.3–3cm) long, dark green above and pale green beneath, and arranged in spirals or two ranks. The reproductive organs are situated in small roundish heads in the leaf axils. Male and female flowers open in early spring and are usually borne on separate trees. The seed is partly enclosed by a bright scarlet, fleshy cup called an *aril*. Birds are the main distributors.

Yews can send down so-called aerial roots to support the crown, and this can even be witnessed inside the hollow (or hollowing) trunks of many ancient yews. At first, a tender root grows downward through the crumbling old hardwood while it is decomposed by fungi. But over centuries, it can grow into a handsome new trunk that stands inside the hollow shell of the old one.

Yews grow extremely slowly – at about half the rate of many other European tree species. Slower-growing even

**RIGHT**: *The morning sun breaks through the branches of the yews on Hambledon Hill, the site of an Iron Age fort in Dorset, England.*

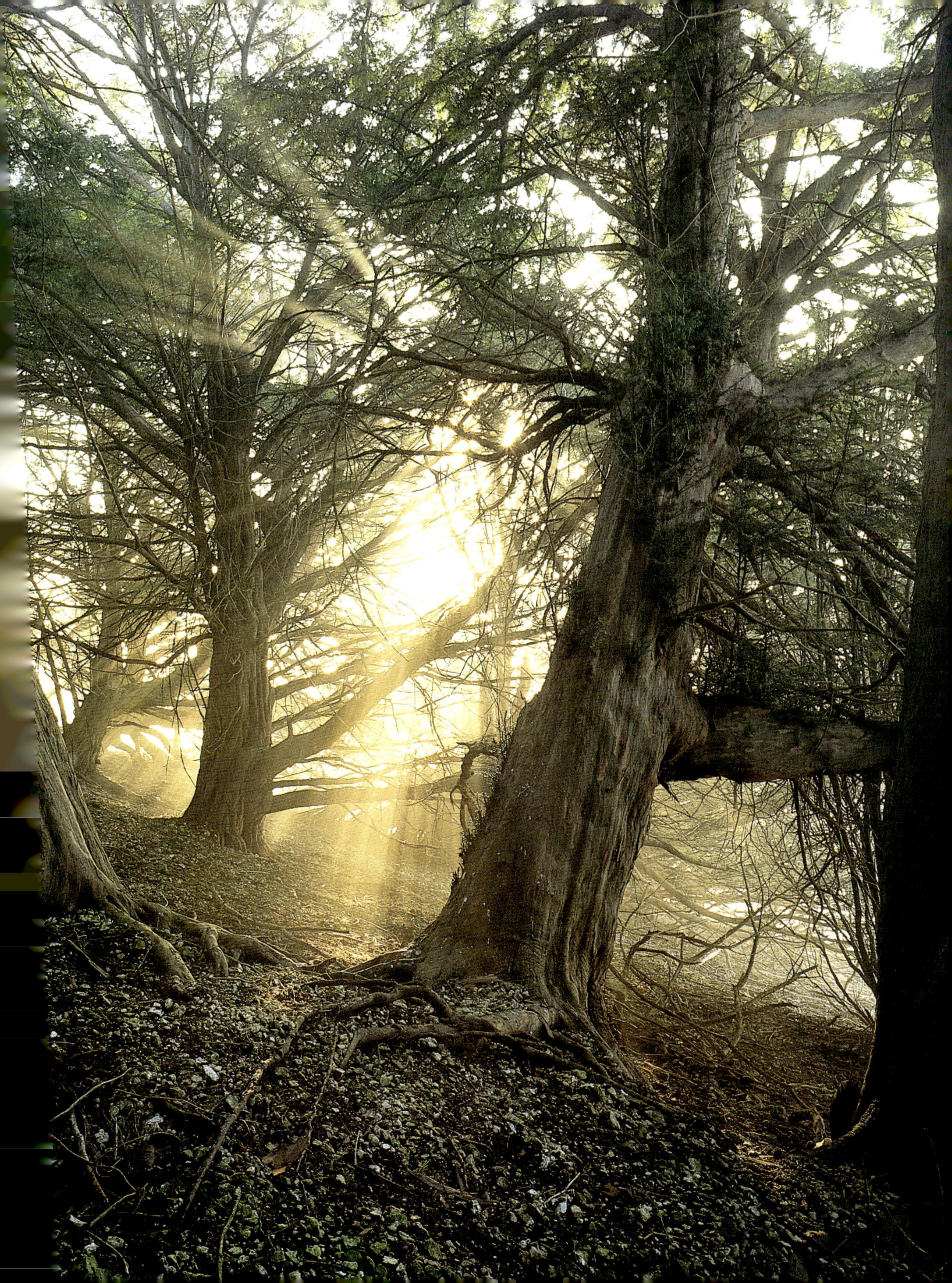

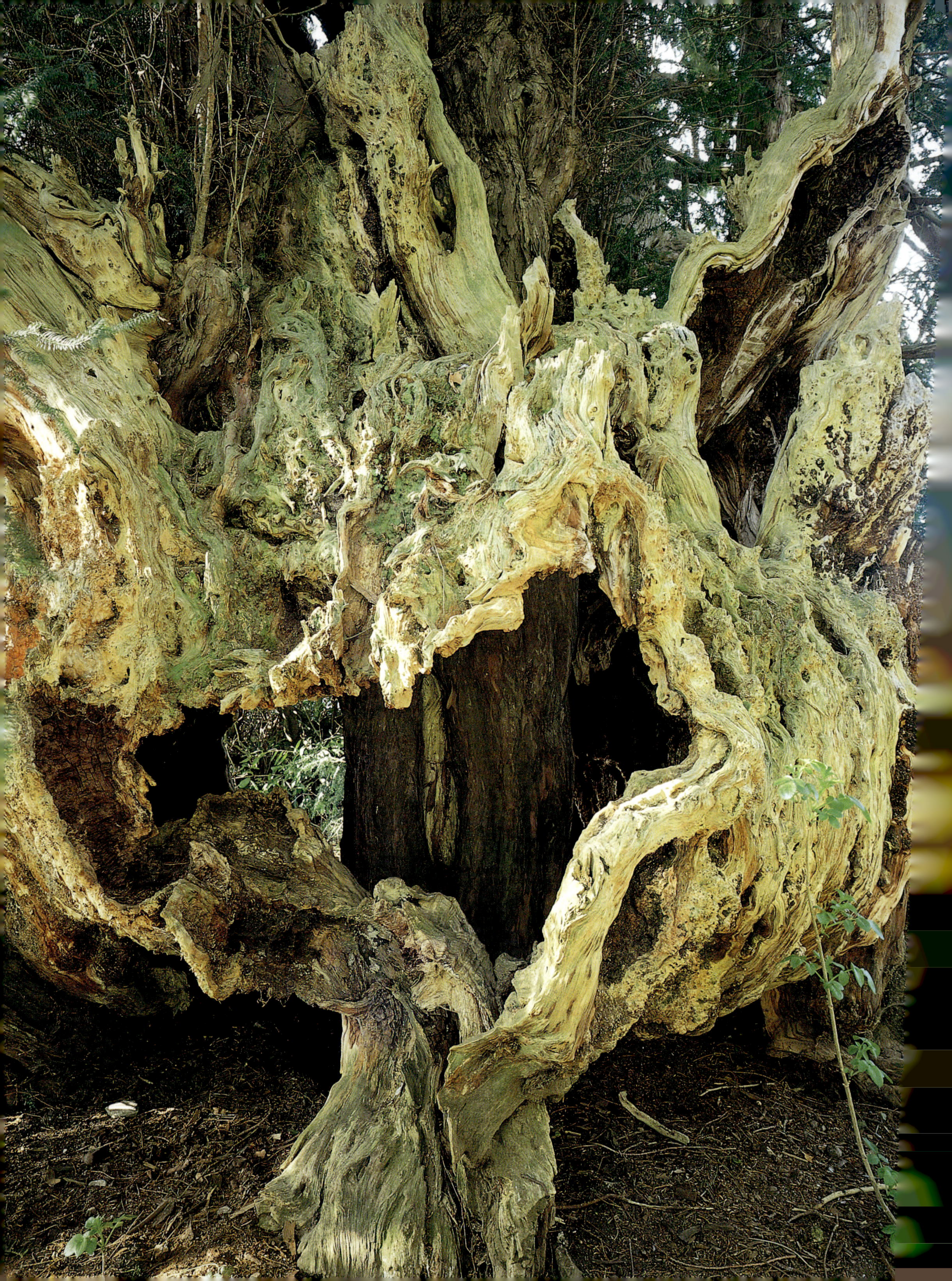

OPPOSITE: *The great longevity of the yew tree often leads to the loss of its heartwood, leaving a fascinatingly shaped hollow of huge girth.*

than the protected trees in parks and churchyards are those in the wild – in forests or rocky areas, such as southern France. As trees in general die when they have outgrown themselves, slow growth is a recipe for long life, of which the yew, indeed, is a master.

The age of yews cannot be assessed easily, mainly because the trunks of almost all old trees eventually become hollow. This is not a sign of weakness or final decay: a hollow tube is much stronger and more flexible (for example, in high winds) than a solid one – every engineer knows this, and trees know it too. But unfortunately, the hollowing process destroys the "rings" that help us to discover trees' ages. Furthermore, an interior root which grew for centuries in the hollowing old trunk will eventually develop into a firm new trunk that slowly takes over the supply of the crown. Many centuries later, when the old shell will have withered away, nobody will be able to guess that the apparently young tree had an entire lease of life before, and thus is at the very least a millenium older than its girth would suggest.

Nevertheless, there is a yew in Borrowdale (Cumbria, England) that has been proven "dendralogically" to be 1,500 years old. And Professor Pridnya, curator of the Caucasian Nature Reserve in Georgia, attests that yews can live in excess of 3,000 years. The Fortingall Yew in Argyllshire, Scotland, is said to be the oldest tree in Britain, and probably Europe, at an estimated 5,000 years old.

## Practical Uses

All cultures have appreciated the qualities of the slow-grown, hard but flexible, fine-grained and water-resistant yew wood, also called "iron wood" because yew fence poles are said to outlast metal ones. When the original yew foundations of some buildings in Venice were replaced in the 1950s, the refurbished yew beams were sold to the building trade. The oldest man-made artifact (a spear thought to be c.150,000 years old ) is of yew; so are the oldest musical instruments. In ancient Ireland, household items, such as bowls and spoons, were carved from yew.

The yew longbow goes back at least 5,300 years (one was found with the so-called "Alpine iceman"), but made political history between the 13th and 16th centuries when skilled, professional archers won crucial battles for the English against Scotland and, particularly, against France. The yew stands of the British Isles were soon depleted, and the English monarchs began to import yew wood, first from Spain, then from the Hanseatic towns of the North and Baltic seas. The yew populations of Europe never recovered from this period of intense trade.

## Natural Healing

Every part of the yew, except the red aril, is poisonous because it contains taxicantin. Eating as little as 50–100 grams of chopped leaves would be fatal for an adult. However, taxicantin poisoning is very rare – all 10 reported fatal cases in the 20th century were deliberate.

In the early 1980s, paclitaxel (formerly taxol), a substance derived from yew bark, was discovered to be a potent anti-cancer drug. After pharmaceutical companies had subsequently raided almost all the yew stands (*T. brevifolia*) in the United States, a newly-discovered method of part-synthesizing the drug from a related substance in the leaves saved the last trees. To meet worldwide demand, China has

OPPOSITE: *A familar sight in the British Isles: the venerable yew in the churchyard. This one is to be found in Dorset, England.*

planted 2 million yews near Yantai in northeast China, and is presently planting another 5 million on the slopes of Sichuan, also partly as an anti-erosion measure.

## Culture, Myth and Symbol

Many ancient Celtic communities and tribes named themselves after the yew (for example, the Eurobones and the Eburovices in Gaul), which indicates the significant sacred status of this tree. The Ibero-Celts, native to Spain, got their name from merging with their non-Celtic neighbours, the Iberians (from *ibe* "yew"). These Celts were the first Celtic invaders of Ireland, the ancient name of which is *Ierne*, "Yew Island". A second kingdom named *Iberia* also existed in medieval Georgia, Asia, where the yew is still today called the "Tree of God".

In tenth-century Wales, the penalty for cutting down a consecrated yew was one pound – far more than most people earned in a lifetime. The consecrated trees in question are those found in churchyards. And these Christian churches were erected on sacred sites of the previous, pagan religion. In the British Isles, particularly in Wales, there are many small churchyards that still display a circular and sometimes elevated geography, which is even older than Celtic earthworks. These sites go back to Bronze Age tumuli or even Neolithic burial mounds. Indeed, the religious significance of the yew is as old as the Stone Age.

The 13th rune in the *old futhark*, the oldest Norse rune alphabet, is called *ihwaz* or *eiwaz*, both variations meaning "yew", and representing death and rebirth. A second rune for this tree, from a younger Scandinavian rune set, *yr*, is *identical* with the Stone-Age symbol for the roots of the Tree of Life. The Nordic Tree of Life, Yggdrasil, not only represents the central pole, the foundation and the unity of the universe, but is also connected intimately with the spiritual search for divine knowledge. In the Icelandic scriptures, the *Edda*s, Yggdrasil is described as a "winter-green needle-ash". Unfortunately, over the past few hundred years this has been interpreted as meaning that Yggdrasil was an ash tree. But the ash is *not* evergreen, *nor* has it needles. And, while the Nordic *ask* can mean "ash", it can also mean "sharp" or "pointed". So was Yggdrasil, in fact, a yew tree?

In myth, Odin, the god of wisdom, hangs himself from Yggdrasil's branches for nine days and nights, on a vision quest from which he brings back runes – the magical

---

**Symbolism**: the Tree of Life, immortality, rebirth, protection

**Divine Associations**: The Great Goddess (Neolithic), Dione (pre-Greek), Artemis (Phrygian and ancient Greek), Persephone, Hecate (ancient Greek), Astarte (Syrian), Odin (Norse)

**Astrological Associations**: Saturn and Pluto

**Superstition**: That someone might die just from sleeping underneath a yew is an idea that has been reappearing in literature ever since the Greek physician Dioscorides first mentioned it in c.77CE.

**Historical Spotlight**: Charles Darwin, the great English naturalist (1809–82), sometimes rested under the great yew in St Mary's churchyard in Downe, Kent, and here he wanted to be buried. However, public opinion preferred a high-status burial for him at Westminster Abbey, London.

alphabet – to share with humankind. Odin climbing the Universal Tree is an exponent of the truth-searching shaman – a tradition found throughout Eurasia. But while the yew has disappeared from central Siberia, it still grows in western Asia. In Japan, too, the yew tree (*T. cuspidata*) is connected with the creator gods and their abodes on mountain tops. Here, also, is it called *ichii*, the "Tree of God".

Yggdrasil denotes the "steed of Odin", but it can also mean "I-carrier" – the supporter of the conscious self. The oldest European names for the yew go back to the Germanic *iwe* (*iwa*), which is related to *ihhe* (*ihha*), the first person singular. And in Anglo-Saxon *ih* means both "I" (the conscious self) and the yew tree. Furthermore, *iwe* is even more closely related to *ewi* (in modern German, *ewig*), which means "eternal". Another Anglo-Saxon name of the yew tree, *eo*, stems from Old High German *eo*, also meaning "eternal" and "always". Somehow, the yew tree has always reflected eternal consciousness.

The Germanic peoples connected the yew with the midwinter solstice on December 21st. The Saxons celebrated

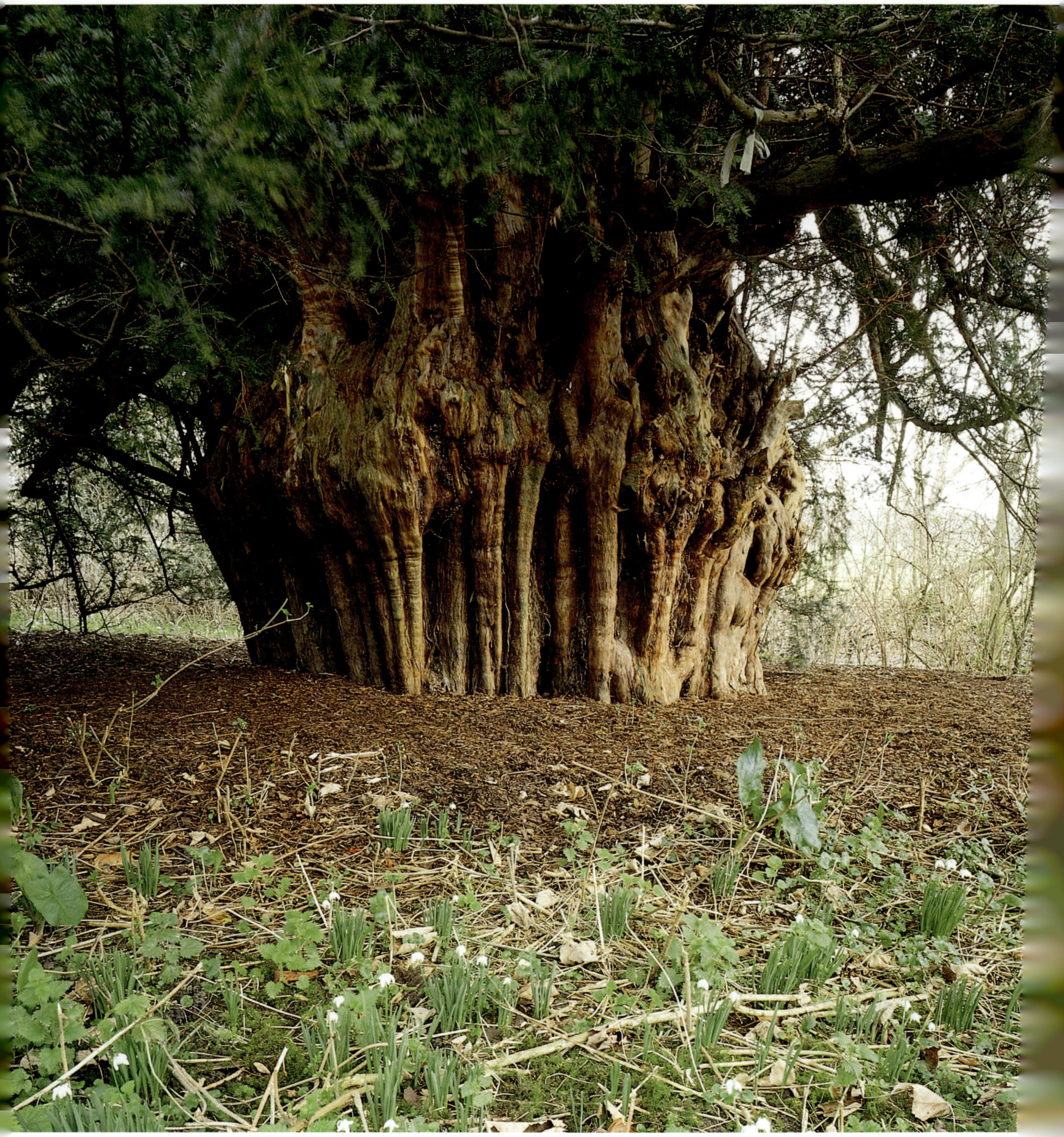

## YEW *(Taxus baccata)*
### NORTHERN HEMISPHERE

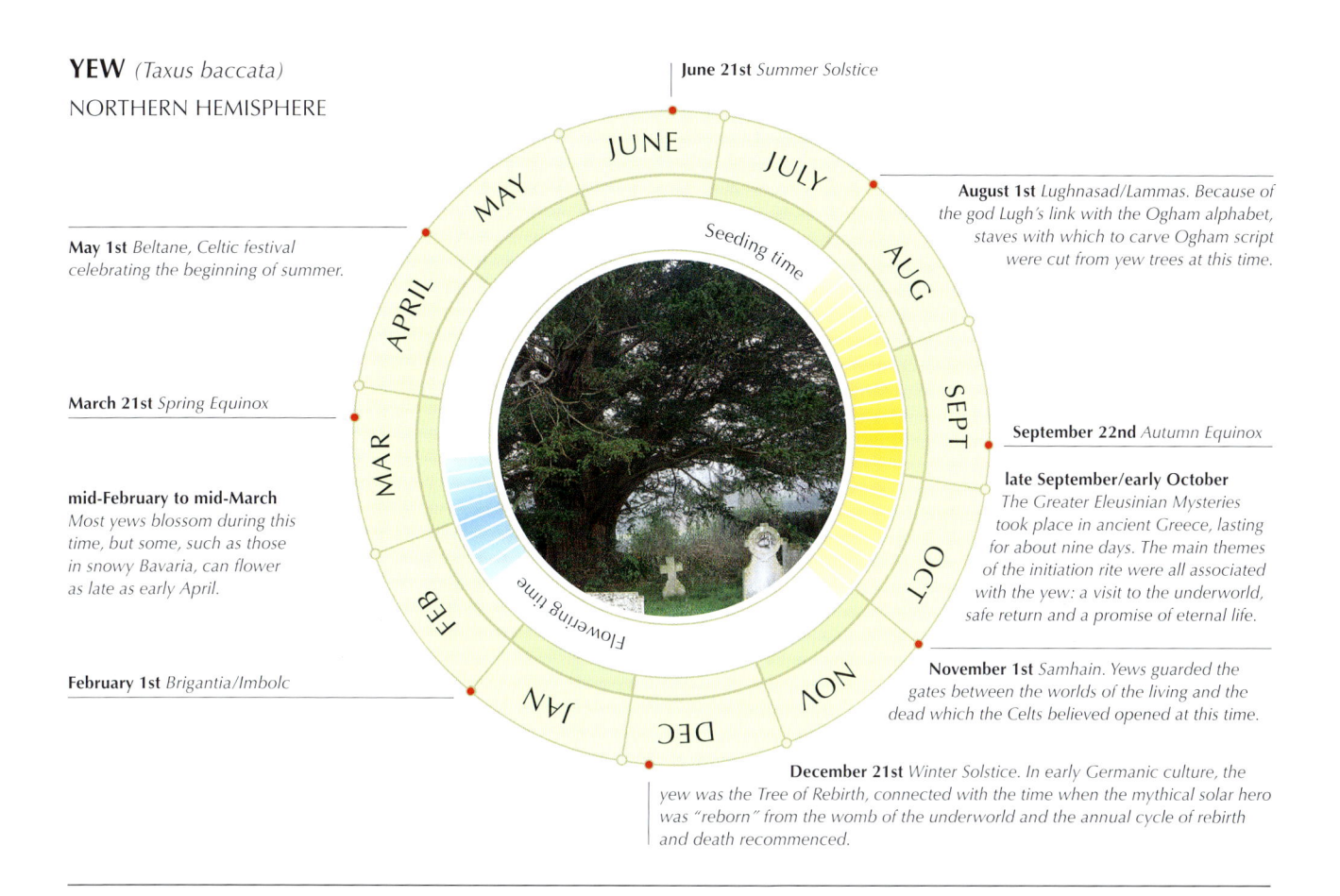

**June 21st** *Summer Solstice*

**August 1st** *Lughnasad/Lammas. Because of the god Lugh's link with the Ogham alphabet, staves with which to carve Ogham script were cut from yew trees at this time.*

**May 1st** *Beltane, Celtic festival celebrating the beginning of summer.*

**March 21st** *Spring Equinox*

**September 22nd** *Autumn Equinox*

**late September/early October**
*The Greater Eleusinian Mysteries took place in ancient Greece, lasting for about nine days. The main themes of the initiation rite were all associated with the yew: a visit to the underworld, safe return and a promise of eternal life.*

**mid-February to mid-March**
*Most yews blossom during this time, but some, such as those in snowy Bavaria, can flower as late as early April.*

**November 1st** *Samhain. Yews guarded the gates between the worlds of the living and the dead which the Celts believed opened at this time.*

**February 1st** *Brigantia/Imbolc*

**December 21st** *Winter Solstice. In early Germanic culture, the yew was the Tree of Rebirth, connected with the time when the mythical solar hero was "reborn" from the womb of the underworld and the annual cycle of rebirth and death recommenced.*

---

the three longest nights of the year as the *modraneht* – the "Mother Nights" – to pay respect to the dark and still womb of the Great Goddess who gives birth to everything on earth. The Norse celebrated the solstice over an even longer period – for the 13 nights of Yuletide.

By contrast, the Celtic calendar connects the yew with the festival of Samhain (November 1st), when the gates between the world of the living and the world of the dead were said to be open. The ancient Greeks, too, saw the yew as a gate to the underworld, and hence a guardian of the soul. Indeed, we find this association cross-culturally, and this is the reason why the yew has been such a familiar sight at ancient burial mounds and in contemporary graveyards alike. However, the yew is not the "tree of death", as some 18th- and 19th-century poets called it. On the contrary, it is the Tree of Life, and has been employed in various ways in burial rites to counter-balance the power of death.

In the history of religion, transformation and rebirth have always been the realm of the female aspect of God. In Judaic myth, it is Channa or Anna, who represents divine mercy; in Christianity, it is Mary, the mother of Jesus. In older religions, it is the many faces and names of the Great Goddess, whose associations with the yew can be easily traced. Her gifts are justice, compassion, forgiveness, contemplation, insight and inner peace.

**OPPOSITE**: *The yew at Ankerwyke is one of the most venerated trees in the British Isles. The Magna Carta, which formed the basis for the constitutions of many countries including the USA, is believed to have been sworn here in 1215. In 1992 environmentalists met at the site to assert the right of all creatures to live according to their natures.*

# Linden  Tilia

*Tilia* is a genus of about 40 species of large deciduous trees in the northern temperate hemisphere. Known by their Anglo-Saxon name, *linden*, they are also popularly called "lime" trees.

The small-leaved European lime (*T. cordata*) reaches 100ft (30m) and has a fissured bark. The leaves are heart-shaped, often broader than long (2½in/6cm), and sharply and finely serrate. In July the fragrant, creamy-yellow flowers are borne in numerous clusters, which have five to seven flowers each. The small round fruits are sometimes ribbed.

The large-leaved European lime (*T. platyphyllos*) reaches 130ft (40m). The roundish-ovate leaves are up to 5in (12.5cm) long, regularly serrate, and downy beneath, especially on the veins. The cymes have three, rarely four to six flowers; the round or pear-shaped fruits are five-ribbed. The common lime (*T. europaea*) is a hybrid of the above two. A vigorous and long-lived tree with heart-shaped leaves, it is easily recognized by the multitude of suckers it produces around its base. All European species drop sticky "honey dew" in late summer, exuded by small insects (aphids).

The American lime or basswood (*T. americana*) grows to 130ft (40m), and has heart-shaped leaves 4–8in (10–20cm) long.

## Practical Uses

Linden trees are an abundant nectar source for bumble- and honey-bees, hence their alternative American name, "bee trees". Tolerance to pruning made the linden popular with farmers from ancient times. The trees were lopped every five to eight years to provide leaf fodder for cows. Linden leaves are not as tasty as ash leaves, but they are easier to chew and to digest. Both are rich in fatty acids and increase the fat content in milk, which thus yields more butter. The tradition of giving leaf fodder is ancient – evidence from Neolithic times (4300BCE) has been found in Lucerne, Switzerland.

The young spring leaves and shoots of the linden have also been a traditional part of the human diet. They can be added to any salad.

ABOVE: *Lime trees are most commonly found today in formal settings, in public parks and along the sides of roads.*

OPPOSITE: *In the autumn, the foliage of the linden tree turns to soft hues such as cream and light yellow.*

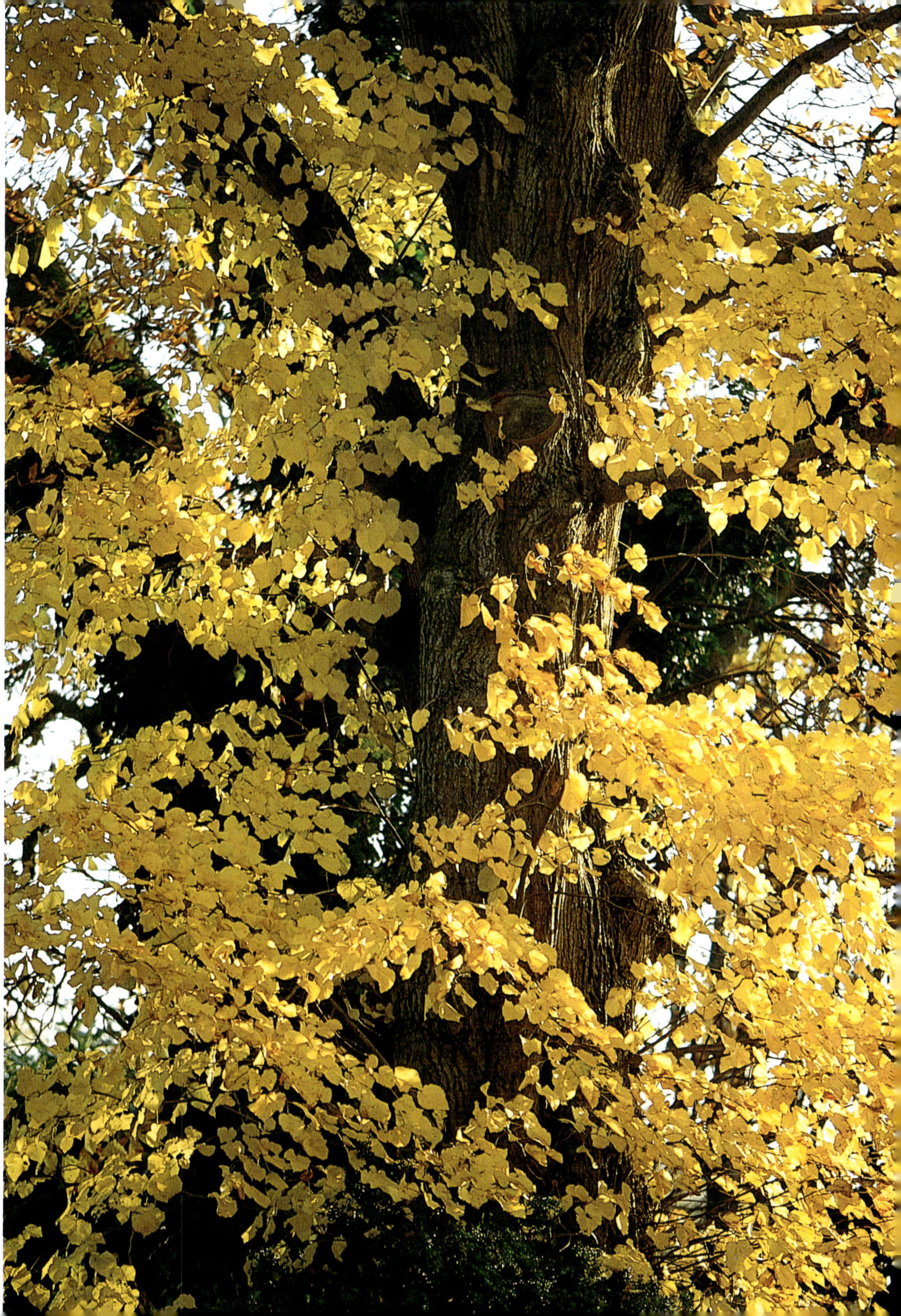

*ABOVE: Although lauded for its healing qualities, stories about the linden also link it with inner earth's upredictable "dragon" powers.*

Another of the linden's vastly important contributions to human life was the fibre of its inner bark – the bast. This was the main material used by both Native North Americans and Europeans to make ropes, strings, fishing nets and so on, until the fibres of hemp (*Cannabis*) replaced those of trees. (Hemp, known in China since c.2500BCE, arrived in central Europe around 400CE. Anglo-Saxons in Britain began to cultivate it between 800 and 1000CE.) Today the linden is a popular tree in parks and avenues all over Europe and North America.

## Natural Healing

Linden has a long history of medicinal use in Europe, most notably for soothing tension and irritability. It is also a heart tonic. The flower tea makes an excellent daily drink as it has a beneficial effect on the blood, helping to reduce cholesterol as well as high blood pressure. It makes a useful drink for children (sweetened with honey), to calm agitation and promote peaceful sleep. The hot tea soothes diarrhea and clears congested sinus conditions. Externally, the flower tea soothes inflammatory skin problems. (In German, the very word for "to soothe", *lindern*, is closely related to the name of the tree.)

## Culture, Myth and Symbol

Many European place names (such as Lincolnshire in England and Leipzig in Germany) and family names (for example, Linne, the father of modern botanical taxonomy) attest to the "lime light" this tree once enjoyed.

In Germany during the 18th and 19th centuries, the traditional *Dorflinde*, "village linden", was celebrated widely in poetry and art. It was the traditional hub of village life, where people would meet or sit on benches in its shade. As the *Tanzlinde*, "dance linden", it also constituted the central point in village feasts (and on May Day saved people the

*LEFT: An ancient coppice stool of small-leaved lime trees in the Lake District in northern England. Patches of woodland like this can be more than 1,000 years old.*

work of carrying a birch tree into the village). However, a more serious task for the linden was to be the location of the local court of law. This custom dates back to pre-Christian times, when tribal gatherings were held underneath sacred trees. It is revealing that the ancients gathered, discussed and judged underneath the "female" linden which represents mercy, rather than the "male" oak tree, the territory of the thunder god Donar (Thor). For the ancient Germanic and Norse peoples, the linden was sacred to Freya, the Mistress of the Earth, and Frigga, the Mother Goddess and patroness of childbirth and fertility.

Baltic peoples, such as the Estonians, kept linden trees sacred right through the Christian age into modern times. And in Christian Bulgaria, linden trees are prime locations for shrines to Mary, the mother of Jesus.

In Greek myth, Phylira, daughter of the sea god Oceanus, lies with Chronos, the deity of the planet Saturn, and conceives Chiron, the learned satyr who is half man, half horse. Then she is metamorphosed into the linden tree.

Later, Chiron taught his secret knowledge about the healing powers of nature to the first physician, Asclepius, who became the father of medicine. Hence the "grandmother" of medicine is the linden, the "soothing tree". And since the true healer is love, the closeness of Phylira's name with Greek *philein*, "to love", might not be accidental.

Asclepius learned more secrets from a serpent in a tomb, which is commemorated in the Staff of Asclepius – an ancient symbol showing a serpent winding around a linear staff, and the emblem of medicine to this day. In the serpent we recognize the guardian of the Tree of Life (see Introduction pp.8–13), and in Norse myth the guardian of eternal life is a dragon. When the hero Sigurd slays this dragon he bathes in its blood to become invincible. However, a leaf from a linden tree close to the dragon's lair lands between Sigurd's shoulder blades, preventing him from being totally immersed in the blood and thus creating a weak spot which eventually brings about his downfall. In this myth the dragon represents the life force of the earth itself.

**Symbolism**: Healing and peace

**Divine Associations**: Phylira (ancient Greek), Freya, Frigga (both Germanic)

**Astrological Associations**: Venus and Jupiter

**Historical Spotlight**: In the Middle Ages, the linden became a symbol of freedom in France and Switzerland. The French planted many lindens to commemorate the end of the Wars of Religion, marked by the Edict of Nantes (1598) in which Henri IV granted French protestants religious freedom.

OPPOSITE: *This ancient elm in Brighton has a healthy crown and is one of the two largest elms in the UK to have survived Dutch-elm disease.*

# Elm *Ulmus*

The genus *Ulmus* comprises about 18 species of deciduous, hardy trees native to the northern temperate zone. The alternating leaves are simple, toothed and usually asymmetrical at the base. The inconspicuous, bisexual flowers are borne in clusters on naked twigs in early spring. The disk-like fruit has a wing surrounding the single seed.

The English elm (*U. procera*) is a stately tree native to western and southern Europe. The leaves are 2–4in (5–10cm) long, coarsely toothed and have ten to 12 pairs of lateral veins. The wych elm (*U. glabra*) is a wide-spreading noble tree native from Europe to Siberia. It has large leaves, 4–8in (10–20cm) long, with 12 to 18 pairs of lateral veins. The upper side of the leaves of both species is distinctly rough to the touch. The American elm (*U. americana*) has leaves up to 6in (15cm) long, and deeply notched fruits.

Outbreaks of Dutch elm disease have destroyed almost all the mature elms in Europe and America. Young trees still flourish, but as soon as the bark reaches a certain thickness, the elm bark beetle *(Scolytus)* returns, infecting the tree with the fatal fungus *Ophiostoma*.

## Practical Uses

Elm is the supreme tree in the leaf fodder tradition, which dates back to the Stone Age. The leaves, which are rich in minerals, starch and proteins, have been even more popular with farmers (or rather with their livestock) than those of the linden and the ash.

In pre-industrial western Europe, elm wood was used for furniture, water-pipes, water-wheel boards, cart wheels and coffins. The Minoans of Crete made chariot wheels from elm and the Greeks used it for temple door posts and lintels.

## Natural Healing

Both Native North Americans and Europeans have made infusions from the inner (root) bark to treat colds and coughs, diarrhea, internal bleeding and fever. This is also applied externally on wounds. The Choctaw and Iroquois tribes drink elm infusions to soothe menstrual problems. Modern Western herbal medicine mainly uses the slippery elm (*U. fulva*), which has the highest mucilage content and hence is more soothing to irritated mucous membranes. The tree essence energizes the mind and balances the heart.

## Culture, Myth and Symbol

In England the elm was used traditionally for coffins, and the ancient Greeks planted it in graveyards. According to Virgil the tree was found in the underworld. It also stood at crossroads leading to the fairy world, hence its English folk name *elfin wood* (and German *Elfenholz*). In Scandinavia, the Baltic and northern Germany, the elm was one of the *Vartraed* – a guardian of the farmyard and a supernatural gate between the worlds of humans and nature spirits.

When Orpheus, the Greek hero and patron of music, mourned the death of Eurydice, an elm grove sprang up from the sound of his lyre. On his return from the underworld, he found shelter under an elm, where he played while all animals of the wood gathered, enchanted by the music.

**Symbolism:** Communication and relationships

**Divine Association:** Orpheus (ancient Greek)

**Astrological Associations:** Mercury, Saturn

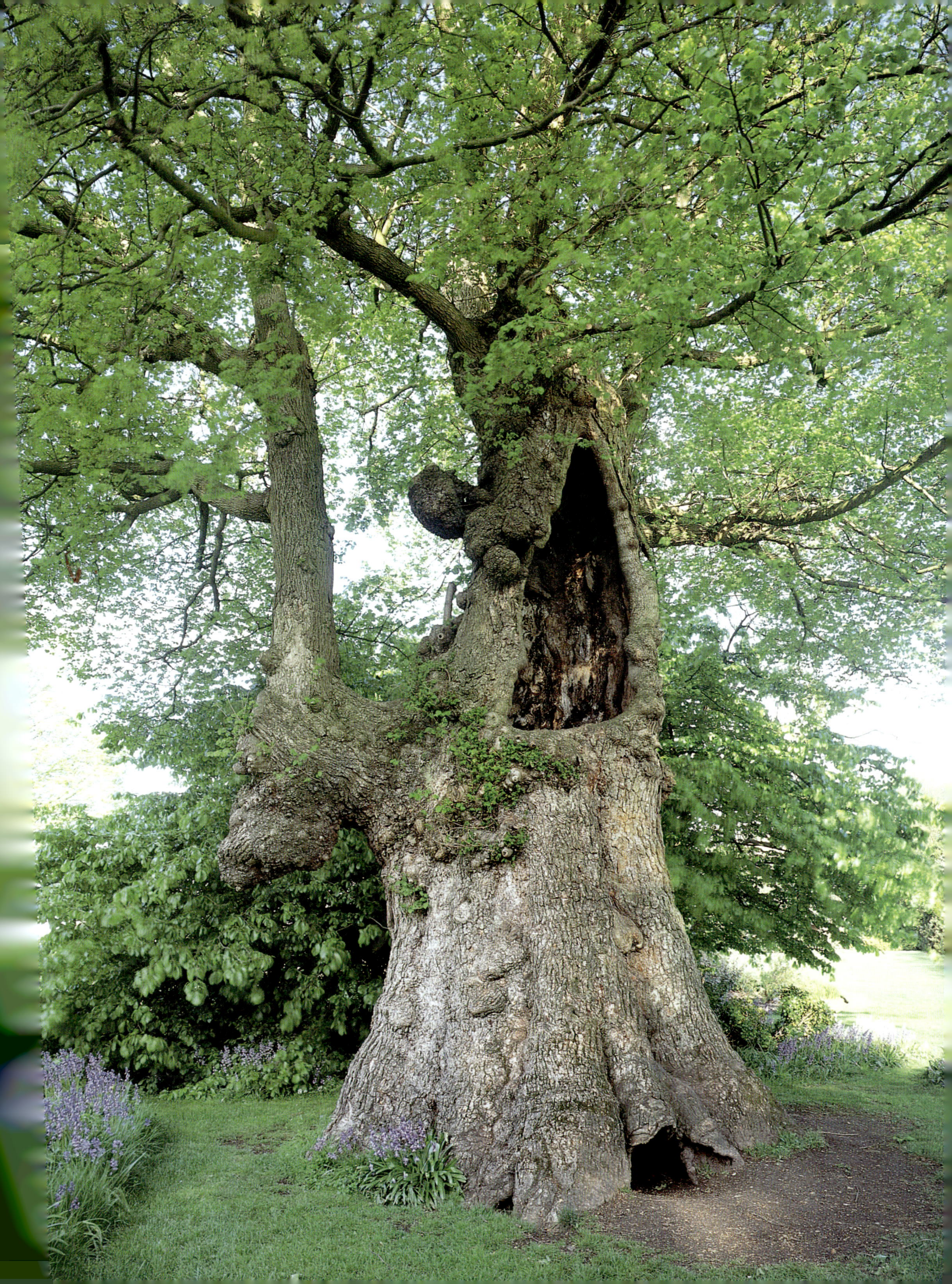

# Botanical glossary

**acuminate** tapering to a fine point

**acute** sharply pointed

**anther** the pollen-bearing part at the tip of the stamen

**apex** the tip, the distal end

**appressed** lying flat and close against

**auricle** ear-shaped expansion at the base of a leaf

**axillary** upper angle between midrib and vein, or stem and branch

**bast** soft, woody fibre from the stems of dicotyledonous plants (such as flax, hemp and jute), also from the old ploem cells underneath the bark of some trees (such as linden). These fibre bundles are often several feet long and consist of overlapping cellulose fibres and a cohesive gum (or pectin).

**bipinnate** twice pinnate (the primary leaflets being again divided into secondary leaflets)

**bole** different word for tree trunk

**boreal forest** also called taiga vegetation. A forest that occupies approximately 17 percent of the earth's land surface area in a circumpolar belt in the northern hemisphere. The trees are mainly conifers (pine, spruce, larch), with some birch and poplar, and reach the highest latitudes of any trees.

**bract** a modified leaf at the base of a flower cluster, stalk or shoot

**calyx** outer part of the flower, the sepals

**compound** composed of two or more similar parts

**conifer** cone-bearing tree

**cordate** heart-shaped

**cultivar** the cultivated variety of a species, often with superior production qualities as a result of plant-breeding by farmers

**cyme** flat-topped or dome-shaped flowerhead with the inner flowers opening first

**deciduous** not persistent, falling at end of a functional period (petals), or seasonal (leaves on deciduous trees)

**dentate** toothed with sharp, rather coarse teeth directed outward

**dioecious** male and female flowers on different plants

**doubly toothed** having teeth which themselves have teeth

**drupe** a stone fruit. One (rarely two) seed(s) enclosed in a hard shell, which is, in turn, enclosed in a fleshy and fibrous layer – for example, almond, peach and walnut

**elliptic** widest about the middle, narrowing equally at both ends

**entire** undivided and without teeth (that is, with a continuous unbroken margin)

**epiphyte** a plant growing on another plant, but not taking nourishment from it

**evergreen** with foliage that remains green during winter

**fascicle** a dense cluster

**filament** the stalk of a stamen

**genus** a biological classification ranking between family and species, consisting of structurally or phylogenetically related species (see species). For example, the aspen and the cottonwood are different species within the genus *Populus*.

**glabrous** hairless

**glaucous** covered with a bloom (a fine whitish/purplish powder)

**globose** more or less globular (spherical)

**indehiscent** fruits that do not open

**involucre** a whorl of small leaves surrounding a flower

**keel** a central ridge

**lanceolate** shaped like the blade of a spear; long, tapering to the apex

**lateral** on or at the side

**legume** also called pod fruit. Plants of the pea family (*Leguminosae*), which release their seeds by splitting open along two seams for example, alfalfa, bean, clover, peanut, soybean.

**linear** long and narrow, with parallel sides

**lobe** leaf or petal segment, divided from adjacent segments by sinuses

**lobule** a small lobe

**monoecious** male and female flowers separate, but on the same plant

**oblong** longer than broad, with nearly parallel sides

**obovate** inversely ovate

**obovoid** inversely ovoid, attached at narrow end

**orbicular** almost circular in outline

**ovate** broadest below the middle (like a hen's egg)

**ovary** the basal, ovule-bearing part of the pistil

**ovoid** egg-shaped solid body, with the point of attachment at the broader end

**ovule** the body which, after fertilization, becomes the seed

**palmate** with lobes or leaflets radiating from a point; hand-shaped

**panicle** a branching raceme

**pedicle** the stalk of an individual flower in an inflorescence

**peduncle** the stalk of a flower cluster or of a single flower

**persistent** remaining attached

**petiole** the leaf-stalk

**pinyon** seed of one of the pinyon pines

**pinnate** with leaflets each side of a central stalk

**pistil** the female organs in a flower: ovary, style and stigma

**polygamodioecious** essentially dioecious, but with some bisexual flowers among the unisexual ones

**pome** the fleshy fruit of plants of the rose family (for example, apple, pear, hawthorn), formed by a fusion of an inferior ovary with the base of the sepals and petals

**puberulent** minutely pubescent

**pubescent** covered with short, soft hairs; downy

**raceme** an inflorescence of stalked flowers borne on a common, unbranched stalk

**receptacle** swollen end of a stalk bearing a flower

**scabrous** rough to the touch, with small rough projections

**sepal** one of the segments of the calyx, usually green

**serrate** saw-toothed

**sessile** without a stalk

**shrub** any woody plant that has several stems (none dominant) and is usually less than 10ft (3m) tall. When much-branched and dense, it might be called a bush.

**sinus** the recess or space between lobes

**species** a biological classification denoting related organisms that share common characteristics and are capable of interbreeding.

**spinescent** with a spine or sharp tip at the end (of a branch or leaf); having spines, spiny

**stamen** the male organ of a flower (comprising filament and anther)

**stigma** female organ in a flower which receives the pollen, at the end of the style

**style** the middle part of the pistil between the ovary and the stigma

**suckering** producing underground stems

**temperate forest** vegetation type with an almost continuous canopy of broad-leaved trees, occuring between approximately latitudes 25° and 50° in both hemispheres. Classified into two groups: deciduous and coniferous.

**temperate zone** the climatical zone between the subpolar and the subtropical. In the temperate regions are the great deciduous and coniferous forests of the world are found.

**terminal** at the tip, apical

**ternate** in threes

**vesicle** a small bladdery sac or cavity filled with air or fluid

**whorl** three or more flowers or leaves arranged in a circle around an axis

# Introduction to natural healing

This brief introduction to Traditional Chinese Medicine, Ayurveda, flower and tree essences, is an accompaniment to the text on Natural Healing found throughout the book.

## Traditional Medicine

While modern Western (allopathic) medicine is generally based on physical and chemical observations and the treatment of specific symptoms, the focus of traditional-based healing systems (both Eastern and Western varieties) is on using "nature" to correct or heal any imbalance or "dis-ease" in the body. Traditional techniques take a holistic approach, considering the energetic properties of our bodies, our food and drink, our environment and their interactions.

According to Eastern medicine (and traditional cooking), individual foods have "temperatures": they are either hot, warm, neutral, cool or cold. These terms do not refer to the physical temperature of the food, but are a measure of the effects of the food on the body after digestion. Cooling foods move energy inward and downward, cooling the upper and outer parts of the body first. Warming foods direct energy upward and outward, warming us from the inside out. Warmer foods speed us up, cooler foods slow us down.

Food preparation methods have an effect on these qualities. Foods eaten raw are at their most cooling, while boiling is neutral, stir-frying is warming, baking is more warming, and grilling and barbecuing are the most heating.

## Traditional Chinese Medicine

Traditional Chinese Medicine (TCM) is based on the philosophy of *yin* and *yang*. Yin is the female principle, described as passive and dark, and represented by the earth. Yang is the male principle, described as active and light, and represented by the heavens.

TCM describes food by the temperatures, and by a second set of qualities, the *flavours*. Each of the five flavours arise from one of the five elemental powers, and enters one of the 12 major meridian pathways, directing its effect toward particular organs.

The *salty* flavour belongs to the water element and enters the kidney. It moves inward and downward. It moistens, softens and detoxifies. The *sour* flavour belongs to the wood element and enters the liver. It stimulates contraction and absorption, having a gathering and astringent effect, useful for conditions involving the loss of body fluids (for example, sweating, diarrhea). The *bitter* flavour belongs to the fire element and enters the heart. It moves downward and drains and dries. It improves appetite, stimulates digestion, and strengthens the respiratory tract. The *sweet* flavour belongs to the earth element and enters the spleen. It harmonizes all the flavours and gently stimulates the circulation. The *pungent* flavour belongs to the metal element and enters the lung. It disperses stagnation and stimulates the circulation of blood as well as energy.

These flavours are summarized in the table below.

| Flavour | Element | Organ | Function |
|---|---|---|---|
| salty | water | kidney | moistens; softens; detoxifies |
| sour | wood | liver | increases absorption of fluids |
| bitter | fire | heart | improves digestion; aids breathing |
| sweet | earth | spleen | stimulates circulation |
| pungent | metal | lung | disperses stagnation; gives energy |

## Ayurveda

Created in India, the medicinal system of Ayurveda can be traced back thousands of years, and, like TCM, it takes into account the patient's body, mind and spirit, instead of merely addressing symptoms. The sages who founded Ayurveda understood the world in terms of five major elements (fire, water, air, ether and earth), which, combine with each other to shape the three vital energies, the *doshas*. Each *dosha* has specific functions in the body, but it is their interplay which is important. Our health, well-being and all our physical, mental and emotional characteristics are determined by maintaining these *doshas* in harmonious balance.

Each *dosha* is a combination of two elements, with one predominating over the other:

*Vata*  a combination of the air and ether elements, with air predominating.
*Pitta*  a combination of the fire and water elements, with fire predominating.
*Kapha*  a combination of the water and earth elements, with water predominating.

The table below shows the main qualities of the *doshas*.

| *Vata* | *Pitta* | *Kapha* |
| --- | --- | --- |
| air and ether | fire and water | water and earth |
| light | light | heavy |
| cold | hot | cold |
| dry | oily | oily |
| rough | sharp | slow |
| subtle | liquid | slimy |
| mobile | sour | dense |

The qualities of the *doshas* do not apply only to food, but to all creation. Trees, too, can be described in these terms. For example, the birch, with its slender trunk, light foliage, and rapid growth is considered *vata*. The holly, with its sharp and spiky leaves, is *pitta*. And the walnut, with its massive trunk, thick bark and slow growth, is *kapha*. However, the qualities of the *doshas* should never be considered in isolation, but in a state of constantly changing interaction.

## Flower and tree essences

Like homeopathic remedies, all flower and tree essences are considered to be "vibrational" medicine, but they are made purely from plant and tree flowers. The flowers are harvested when they are in peak condition and dried in the sun. Next, the essence is extracted, diluted in water and preserved with alcohol to make a tincture. This is further diluted in spring water to make a solution that can be ingested to help to treat any imbalances and improve general well-being.

*Bach Flower Remedies*

There are a number of systems of flower essences, but Bach is probably still the best known. It comprises a range of 38 complete essences or "remedies", along with one combination (Rescue Remedy, which is a mixture of five of the other essences). These were first collected by Dr Edward Bach in the 1920s and 1930s, and used to address negative emotions underlying disease states.

*Tree Essences*

These are similar to flower essences but consist solely of potentized water from the flowers of trees.

# Further reading

**Bakhru**, H.K., *Foods that Heal*. Orient Paperbacks, New Delhi (1996).

**Balbuena**, Enrique, "Oak Open Forests ('Dehesa' or 'Montado') of *Quercus rotundifolia* Lam. and *Quercus suber* L. in the Iberian peninsula and their Products", in *Proceedings – Fourth International Oak Conference Fall 2003*. Issue 15/Spring 2004, International Oak Society, Browns Valley, California (2004).

**Baldwin**, Edwin, *Sacred Mountains of the World*. University of California Press, (1997).

**Bartram**, T., *Encyclopedia of Herbal Medicine*. Robinson, London (1995).

**Borgeest**, Bernhard, *Ein Baum und sein Land – 24 Symbiosen*. Rowohlt, Hamburg (1997).

**Brosse**, Jacques, *Mythologie der Bäume*. Walter-Verlag, Düsseldorf (1994).

**Brown**, Joseph Epes (ed.), *The Sacred Pipe – Black Elk's Account of the Seven Rites of the Oglala Sioux*. University of Oklahoma Press 1953, reprinted by Penguin, Baltimore (1971).

**Caldecott**, Moyra, *Myths of the Sacred Tree*. Destiny, Rochester, Vermont (1993).

**Campbell**, Joseph, *The Masks of God: Primitive Mythology*. Penguin Compass, New York (1959).

**Campbell**, Joseph, *The Masks of God: Oriental Mythology*. Condor, London (1962).

**Campbell**, Joseph, *The Masks of God: Occidental Mythology*. Penguin Compass, New York (1964).

**Car-Gomm**, Philip, *The Elements of the Druid Tradition*. Element Books, Shaftesbury (1991).

**Chetan**, Anand and Bruton, Diana, *The Sacred Yew*. Arkana, London (1994).

**Cook**, Roger, *The Tree of Life – Image of the Cosmos*. Thames and Hudson, London (1992).

**Chevalier**, A., *The Encyclopedia of Medicinal Plants*. Dorling Kindersley, London (1998).

**Conway**, P., *Tree Medicine*. Piatkus, London (2001).

**Culpeper**, N., *Complete Herbal*. Wordsworth Reference, Hertfordshire (1995).

**Dash**, V.B., and Junius, A.M.M., *A Handbook of Ayurveda*. Concept Publishing, New Delhi (1987).

**Diederichs**, Ulf (ed.), (transl. Felix Genzmer, Gustav Neckel) *Germanische Götterlehre: Nach den Quellen der Lieder und Prosa-Edda*, Diederichs, Cologne (1984).

**Earwood**, Caroline, *Domestic Wooden Artefacts in Britain and Ireland from Neolithic to Viking Times*. University of Exeter Press (1993).

**Faulkner**, R.O., *The Ancient Egyptian Book of the Dead*. British Museum Press, London (1985).

**Felter**, H.W., and Lloyd, J.U., *King's American Dispensatory 18th ed*. Portland (1898).

**Fife**, Hugh, *Warriors and Guardians – Native Highland Trees*. Argyll Publishing, Argyll (1994).

**Fischer-Rizzi**, Susanne, *Blätter von Bäumen*. Hugendubel, Munich (1996).

**Fuhrmann**, M. (transl.) *Tacitus: Germania*. Reclam, Stuttgart (1995).

**van Gelderen**, D.M., and van Hoey Smith, J.R.P., *Conifers – The Illustrated Encyclopedia, vol 2*. Timber Press, Oregon (1996).

**Gerard**, John, *The Herbal*. (First printed 1597.) Dover Publications, New York (1975).

**Graves**, Robert, *Greek Myth Vol. I and II*. Penguin, London (1975).

**Graves**, Robert, *The White Goddess*. Faber and Faber, London (1999).

**Green**, M.J., *Dictionary of Celtic Myth and Legend*. Thames and Hudson, London (1992).

**Grieves**, M., *A Modern Herbal*. Tiger Books International, London (1998).

**Gupta**, Sankar Sen (ed.), *Tree Symbol Worship in India*. Indian Publications, Calcutta (1965).

**Hageneder**, Fred, *The Heritage of Trees – History, Culture and Symbolism*. Floris, Edinburgh (2001).

**Hageneder**, Fred, *The Spirit of Trees – Science, Synthesis and Inspiration*. Floris, Edinburgh (2000), and Continuum, New York (2001).

**Hartzell**, Hal, *The Yew Tree – A Thousand Whispers*. Hulogosi, Oregon (1991).

**Harvey**, H. Thomas, *The Sequoias of Yosemite National Park*. San Jode State University (1978).

**Hillier**, J. *The Hillier Manual of Trees and Shrubs*. 6th edition, David and Charles, Winchester (1991).

**Howkins**, Chris, and Sampson, Nick, *Searching for Hornbeam – A Social History*. Chris Howkins, Surrey (2000).

**Howkins**, Chris, *Sweet Chestnut – History, Landscape, People*. Chris Howkins, Surrey (2003).

**Hutton**, Ronald, *The Pagan Religions of the Ancient British Isles – Their Nature and Legacy*. Blackwell, Oxford (1991).

**Hutton**, Ronald, *Shamans – Siberian Spirituality and the Western Imagination*. Hambledon and London, London/New York (2001).

**Hyde Bailey**, Liberty, *Hortorium* (Cornell University), *Hortus Third – A Concise Dictionary of Plants Cultivated in the United States and Canada*. MacMillan, New York (1976).

**van Ingen**, G., Visser, R., Peltenburg, H., van der Ark, A.M., and Voortman, M., "Sudden Unexpected Death Due to Taxus Poisoning. A Report of Five Cases, with Review of the Literature". *Forensic Science International*. 56, 81–87, (1992).

**Kindel**, Karl-Heinz, *Kiefern in Europa*. Fischer, Stuttgart (1995).

**Knight**, W.F.J. (transl.), *Virgil: The Aeneid*. Penguin, London (1958).

**Krenzelok**, E.P., Jacobsen, T.D., and Aronis, J., "Is the Yew Really Poisonous to You?", *Journal of Toxicology – Clinical Toxicology*. Issue 36, 219–223, (1998).

**Kusmirek**, Jan, *Liquid Sunshine – Vegetable Oils for Aromatherapy*. Floramicus, Glastonbury (2002).

**Lad**, Vasant, *Ayurveda – The Science of Self-Healing*. Lotus Press, Wilmot (WI) (1990).

**Larson**, D.W., et. al., "Ancient Stunted Trees on Cliffs", in *Nature*. Vol. 398, (1999).

**Lewington**, Anna, *Plants for People*. Natural History Museum Publications, London (1990).

**Lewington**, Anna, and Parker, Edward, *Ancient Trees – Trees that Live for a Thousand Years*. Collins and Brown, London (1999).

**Lindner**, David, *Traumzeit – Das Geheimnis des Didgeridoo*. Traumzeit, Schönau (2004).

**Lindner**, David (ed.), *The Didgeridoo Phenomenon – From Ancient Times to the Modern Age*. Traumzeit, Schönau (2004).

**Littleton**, C. Scott (ed.), *The Sacred East – Buddhism, Hinduism, Confucianism, Daoism, Shinto*. Duncan Baird Publishers, London (1996).

**Littleton**, C. Scott, *Understanding Shinto*. Duncan Baird Publishers, London (2002).

**Lu**, Henry C., *Chinese System of Food Cures, Prevention and Remedies*, Sterling Publishing, New York (1986).

**Mabey**, Richard, *Flora Britannica – The Definitive New Guide to Wild Flowers, Plants and Trees*. Chatto and Windus, London (1997).

**Machatschek**, Michael., *Laubgeschichten – Gebrauchswissen einer uralten Baumwirtschaft, Speise- und Futterlaubkultur*. Böhlau, Vienna (2002).

**Mails**, Thomas E, *Sundancing – The Great Sioux Piercing Ritual*. Council Oak Books, Tulsa/San Francisco (1978/1998).

**Mannhardt**, Wilhelm, *Der Baumkultus der Germanen und ihrer Nachbarstämme, Mythologische Untersuchungen*. Gebrüder Bornträger, Berlin (1875).

**Mannhardt**, Wilhelm, *Antike Wald und Feldkulte aus nordeuropäischen Überlieferungen*. Gebrüder Bornträger, Berlin (1877).

**Markale**, Jean, *The Druids: Celtic Priests of Nature*. Inner Traditions International (1999).

**Matthews**, John, *Taliesin: Shamanism and the Bardic Mysteries in Britain and Ireland*. Aquarian Press, London 1991.

**Matthews**, John (ed.), *The Druid Source Book*. Blandford Press, London (1996).

**May**, John, "Cork in Crisis", in *Tree News*. Spring/Summer 2004, The Tree Council, London (2004).

**Milner**, J. Edward, *The Tree Book – The Indispensable Guide to Tree Facts, Crafts and Lore*. Collins and Brown, London (1992).

**Mitchell**, Alan, *A Field Guide of Britain and Northern Europe*. Collins, London (1974).

**Moerman**, Daniel E., *Native American Ethnobotany*. Timber Press, Oregon (1998).

**Mooney**, James, *James Mooney's History, Myths, and Sacred Formulas of the Cherokees*. Bright Mountain Books, Fairview, North Carolina (1992).

**Morrison**, Judith H., *The Book of Ayurveda*. Gaia Books, London (1994).

**Murphy**, Arthur (transl.) *Tacitus: Historical Works, Vol II*, J.M. Dent, London (c.1915).

**National** Audubon Society, *Field Guide to North American Trees, Western Region and Eastern Region*, Knopf, New York (1998).

**Naumann**, N. *Die Mythen des alten Japan*. C.H. Beck, Munich (1996).

**Ovid**, *Metamorphosen*. Reclam, Stuttgart (1994).

**Pennick**, Nigel, *Rune Magic*. Aquarian Press, Wellingborough (1992).

**Philpot**, J.H., *The Sacred Tree – The Tree in Religion and Myth*. Llanerch Press, Ceredigion (1994).

**Ploetz**, *Der grosse Ploetz – Die Daten-Enzyklopaedie der Weltgeschichte – Daten, Fakten Zusammenhaenge*. 32nd ed., Zweitausendeins/Herder, Frankfurt/Freiburg 1998.

**Porteous**, Alexander, *The Lore of the Forest – Myths and Legends*. Senate (1996).

**Pridnya**, Mikhail V., "Taxus baccata in the Caucasus Region", in *Der Eibenfreund*. Issue 9/2002, Cambiarare, Markgröningen (2002).

**Rackham**, Oliver, *Trees and Woodland in the British Landscape*. J.M. Dent, London (1976).

**Rackham**, Oliver, *Ancient Woodland – Its History, Vegetation and Uses in England*. Edward Arnold, New York (1980).

**Randhawa**, M.S., *The Cult of Trees and Tree-Worship in Buddhist-Hindu Sculpture*. All India Fine Arts and Crafts Society, New Delhi (1964).

**le Roux**, Francoise, and Christian-J. Guyonvarch, *Die Druiden*. Arun, Engerda (1996).

**Sayce**, A.H. *The Religions of Ancient Egypt and Babylonia*. T. and T. Clark, Edinburgh (1903).

**Schulz**, Matthias, "Zauberin im Garten Eden – Die Königin von Saba", in *Der Spiegel*, Issue 16/2001. Frankfurt (2001).

**Schwarzschild**, B Shimon, "The New Green China – Correcting the Spin", in *Der Eibenfreund*. 8/2001, Cambiarare, Markgröningen (2002).

**Smith**, William Robertson, *The Religion of the Semites – The Fundamental Institutions*. Meridian Library, New York (1957).

**Stäubli** H. Bechtold, *Handwörterbuch des deutschen Aberglaubens* (10 vols, first printed in 1927). Walter de Gruyter, Berlin (1987).

**Tresidder**, Jack, *Dictionary of Symbols*. Duncan Baird Publishers, London (1997).

**Weinreb**, Friedrich, *Schöpfung im Wort – Die Struktur der Bibel in jüdischer Überlieferung [Creation in the Word – The Structure of the Bible in Jewish Tradition]*. Thauros, Weiler i. Allgäu (2002).

**Willard**, Dwight, *A Guide to the Sequoia Groves of California*. Yosemite Association, California (2000).

**Wilkinson**, Gerald, *A History of Britain's Trees*. Hutchinson, (1981).

**Wilson**, Ernest Henry, *A Naturalist in Western China*, vols. I and II. Methuen, London (1913).

**Wilson**, Ernest Henry, *Aristocrats of Trees*. The Stratford Company, (1930); unabridged reprint, Dover Publications, New York (1974).

**Wilson**, Earnest Henry, *The Conifers and Taxads of Japan*. Arn. Arb. 8: 1–91, Cambridge University Press (1916).

**Wirth**, Herman, *Die heilige Urschrift der Menschheit*. Mutter Erde Verlag, Frauenberg (1979).

**Wolkstein**, Diane, *The Magic Orange Tree and Other Haitian Folktales*. Shocken, New York (1978).

**Yarden**, L. *The Tree of Light – A Study of the Menorah*. East and West Library, London (1971).

**Zohary**, Michael, *Plants of the Bible*. Cambridge University Press (1982).

## Useful websites

**www.spirit-of-trees.net**
*The author's homepage on the significant impact of trees on human culture and spirituality*

**www.Friendsofthetrees.org.uk**
*A charity to re-establish sacred groves in the British Isles*

**www.saveamericasforests.org**
*A nationwide campaign to protect and restore America's wild and natural forests*

**www.fsc.org**
*The Forest Stewardship Council is an independent, non-profit-making organization devoted to encouraging responsible management of the world's forests through developing standards, a certification system and trademark recognition*

**www.worldwildlife.org/forests** and **www.panda.org**
*Both homepages of the World Wildlife Fund have a section on Forest Conservation*

**www.greenmanessences.com**
*All about traditionally handmade flower and tree essences*

**www.nimh.org.u**
*The (British) National Institute of Medical Herbalists website – a portal for herbal information*

**www.ibiblio.org/herbmed**
*Henriette's Herbal Homepage, a rich source of herbal links and information*

**www.bant.org.uk**
The British Association of Nutritional Therapists

# Index

Note: page numbers printed in *italic* refer to diagrams and captions

**Aborigines** of Australia, 85
Acacia *(Acacia)*, 16–19, 95
Africa, 24, 48, 64, 128
    northern, 110, 138, 166, 170, 172, 182, 194
Alder *(Alnus)*, 32–3
Alder people, 177
Almond *(Amygdalus)*, 32–7
Alpine Iceman, 201
Alpine regions, 103, 120, 142
American beech *(F. americana)*, 86
American elm *(U. americana)*, 210
American larch *(L. americana)*, 120
American lime *(T. americana)*, 206
American mountain ash *(S. americana)*, 190
Anglo-Saxon tree use, 22, 45, 68, 127, 172, *177*, *181*, 193, 203, 206
Anuradhapura, Sri Lanka, 101
Apple *(Malus)*, 124–7
Arabia, 19, 57, 64–5, 128, 141
Armenia, ancient, 152
Ash *(Fraxinus)*, 102–5
Asia Minor, 48, 72, 114, 118, *141*, 150, 172, 190
Asia, tree use, 119, 138, 142, 156
    eastern, 99, 142
    southeastern, 60, 96, 112
    southern, 168
    western, 110, 128, 152
Aspen *(P. termula)*, 158–9
Assyria, 76, 115, 138
Athens, 132–5, *136*
Atlas cedar, 52
Australia, 30, 82–5
Aztec peoples, 196–7

**Baltic** peoples, 119, 182, 201, 210
Banyan *(F. bengalensis)*, 96–9
Baobab *(Adansonia)*, 24–5
Beech *(Fagus)*, 86–9
Birch *(Betual)*, 40–45
Black poplar *(P. nigra)*, 156
Blackthorn *(P. spinosa)*, 166–7
Bodh Gaya pipal, 101
Bohemia, 192
Borrowdale yew, 201
Britain, tree use, 68, 86, 106, 142, 166
    *see also* England; Scotland; Wales
British Channel Islands, 194

**Calcutta** Botanical Gardens, 96
Canaan, City of Almond, 37
Canada, 75, 120, 143
Caucasian Nature Reserve, 201
Caucasus, 102, 170, 172
Cedar *(Cedrus)*, 52–9, 72, 115, 118
Celtic tribes, 66, 103, 105, 119, 127, 158, 177, 201–2, 205
Chaldeans, 55
Cherry *(P. avium)*, 164–5
Chilean pine *(A. araucana)*, 38–9
China, tree use, 60, *63*, 99, 106–9, 124, 128, 194, 201
    ritual and legend, 77, 99, 148, 180
Common juniper *(J. communis)*, 116
Common oak *(Q. robur)*, 172
Common olive *(O. europaea)*, 132
Common walnut *(J. regia)*, 112
Conifer, 106
Cork oak *(Q. suber)*, 174
Cottonwood *(P. deltoides)*, 160–63
Crab apple *(M. sylvestris)*, 124
Crete, 78, 135, 152, 158, 210

Cypress *(Cupressus)*, 54, 72–7, 115
Cyprus, 52

**Date** palm *(P. dactylifera)*, 138–41
Delos, 141, 168
divining rods, 66
Druids, 177, 180, *181*, 193
dyes, 112

**Eastern** cottonwood *(P. deltiodes)*, 160
Egypt, ancient, tree use, 16–19, 76, 94, 138, 194
    ritual and legend, 19, 37, 65, 138
Elder *(Sambucus)*, 182–5
Elm *(Ulmus)*, 105, 210–11
endangered species, 38
England, tree use, 26, 48, *128*, 201, 210
    ritual and legend, 22, 68, 71, 127, 149, *177*, 192
    *see also* Britain
English elm *(U. procera)*, 210
Estonia, 119
Eucalyptus *(Eucalyptus)*, 82–5
Europe, tree use, 86, 102–3, 106, 146, 206, 208
    northwestern, 156
    oldest tree, 201
    ritual and legend, 119, 127
    southeastern, 26, 112, 152, 156, 168
    southern, 48, 110, 190, 194
    western, 110, 166, 175, 210
European beech *(F. sylvatica)*, 86
European hazel *(C. avellana)*, 66
European larch *(L. decidua, L. europaea)*, 120
European limes *(T. cordata; T. platyphyllos)*, 206

**fertilization**, 90, 94
festivals and celebrations
    Feast of Tabernacles, 141, *181*
    of Beltane, *45*, *71*, *181*
    of Blessed Name of the Virgin Mary, 81
    of Green George, *181*
    of Lammas, *177*, *205*
    of "mother nights" 45
    Palm Sunday, *181*
    of sacred palm, 141
    spring or May, 43, 71, 149
    Rogationtide, *177*
    of the rowan, *193*
    Royal Oak Day, *177*
    of Samhain, 205
    of the yew, *205*
    *see also* ritual and symbolism
Fig, common *(F. carica)*, 90–3
Fig, sycamore *(F. sycomorus)* 94–6
Finno-Ugric peoples, 119
Fir *(Abies)*, 142–5
food and drink derivatives
    almond, sweet and bitter 34–6
    for beer brewing, 26
    for bread making, 38
    for coffee substitute, 29
    cooking vessels and, 22
    for flavouring, 122, 166
    food wrappings and, 51
    for marmalade and preserves, 62
    for Mirto, 130
    in North America, 40
    olive oil, 132
    for salads and soups, 86, 105, 206
    tea brewing, 40–42, 70
    for wine fermentation, 112
France, 118, 127, 201, *209*

# INDEX

**Germanic** tribes, tree use, 43, 46, 103, 119, 170, 192, 203, *205*, 209, 210
Germany, tree use, 29, 62, 142
    ritual and legend, 127, *127*, *167*, 185, 208
Ginkgo *(G. biloba)*, 106–9
Glastonbury, 127, 149
Glastonbury thorn, 68, 71
Goat willow *(S. caprea)*, 178
gods and goddesses
    Achilles, 103
    Adonis, 65, 145
    Aesclepius, 75
    Aphrodite (Venus), 130–31, 168
    Apollo, 123
    Artemis, 130, 141, 145, 180
    Athena, 132–5
    Attis of Syria, 65, 148–9
    of the Aztecs, 197
    Baal, 57, 141
    Belili of Sumeria, 180
    Brigid of Ireland, 42, *177*, 193
    Car/Carya, 46, 114
    Cardea, 71
    Carmenta, 115
    Culhwych and Olwen of Wales, 71
    Cybele of the Phrygians, 36, 148
    Demeter, 124
    Diana of Tusculum, 89
    Dionysus, 93, 114, 145, 168
    Dziwitza and Boruta, 143
    Ea/Enki, 55–7
    Earth Mother of Paleolithic age, 43
    Europa, 152
    Fagus, 89
    of fertility, 145
    Great Goddess, 166
    Hathor/Nuit, 94–5
    Hecate, 180
    Hera, 71, 81, 168, 170, 180
    Herne the Hunter, 176

    Iduna, 127
    Isis, 65
    Jupiter, 89
    Lugh, 43–5
    Marian of the Pelasgian, 81
    Mars Silvanus, 176, *177*
    Merlin of Breton, 149
    of Native North Americans, 23
    Nephtys, 138
    Nuadu of Ireland, 105
    Olwen of Wales, 71
    Oracle of Delphi, 123, *123*, 135
    Orpheus, 210
    Osiris, 19, 37, 194
    Pan, 148
    Pehuenche of Chile, 38
    Persephone, 168–9, 180
    Phoroneus, 32
    Phylira and Chiron, 209
    Poseidon, 105, 132
    Silvanus, 66, 176
    Tane Mahuta of the Maori, 30
    Velkhanos (Vulcan), 158
    Walleechu of Patagonia, *19*
    of war and weather, 175
    White Goddess(es), 36, 42–3, 45, 71, 182
    Zeus, 51, 152
    *see also* myths and legends
Grandfather-Grandchild tree, 109
Greece, ancient, tree use, 32, 75–6, *93*, 114–15, 118, 146, 175, *177*
    ritual and myth, 36, 65, 75, 81, 103, 105, 114, 130, 132–5, *136*, 141, 145, 205, 209
Greek myrtle *(M. communis)*, 130

**Haiti**, 63
Hawaii, 19
Hawthorn *(Crateagus)*, 68–71
Hazel *(Corylus)*, 66–7
healing properties *see* medicinal properties
Himalayas, 52

historical and literary figures
    Abu Bekr, 141
    Alexander the Great, 76–7, *99*
    Black Elk of the Sioux, 162
    Buddah and Bodh Gaya, 100–1
    Busteq, Ogier Ghistlain de, 29
    Charles II, King, *177*
    Cook, Captain, *30*
    Culpeper, Nicholas, 194
    Darwin, Charles, *19, 202*
    Deborah (Jewish judge), 141
    Dioderus Siculus, 64
    Friedrich Wilheim, Duke, *167*
    Gallus, Cyprianus, 127
    Graves, Robert, 81
    Hatshepsut, Queen of Egypt, *65*
    Henry IV and Edict of Nantes, 209
    Hesiod, 122
    Hippocrates, 103
    Jesus Christ, 63, 64, 65, 71, 110, *110*, 136–7, 141, 149, 167, 185, 205, 206
    Joan, Queen of Aragon, *51*
    Josiah, King, *37*
    Julius Caesar, 120, *141*
    Kampfer, Engelbert, 109
    Li Wen-po, Prince, 106
    Menzies, Archibald, 189
    Montezuma II, Emperor, 196
    Ovid, 65
    Paracelsus, 62
    Philostratus, 55
    Pius II, Pope, *66*
    Pliny, 124
    Pliny the Elder, 177
    Servius, 23
    Smith (English botanist), *109*
    Snefru, Pharaoh, 55
    Solomon, King, 55, 135–6, 169
    Strabo, 130
    Suleman, court of, 29
    Sun King of France, 62
    Theodosius, King of Syria, *72*

    Tuthmosis I, Pharaoh, 194
    Virgil, 62, 130, 210
    Wilson, E. H., 99
    Wuti, Emperor of China, *63*
    Xerxes, King, *93, 152*
    *see also* literary references
Holly *(Ilex)*, 110–11
Holm oak *(Q. ilex)*, 172
Hornbeam *(Carpinus)*, 46–7
Horse chestnut *(Aesculus)*, 26–9

**Iberian** peninsula, 172
Iceland, *193, 202*
India, 64, 96, 100
Iran, 34, 76, 78, 112
Iraq, 77, 115, 138
Ireland, 42, 66, 105, *177*, 180, 192–3
Israel, 34, 90
Israelite/Jewish tribes, 19, 36–7, 169, 181, *181*, 195
Italy, 72, 127, 201

**Japan**, 77, 109, 154, 164–5, 202–3
Jericho, 65, 141
Jerusalem, *110, 149*, 167
    Temple of Solomon, 55, 81, 135–6, 169
Juniper *(Juniperus)*, 54, 72, 115, 116–19

**Kampfer**, Engelbert, 109
Kauri *(A. australis)*, 30–31
Korea, 109
Krishna-bor *(F. bengalensis* var. *Krishnae)*, 96

**Larch** *(Larix)*, 120–23
Laurel *(Laurus)*, 122–3
Lawson false cypress, 72, 77
leaf fodder, 86, 178, 206, 210
Lebanon, trees of, 54, 55, 57–8, *58*

Linden *(Tilia)*, 206–9
literary references
    Babylonian tablet text, 55
    *Bhagavad Gita,* 99
    Biblical,
        New Testament, 65, 136–7
        Old Testament, 36–7, 58, 65, 93, 127, 136, 137, 141, 150, 169, 176, 195
    birch bark manuscript, *43*
    *Book of Kings,* 76
    *Book of the Dead,* 94
    *Dinnshenchas,* 66
    *drys/drus* etymology, 177
    *Eddas,* 105
    *Epic of Gilgamesh,* 57–8, 130
    *Herball* (J. Gerard), 78
    Hittite text, 71
    *King's American Dispensatory,* 130
    *Koran,* 135, 141
    *nagarunga,* the term, 60
    Norse rune alphabet, 202
    "Orosu", 77
    *Peaceful Giants,* 189
    *Pen Tsao Kang Mu,* 106
    poetry, 109, 180, *181*
    and printing press, *46, 89*
    "The Juniper Tree", 119
    *Upanishads,* 99
    *Vedas,* 43
    and writing, art of, 115
    and writing runic talismans, 89
    *Wulfdietrich Saga,* 32
    *see also* historical and literary figures
London plane *(P. acerifolia),* 152

**Madagascar,** 64
Mallorca, 81
Maori tribes, 30, 154
Maple *(Acer),* 20–23
"masting" livestock, 172
maypoles, 43
medical practices
    aromatherapy, 55
    ayurvedic, 36, 55, 62, 90, 99, 100, 112, 124, 138, 170
    Bach Flower Remedy, 89, 110, 120, 124, 146, 158
    Chilean, 38
    homeopathic, 42, 105
    Kundalini yoga, 37
    sauna, 40
    Taoist, 37, 77
    Traditional Chinese, 62–3, 81, 90, 106, 112, 124, 128, 132, 138, 146, 164, 170
    Western herbal, 210
medicinal properties
    for Alzheimer disease, 106
    analgesic, 64, 156, 160, 170
    anti-bacterial, 77, 89, 142
    anti-inflammatory, 32, 64, 78, 156, 158, 160, 166, 178
    anti-viral, 182
    for arthritis, 85, 119, 123, 154, 178, 194
    for asthma, 106
    for bowel complains, 32, 66, 72, 78, 90, 99, 103, 112, 128, 138, 154, 158, 175
    for burns, 194
    cancer inhibitors, 64, 106, 201
    for circulation, 106, 112, 142, 146, 208
    and contraceptive properties, *119*
    for cough relief, 51, 90, 106, 112, 123, 128, 142, 146, 164
    "date coffee", 138
    diuretic, 103, 166, 194
    for "detox," 40–2, 124
    for diabetes, 90
    for earache, 100, 123, 189
    for eyes, 36, 78, 152
    for gastric/digestive complaints, 112, 119, 123, 132, 138, 168, 192
    for gout, 42, 103, 119, 124, 142, 156
    for hemorrhoids, 26, 175
    for impotence, 112
    for kidney complaints, 156
    for lice, 150
    for lymphatic conditions, 112
    for menstrual problems, 210
    for migraine, 106
    for nervous system, 119
    nutritional/mineral, 19, 22, 24, 51, 62, 66, 86, 90, 112, 124, 146, 170
    Olbas oil, 82
    poison antidote, 175, 192
    for prostate problems, 156
    for pulmonary disorders, 55, 68–70, 124, 132, 138, 208
    as purgative, 182
    for respiratory conditions, 119, 142, 146, 150
    for rheumatism, 32, 42, 103, 124, 142, 154, 156
    for sinus complaints, 182, 206, 210
    for the skin, 32, 36, 40, 55, 78, 112, 120, 123, 142, 154, 175, 208
    for sores and wounds, 51, 99, 100, 175, 192
    for sprains and bruises, 29, 123, 170, 182
    for toothache, 152
    toxins and, *29,* 62–3, 106, 110, 119, 168, 201
    for urinary/bladder complaints, 46, 55, 106, 112, 119
    for vaginal infections, 78, 100
    for varicose veins, 26, 29, 72, 194
    for wart treatment, 90
    for well-being, 51, 55, 70, 110, 120, 178, 192, 208
    for worms, 168
Medina, 141
Mediterranean regions, 72, 116–18, 142, 148, 150, 154, 194
Mesopotamia, 158
Minoans, 210
Monkey-puzzle *(A. araucana),* 30, 38–9
Monterey pine *(P. radiata),* 146
Montezuma cypress *(T. mucronatum),* 196–7
moon priestesses, 180
Moon Tree, 76
Morocco, 135
Mulberry *(Morus),* 115, 128–9
musical instruments, 22, 82, 164, 180–1, 201
Myrrh *(C. myrrha),* 64–5
Myrtle *(Myrtus),* 130–1
myths and legends
    abode of the *Saeligen,* 120
    of Aeneas, 130–1
    Arthurian, 66, 127, 176
    of Asclepius, 209
    behind laurel wreath custom, 123
    relating to Christianity, *110, 149, 166, 185*
    Creiddylad of Wales, 110
    death and, 19, 145
    of Diarmuid and Grainne, 193
    of the elder spirit, 182
    of the Flute of North America, 75
    Freya and Frigga of Norse tradition, 42
    the gate to other dimensions, 119
    Germanic, 43, 46
    Gilgamesh of ancient Near East, 57–8
    Glastonbury thorn, 68, 71
    golden apples of Hesperides, 81, 127
    Green Man, 110, 143, 176
    Heimdall of Norse tradition, 46
    of Heracles, 152, 158
    Holy Family of Andalusia, 63

# INDEX

of the house spirit, 182–4
of the Hydra, 152
King Bran of Wales, 32
of Konohana Sakuya Hime, 164
of Lady of the Forest, 42
Magic Orange Tree of Haiti, 63
Mithra and Mao of Persia, 77
of Phaeton, 156
Rata's Waka, 154
relating to fertility, 124–6
of Rhoeo, 168
Robin Hood, 176
Ruminal Fig tree of Rome, 93
sanctuaries and, 70–71, 76–7
of Sigurd, 209
of Yggdrasil, 202
*see also* gods and goddesses

**Native** North Americans *see* North Americans, Native
Near East, 150, 152
Nebudda River banyan tree, 99
Nepal, 100
New Zealand, *30*, 30, 154, *154*
Nordic tribes, tree use, 42, 46, 105, 192, 202, 209
North America, 72, 86, 102, 116, 128, 164, 190, 196
   California, 132, 138, 186–9
   Mexico, 196–7
North Americans, Native, tree use, 22, 40, 72, 119, 124, 143, 146, 186–9
   Algonquin, 120, 142
   Apache, 112
   Bella Coola, 142, 158
   Blackfoot, 146, 158
   Brule, 75
   Cheyenne, 158
   Chippewa, 23, 66
   Choctaw, 160, 210
   Cree, 142
   Hopi, 146–8, 158
   Iroquois, 23, 48, 110, 120, 210
   Kashaya, 188

Kawaiisu, 148
Kiowa, 23, 112
Kwakiutl, 142, 143
Lakota (Sioux) tribe, 75, 146, 160, 162
Malecite and Micmac, 142
Mendocino, 188
Navajo, 72, 75, 148, 158, 160
Ojibwa, 40, 66, 142
Omaha, 160
Paiute, 142, 146
Pawnee and Ponka, 160
Pima, 19
Quebec, 120
Salteaux, 23
Seminole, 196
Seminole tribe, 110
Shuswap, 158
Sioux *see* Lakota
Thompson tribe, 158
Tolowa, 188
Tsalagi, 22, 46, 48, 86, 110, 112, 142, 186
Tsimshian tribe, 143
Yurok, 188
Norway maple *(A. platanoides)*, 20
Norway pine *(P. abies)*, 142, 143, 145

**Oak** *(Quercus)*, 110, 150, 172–7
Olive *(Olea)*, 102, 132–7
Oman, 141
Orange *(C. sinensis)*, 60–3
orangeries, 62
Oriental beech *(F. orientalis)*, 86
Ostyak people, 120

**Pakistan**, 96
Palestine, 94, 127
Palm, date *(P. dactylifera)*, 138–41
Pande, Dr Alka, 99
Patagonia, *19*
Patrician Tree, 131
Peace Tree, 143

Pear *(Pyrus)*, 170–71
Pehuenche tribe of Chile, 38
Pelagasians, 114–15
Persea, 95
Persia, 76, 130, 152
Philippines, 30
Phoenician juniper *(J. phoenicea)*, 116, 118
Phrygia, 36, 148–9
Pine *(Pinus)*, 146–9
Pipal or Bo *(F. religiosa)*, 100–101
Pistacia nut tree *(P. vera)*, 150
Plane *(Platanus)*, 152–3
Plebian Tree, 131
Pomegranate *(P. granatum)*, 168–9
Poplar *(Populus)*, 156–7
Portugal, 60, 82
Pridnya, Professor, 201
Pureora Forest Reserve, *154*

**Quaking** aspen *(P. termuloides)*, 158
Quince *(Cydonia)*, 78–81

**Red** cedar *(Thuja plicata)*, 75
Redwood *(Sequoia)*, 186–9
ritual and symbolism, religious, 71, 127, *177*, 192
   burials, 19, 22, 24, 43, 75, 77, 94–5, 148, 158, 202, 210
   Canaanite, 36–7, 81
   didgeridoo playing, 85
   Eleusinian initiation, 130
   marriage, 81, 114, 127, 164
   myrrh related, 64
   of Buddhism, 99, 100–101, 109
   of Christianity, 37, 43, 51, 63, 81, 110, 115, 136, 166
   suppressing custom, *123*, 167, 185
   of Hinduism, 99, 100
   of Islam, 135
   of Israel/Judaism, 19, 36–7, 65, 136

of Native North Americans, 23, 72, 75, 162–3, *163*
of Taoist tradition, 148
of the Maori, 30
*Para Adumma*, Hebrew, 58
rain-making, 105
runic, of Germanic tribes, 89
shamanistic, 45, 166–7, 168
smoke offerings, 119
thanks for water, African, 24
*see also* festivals and celebrations
Roman Empire, 120, *120*, 170
Rome, ancient, tree use, 64, 118, 132
   ritual and myth, 23, 66, 71, 89, 93, 115, 131, *141*
Rowan *(Sorbus)*, 190–3
Rumania, 127, *181*
Russia, 40–2, *181*, 185

**Sardinia**, 130
Saudi Arabia, 141
Scandinavia, 40, 45, 182, 210
Scotland, 148, 192, 201
   *see also* Britain
Scots pine *(P. sylvestris)*, 146
Semitic tribes, 36, 57
Sessile oak *(Q. petraeal)*, 172
Siberian larch *(L. sibirica)*, 120
Siberian peoples, 120, 143
Sicily, 60
Silver maple *(A. saccharinum)*, 20, 22
Sinai, 19
Slavic peoples, 119, 142
sloes, 166
soap derivatives, 26
South America, *19*, 38, 112, 196–7
Spain, 60, 63, 82, 202
Spruce *(Picea)*, 142–5
Sri Lanka, 100, 101
Sugar maple *(A. saccharum)*, 20, 22
*sugi*, 77
Summer solstice, *177*
Sun Dance ceremonies, 162–3, *163*
Sun Tree, 76

superstition, *105, 110, 115, 127, 167, 181, 185, 202*
Sweden, 192
Sweet chestnut *(C. sativa)*, 48–51
Swiss canton of Aargau, 170
Sycamore *(A. pseudoplatanus)*, 20, 22–3
Sycamore fig *(F. sycomorus)*, 94–6
Syria, *72*
Syrian juniper *(J. drupacea)*, 118

**Tajikistan**, 118
Tamarisk *(Tamarix)*, 95, 115, 194–5
Tasmanian blue gum *(E. globulus)*, 82
Terebinth *(P. terebinthus)*, 150–51

Totara *(P. totara)*, 154–5
totem poles, 75
Tree of God, 150, 203
Tree of Inspiration, 193
Tree of Knowledge, 89, 93, 99, 127
Tree of Life, 99, 127, 138, 152, 196, 202, 205, 209
Tree of Light, 136, 145
Tree of Renewal, 128
Turkey, 29, 55, 71, 148, 152, *152*

**United** States of America
see North America; North Americans, Native
Universal Tree, 99, 202

**Wales**, 32, 66, 71, 110, 193, 202
see also Britain
Walnut *(Juglans)*, 112–15
Watts River eucalyptus, *85*
West Indies, 154
White ash *(F. americana)*, 102
White birch, 40
White poplar *(P. alba)*, 156
White willow *(S. alba)*, 178
Willow *(Salix)*, 95, 178–81
Winter solstice, *45, 177*, 203, 205
World Tree, 46, 55, 81, 100, 105, 120, 128, 135, 143
Wych elm *(U. glabra)*, 210

**Yakushima** national park, 77
Yarrow, 182
Yemen, 141
Yew *(Taxus)*, 89, 105, 118, 198–201
Yew people, 177
Yggdrasil, 105, 202–3

**Zapotecs** of Mexico, 196

## Acknowledgments and picture credits

**About the author**
Fred Hageneder, born in 1962 in Hamburg, Germany, is an author, musician, graphic designer and lecturer, who has studied trees passionately since 1980 in conjunction with comparative religion, cultural history, mythology and archeology. He has given lectures on the spiritual and cultural history of trees in various ecology centres in Germany and Switzerland, and at the Abant Izzet Baysal University in Turkey. His previous publications are *The Spirit of Trees* (2000), a holistic appraisal of one of the earth's most visible and influential creations, and *The Heritage of Trees* (2001), exploring the cultural relationships between humanity and trees.

He is a member of the AYG (Ancient Yew Group), an independent research group, and co-founder of Friends of the Trees (www.Friendsofthetrees.org.uk), a registered charity, which aims to promote modern tree sanctuaries as oases of peace as well as cross-cultural and inter-faith meeting places. He also plays traditional harps and has composed music for various (European) tree species.

Fred lives in the Cotswolds, England. For more on his work, visit www.spirit-of-trees.net.

**Acknowledgments**
My deepest thanks, first of all, to my partner Vijaya, for all her understanding and support, and to Edward Parker for his awe-inspiring photography. Special credits to Steven Ash, Robert Standing Bear and Laurinda Reynolds for their informative and inspiring words about Native American traditions. For their professional support, I would like to thank Roselle Angwin for reading and editing the typescript before submission, Mary Sharma on matters of nutrition, Nathan Hughes on medical herbalism, and Scott Messenger for discussing astrological associations.

Many thanks to Chris Worrall, Christine Konrad and Martin Trilk, and Sangita and Sam Squires. And to everyone at Duncan Baird Publishers for making this book possible.

*Fred Hageneder, 2005*

**Picture credits**
All photographs by Edward Parker, except the following:
**Page 9** Arni Magnusson Insitute, Reykjavik/The Bridgeman Art Library; **10** Deriel-Medina, Thebes/The Bridgeman Art Library; **64** John Feltwell/Garden Matters; **74–5** F.H.C. Birch/Sonia Halliday Photographs; **76** Max Alexander/Duncan Baird Publishers; **78–9** John Feltwell/ Garden Matters; **91** John Ferro Sims; **96–7** Inga Soence/Holt Studios; **101** Robert Preston/Alamy; **137** John Ferro Sims; **159 below** Archie Miles; **169 above** John Ferro Sims; **184** Mike J. Thomas/Frank Lane Picture Agency.